THE PACIFIC WAR

To My Favorite
"Dogface"
From Your Favorite
"Jarhead"

Semper Fi

Mike

April 2019

CAMPAIGNS OF WORLD WAR II

THE PACIFIC WAR

Pearl Harbor • Singapore • Midway • Guadalcanal • Philippines Sea • Iwo Jima

ANDREW WIEST & GREGORY L. MATTSON

amber
BOOKS

This Amber edition first published in 2018

First published in 2001

Published by
Amber Books Ltd
United House
North Road
London N7 9DP
United Kingdom
www.amberbooks.co.uk
Appstore: itunes.com/apps/amberbooksltd
Facebook: www.facebook.com/amberbooks
Twitter: @amberbooks

ISBN 978-1-78274-618-8

Printed in the United States

Photo credits:
All photographs TRH Pictures except the following:
Popperfoto: 6, 8, 9, 10, 11(t), 12-13, 13(b), 16(t), 17(t), 20(t), 22(t), 26, 27, 76, 79(b),
82, 89, 91, 100.
Camera Press: 54, 55, 56, 58-59, 60, 61, 62, 64-65, 66, 71, 72, 183.

Artwork and Map credits:
Aerospace: 25, 34, 48, 80, 84/85, 88, 90/91, 98, 110/111, 127, 133, 135, 136, 154, 164,
166, 172, 178, 197, 204, 211, 215, 219, 233, 238, 244, 250. De Agostini: 14, 22, 36, 37,
45, 57, 64, 71, 96, 113, 122, 150, 161, 189, 195, 199, 206, 212. Peter Harper: 95, 106,
116, 140, 142, 208, 221, 230.

CONTENTS

CHAPTER ONE

THE APPROACH OF WAR

Japan's 'Way of the Warrior' and the 'Manifest Destiny' of the United States placed the two powerful nations on a collision course that would lead to world war.

The conflict in the Far East during World War II followed a very different path from the better-known conflict in Europe. Although there were ties between the two conflicts, historians consider the fighting in the theatres of the Pacific and Asia to be entirely separate to the struggle which was going on at the same time in the West. Two factors dictated the coming of war in the East, and the course it took: the culture and military desires of the Japanese Empire, and the westward expansion of the United States. Although several nations – from Australia to Great Britain – took part in the fighting there, the main contenders were Japan and the United States, and each wanted dominance over the Pacific.

Driven by a desire for international greatness, it was the Japanese who first launched the war in Asia. In 1931 they attacked the economically vital area of Manchuria in an effort to solidify their influence there. From that point onwards, the war slowly escalated, transforming into a bewildering and brutal array of conflicts. Although war in Asia involved Japan's harsh attempt to conquer China, in another sense it was a colonial war which pitted Japan against the Pacific forces of tottering European empires. Finally, and most importantly, the war between Japan and the United States would decide who would be the dominant world superpower for the rest of the twentieth century.

The conflict in the East was also different from that in Europe in the way that it was carried out. Although it was a land war, it did not involve great armoured thrusts; in fact, the Japanese did not even have one armoured division. The conflict in the East was an infantry struggle, often involving units clashing in tropical jungles and, more importantly, much of the war being fought at sea using naval air power. Therefore the motivation and prosecution of the Pacific War differed so much from the war in Europe that it constituted an entirely separate campaign during World War II.

The rise of Japan

As an island nation located close to the Asian mainland, Japan was often buffeted by storms of conquest and was frequently at war. China, as the dominant military and cultural power of the Far East, regularly tried to impose its military and cultural will over its tiny neighbour. As a result, Japan had developed a unique culture: one which was related to Chinese culture, but at the same time had to fight to retain its individual identity. The result was a nation with a strong martial tradition and which was often suspicious of foreign influence. It did not come into its own until the early twentieth century, when the slow collapse of China was nearly complete.

Until the early modern period, Japan was mired in a chaotic, warlike system of feudal government. Presiding over the nation was the semi-divine emperor. Although descended from the Sun Goddess, the emperor – as in most feudal systems – had little tangible power. The true ruler of Japan was the shogun, or the chief military advisor to the emperor. Even his rule was tentative, for the important families of Japan were almost constantly at war, vying for greater power and influence. Feudal warfare on this scale led to the rise of an important warrior class in Japan: the samurai. These warriors lived by the strict code of Bushido, which stressed courage, honour, self-sacrifice and a contempt for death. To a samurai, surrender was the ultimate disgrace; it was far better to die an honourable death in battle or to take one's own life. Samurai venerated their distant emperor and all wanted to earn a place in his favour through their bravery.

Originally, the samurai and their warrior code had a limited influence, but by 1939 their ideas had spread to the Japanese military as a whole and were to greatly influence the nature of the conflict in the Pacific.

As Japan muddled through its period of feudal turmoil, the situation became even more complicated with the arrival of the Portuguese in 1543. These visitors brought not only increased trade but also disruptive foreign influences to Japan, including firearms and the introduction of Christianity. In 1600, a convincing victory by the Tokugawa clan ended the military chaos and, feeling that foreign influence had already done enough to disrupt Japanese life, the Tokugawa shogunate decided to cut Japan off from the outside world, even going to the extreme of expelling all foreigners and outlawing firearms as being disruptive to the social system. For the next 250 years, the Tokagawa shoguns ruled the country as an insular military dictatorship.

The coming of change

Japan shed much of its feudal veneer during the Tokugawa period and managed to come together as a nation. However, the insularity of its system made it weak in comparison to more technologically advanced Western nations. This became clear in 1853 when an American fleet, under Commodore Matthew Perry, entered Tokyo Bay. By this time, the United States, too, was coming of age. With a firm belief in American exceptionalism, the nation had followed its 'manifest destiny' as far west in North America as was possible. Undaunted, the Americans did not stop there, but now sought to spread their power and benevolent rule across the vast Pacific to Japan. The Japanese, realising their technological weakness, eventually gave in to American pressure, re-opening their society to trade and even granting Americans special concessions and legal standing. A swift and powerful backlash was soon to follow this controversial decision, leading to an armed popular uprising in the 1860s.

By 1867, the shogun's forces had been defeated by those loyal to the emperor. In the period that followed, known as the Meiji Restoration, the emperor returned to a direct rule over Japan, while his followers tried to make sense of a society which had been re-opened to foreign influence after years of isolation. Unlike China – which rejected

BELOW

A young Emperor Hirohito wearing his ceremonial robes of state. The coming of the Meiji Restoration in Japan once again placed national power into the hands of the emperor – but Hirohito was supposed to remain above politics, as befitted his semi-divine status. Thus the Emperor had little real control over his military subordinates.

Western values – the Meiji Restoration recognised the physical strength of the West and embraced Western ideas, technology and institutions as its own. Politically, the emperor held all power, but he was supposed to be aloof and above politics, as befitted his semi-divine status. The Japanese based their new government upon that of Imperial Germany, now including an elected Diet, or Parliament, in their political system. However, the Diet was left with little real authority. The all-important cabinet did not have to answer to the Diet; cabinet members answered only to the emperor. Since the emperor was above politics, the cabinet was free to rule the nation with dictatorial authority. Within it, the Japanese military forces held great power; they chose the heads of the war and navy ministries, and their resignation could destroy any cabinet that was found to be unacceptable to the military.

The Meiji Restoration also ushered in economic and military changes. The government recognised the power of industry and worked hard to bring on a controlled Industrial Revolution in Japan. The results were astounding, especially within armament production, and quickly catapulted Japan to a great power status. The Japanese also revamped their military forces, basing their new army on the German model and their navy on that of the British. By the early 1900s, Japan now possessed a first-class navy and army; in fact, all male citizens were subject to a compulsory military training programme. The miracle was complete; Japan had been almost totally transformed.

While Western nations were sceptical about Japanese strength, Japan was trying to emulate the West and become a colonial power in its own right. Many members of the Japanese cabinet believed that a modern nation had to expand, or it would die. To them, the most logical place for expansion was the Asian mainland. Setting their colonial sights on Korea and Manchuria, they had little to fear from China, whose position was steadily weakening. There was, however, one serious problem: Korea and Manchuria were also coveted by the Russians.

ABOVE
Four samurai wearing their traditional costume. Warriors such as these bequeathed their code of Bushido, which stressed bravery and abhorred surrender, to the nation of Japan.

Russia and Japan were now heading towards a clash. After threats and negotiations between the two failed, the Japanese decided to settle the matter with military force, launching a surprise attack on the Russian Pacific Fleet stationed at Port Arthur. The Russians were not used to attacks without warning, but such attacks were accepted as part of the Japanese warrior tradition; only after this did the Japanese declare war. The ensuing land war in Asia – the Russo-Japanese War – was a hard-fought affair which was eventually won by the Japanese when Russia dissolved into revolution. The Japanese were elated. For the first time in history, an Asian nation had defeated a European nation. Thus, in only 50 years, the Japanese had gone from abject defeat to resounding victory, beating the West at its own game.

In the wake of victory, Japan set out to achieve empire. There were treaty negotiations, mediated by the American president Theodore Roosevelt, but the Japanese received less than they had hoped for. It seemed that America – which was itself a colonial power – was set on denying them their colonial due. Soon the United States was perceived to be an enemy throughout Japan, and indignation raged. In contrast, Japan did receive special economic and political privileges in Korea and Manchuria which, by 1909, had been transformed into

a Japanese armed occupation of Korea. The United States, although concerned by this development, did not intervene. Thus the Japanese Empire was born.

Japan next took part in World War I on the side of the Allies and, although her actions were mainly limited to mopping up weak German colonial holdings in the Pacific, she emerged from the war victorious and as the foremost Asian military power. However, in the wake of the losses suffered during World War I, the West began to focus on its collective security and disarmament as part of an increasing move towards isolationism. The United States especially concluded that it had seen enough of foreign wars, deciding to rely on negotiations and the League of Nations for security while continuing to pursue its own world goals. In that general atmosphere of postwar caution Japan, too, made moves toward political liberalism and military moderation. In the 1920s she adopted manhood suffrage, joined the League of Nations and negotiated naval treaties with both the United States and Britain that lessened tension in the Pacific. While such moves were quite acceptable to politicians in Japan, they were not acceptable to many powerful members of the military.

Already chafing at humiliating treaty limitations, with the onset of the Great Depression, Japanese military leaders struck

ABOVE
A group of Japanese cavalry officers pose for a photograph after the victory over the Russians at Port Arthur.

LEFT
Poised for aggression. A flying squad of Japanese Marines and a small tank stand ready for action in the international section of Shanghai amid the turmoil of anti-Japanese boycotts in that city.

back. At the highest levels, they urged that Japan once again needed to expand its borders, this time into China. Such a move, partly motivated by a racial hatred for the Chinese, would help to make Japan economically self-sufficient. At the lower levels of the military, however, violence reigned. The military ethos of Japan involves strict discipline, but at that time a tradition known as *gekokujo* gave junior officers the permission to openly defy their superiors if they believed their cause to be just. Senior officers would level few punishments against this kind of defiance, instead often lauding their rebellious junior officers as 'spirited'. During the 1930s, the military forces of Japan, through both violent and peaceful methods, seized near-total control of the government and decided to embark on an expansionist policy that would bring Japan into conflict with the United States. During the approach to that conflict, *gekokujo* would play a prominent role.

Manchuria

Japan had long seen China as a target of imperial expansion, and by the early 1930s the time had come to act. China was now weak, having been wracked by conflict for two decades. After the fall of the Manchu Dynasty in 1911, there had seemed to be a chance for Chinese unity and strength, but the nation had dissolved into chaos under warlords battling for dominance. The most important warlord was Chiang Kai-shek, who eventually became head of the Kuomintang regime and the nominal leader of China. Even though, after the assertion of his control, Chiang faced a considerable threat from Mao Tse-tung's Communist uprising, it seemed

by 1930 that he had matters in hand, and he set about consolidating his authority. To the military leadership of Japan, a strengthened China was a great worry, especially when Chiang decided to make a move towards the control of Manchuria.

Since its victory over Russia, Japan had regarded Manchuria as something of a special preserve; in essence, its informal colony.

BELOW
Yura, *a powerful Japanese cruiser of the* Natori *class. This ship took part in the Japanese attack on and seizure of the Chinese port of Shanghai in 1937 – an act that provoked international condemnation.*

LEFT
Japanese and Russian peace negotiators in the wake of the Russo-Japanese War. Though they had achieved victory over Russia, the Japanese did not obtain all of their territorial goals and blamed much of their failure on the United States.

BELOW
The Japanese resorted to brute force to keep Chinese citizens of Shanghai in line. Here an 'execution patrol' marches through the streets threatening recalcitrants with decapitation. Notice the menacing sword carried by the 'headsman' in the centre of the group.

RIGHT
Cementing the Tokyo/Berlin alliance. Here Hitler youth parade outside a railway station in Tokyo while on a goodwill mission to Japan.

BELOW
A 1st Lieutenant in the Chinese Nationalist Air Force in 1939. Becoming an independent service in the mid-1930s, the force relied heavily on the United States for the supply of aircraft, equipment and training.

Manchuria's value to Japan was enormous, for it was rich in several natural resources that, as a small country, Japan lacked. Some even saw Manchuria as a settlement colony where surplus Japanese population could go once the home islands became too crowded. This assumption was contested in 1930 when the nominal leader of Manchuria, Chang Hsueh-liang, recognised Kuomintang authority over the region. As if this were not enough, China and Manchuria went on to launch a potentially disastrous boycott of Japanese trade. Coming as they did fast on the heels of the Great Depression, these events in Manchuria pushed the Japanese military leaders to breaking point. They could not afford to lose their important colony.

The Shanghai Incident

The Japanese Government decided to follow a two-fold plan. First, it would negotiate with Chang to convince him to rescind his recognition of the Kuomintang. If that failed, Japan would resort to military force. The Japanese maintained an army on the Asian mainland which was tasked with defending Japanese interests in Manchuria and Korea. Known as the Kwantung Army, this large and well-equipped military force numbered among its officers many of Japan's best and brightest military minds. These ultra-nationalist Japanese warriors – the inheritors of the samurai tradition – were reticent to stand by while China made Japan look foolish.

After initial negotiations with Chang had gone nowhere, the officers of the Kwantung Army, in a move of pure *gekokujo*, took matters into their own hands.

On the night of 18 September 1931, a blast shook the Japanese-owned South Manchuria Railway near the city of Mukden. Leaders of the Kwantung Army accused the perfidious Chinese of sabotage and, as a protective measure, sent their troops out all along the railway line. In fact, the Kwantung had planted the bomb in order to provoke military action in Manchuria. Aghast, the government in Tokyo ordered the Kwantung firebrands to cease their operation, but the officers refused. It was a military revolt. Without orders, Kwantung officers in Manchuria called the Japanese Army in Korea to their aid – and they came. The Japanese Government had to face facts; it could no longer control its own army. Its hands tied, it belatedly gave its approval to the military actions against the Chinese. Vindicated, the Kwantung Army now was quick to assert its military authority over all of Manchuria. Chiang Kai-shek chose not to resist but instead to call upon foreign mediation, making the Kwantung's task much easier. By early 1932, the Japanese takeover of Manchuria was complete, and they then proceeded to install a puppet regime, renaming the area Manchukuo.

The Chinese responded by declaring a renewed boycott of Japanese goods, centring

on the Chinese port city of Shanghai. Due to international trade concessions, Shanghai was a city divided; foreigners lived in their own part of the city under their own laws and were guarded by their own troops, whereas Chinese citizens lived in the so-called 'Old City'. To break the back of the boycott against them, Japanese forces trumped up another 'incident', this time involving a Chinese attack on their nationals. As a retaliation for this 'incident', on the morning of 29 January 1932 Japanese bombers raided the Old City, setting it alight with incendiary bombs, killing thousands of women and children and sending over 250,000 refugees streaming into the international sector of the city for protection. On the ground, Japanese forces moved into the Old City, clashed with the Chinese Army and laid waste to the area. Japanese aggression in the so-called 'Shanghai Incident' would only let up two months later in March with the end of the Chinese boycott.

One story from the Shanghai Incident illustrates the meaning and widespread nature of the Bushido code. A Japanese junior officer was wounded in the fighting. His unit retreated but he was discovered by a Chinese officer, an acquaintance who carried him to hospital, where he was treated and recovered from his wounds. The Japanese officer, disgraced because his unit had not achieved victory, then returned to the battlefield, sat down on the spot where he had been wounded and disembowelled himself. His

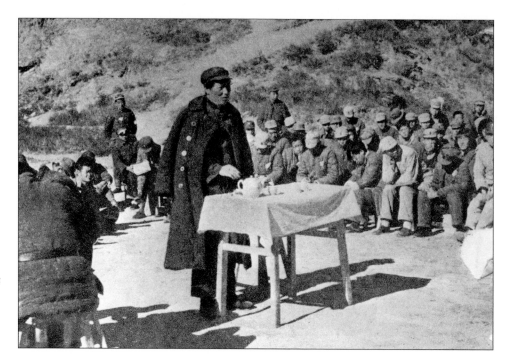

Mao Tse-tung, the leader of the Chinese Communists, rallies his supporters after the fabled 'Long March'. The ongoing struggle between the Communists and the nationalists in China weakened the giant nation and presented the Japanese with an opportunity to seize control.

The prolonged attritional war in China presented the Japanese with a supply and logistics nightmare. Here a Japanese tank makes its way across a rather rickety pontoon bridge during the drive into central China.

story swept through the army like wildfire and he was held up by all as the perfect example of a Japanese warrior.

In their aggression against China, much like Hitler's later actions in Europe, the Japanese had swamped a smaller nation on trumped-up grounds. The Western powers – as in their reactions to Hitler in Europe – chose to take no real punitive action. The Soviet Union was concerned about these developments, but was itself involved in a period of societal turmoil and therefore did nothing to intervene. The League of Nations, under the control of Britain and France, took a few months to consider Japanese actions in Manchuria, eventually condemning them as acts of international aggression. However, the condemnation carried no military punishment and no economic boycott; it was simply an international slap in the face that Japan would not forget. In addition, Japan came to the happy realisation that, militarily, it had

LEFT
Turmoil in Shanghai. As the Japanese moved to conquer the city, foreigners in the international section of Shanghai made ready for the uncertainty of the coming takeover.

BELOW
As these tanks rolling through a village in northern China show, the Japanese held a strong military edge in their war in China. However, the Chinese population was so vast that the Japanese never had enough manpower to conquer the whole country.

nothing to fear from the European colonial powers and it promptly withdrew from the League of Nations to show its indifference to any European threat.

Relations with the United States, however, would present the Japanese with more difficulty. The USA had special economic interest in China and had long championed the 'Open Door' policy of equal access to Chinese trade. The US Secretary of State, Henry L. Stimson, urged vigorous action, but was forestalled by the concerns of President Herbert Hoover. The Japanese marvelled when the USA expressed a mild condemnation of their actions in Manchuria; they were, after all, only engaging in the same type of imperialism that the West had practised for centuries. One Japanese paper responded with the comment, 'America's control of the destiny of Panama is no more essential to the safety of the United States than is Japan's control of Manchuria to the safety of her empire.' However, the lack of military action against Japan was even more surprising. Interpreting Western inactivity as a sign of weakness, and as a humiliation, they were emboldened to seek more territory in China through actions that would in many ways begin World War II.

Japan moves toward war

As Western nations limited themselves to mild condemnations of Japanese actions in Manchuria, the Japanese sought to extend their influence in China ever further. Leaders

Japanese artillery fire at distant targets during the war in China. The experience gained in the Chinese conflict served the Japanese well in their coming struggle with Britain and the United States.

BELOW

The Japanese relied on railroad transportation to supply their war effort in the vast interior of China. Here a Japanese 'railway tank' operates in Manchuria in 1932 – the firepower and durability of such ingenious weapons served to keep much of the Japanese empire in China stable.

of the Kwantung Army were also emboldened by official Japanese support, and quickly moved forces south from Manchuria into the Jehol province of China. As with Manchuria, Chiang Kai-shek's nationalist forces chose not to resist. Japan was able to incorporate Jehol into the puppet state of Manchukuo with little difficulty.

In May 1933 the Kwantung Army invaded the Chinese province of Hopei, near Beijing, but at this point the Chinese nationalists were much more concerned about their ongoing war with Chinese Communists under Mao. Hoping to conserve his forces and thus be able to destroy his Communist adversary forever, Chiang decided to enter into negotiations with the Japanese, rather than fight in Hopei. In return for a peace with Japan, Chiang recognised Japanese control over Manchuria and Jehol and granted the Japanese 'exclusive rights' in Hopei. Chinag hoped that the time this compromise bought

him would be enough to consolidate his forces and ultimately destroy Communism.

The League of Nations had already demonstrated its weakness, doing nothing to stop the continuing Japanese aggression in China. In the United States, Stimson was now urging President Hoover to take measures to halt the Japanese advance, including sending a naval force to Shanghai. Sidetracked by economic issues, and about to be succeeded in office by Franklin D. Roosevelt, Hoover did nothing. A frustrated Stimson had to content himself with veiled, diplomatic threats against the Japanese, which only served to strengthen their resolve. Even though the West had done nothing to hinder Japanese aggression, the tentative peace in China held for nearly four years. In the mean time, the Japanese were consolidating their gains and preparing for a renewed military effort on the Asian mainland.

In China, Chiang and his nationalist forces used the interlude of peace to launch a final effort to crush the tottering forces of Mao Tse-tung in their stronghold in Kiangsi province. The nationalist offensive was so successful that Mao and the Communists fled

Kiangsi for the remote Shensi province. In the fabled 'Long March' of 9654km (6000 miles), many thousands of Mao's supporters perished. Undeterred, Mao reached Shensi, where he was free to begin to rebuild his forces. However, for Chiang the Communists' escape represented something of a failure. It was a greater failure than he could have ever known, for it was to be his last true chance to defeat Mao.

Many nationalists thought Chiang mistaken in pursuing war against the Communists. To these nationalists, Japan was the real, common enemy. It seemed that they would be vindicated when, in 1936, the situation in China changed radically. Chiang was taken captive by nationalist supporters of Manchuria and, in order to secure his release, was forced to agree to a truce with Mao, making common cause with him against the Japanese. From that point onwards, the two factions worked towards an uneasy peace. However, Chiang's hostility towards the Communists proved to be justified, as once the war with Japan broke out in earnest it quickly became clear that they did little of the real fighting. Instead, they used the bitter

ABOVE

A Japanese Type 93 light tank pictured in China in 1935. The Japanese learned that they were lagging far behind their European rivals in both armoured technology and tactics in their short war with the Soviet Union in 1939.

RIGHT
The ruins of a Chinese neighbourhood in Shanghai after the Japanese advance. In their takeover of Chinese cities Japanese troops often committed brutal atrocities against Chinese civilians – but Japan suffered only muted international condemnation.

BELOW
Japanese tanks advance across a river in China in 1941. The armoured arm of the Japanese army always lagged behind in development as the Japanese chose to place emphasis on infantry and the navy.

war against Japan as a period to build up their strength, waiting for their chance to take over the whole of China.

In 1936, Japan finally reached the end of its complacency towards China. Dissatisfied with inactivity on the Asian mainland, in February 1936 several young army officers launched a military coup against the Japanese Government. Before loyal forces could destroy them, the conspirators managed to kill several members of the cabinet and seize some government buildings. Ultimately, the coup failed; however, it did manage to pave the way for a military takeover of the government and new, aggressive policies regarding expansion in China. In a provocative move, the new cabinet – now dominated by the military – adopted a plan called the Fundamental Principles of National Policy. This ordered a massive military and naval build-up, expansion into China and Indo-China and repudiation of all treaties which limited Japanese power. A scant three months later, the Japanese began to solidify their international position by signing a pact with Germany aimed against the Soviet Union. Through the anti-Commintern pact, Japan – which had become something of a

military dictatorship in its own right – closed ranks with Germany. These two revisionist nations were ready to use military force to contest the dominance of the Western democracies in world affairs.

War in China

On the night of 7 July 1937, Japanese and Chinese forces clashed near the Marco Polo Bridge only 32km (20 miles) from Beijing. Although the skirmish had not been staged – as had the Mukden Incident – the military in Japan was quick to seize upon it as reason for invading the rest of China, and they bragged that the job would be accomplished in one month. The Japanese prime minister tried to send a negotiator to the scene in China, but before he could even leave the country, the army arrested him. Once again, the Japanese Army had proven its power. It rushed reinforcements to the scene in China; the war in Asia had begun.

The Kwantung Army, reinforced by troops sent from Japan, quickly faced down the outmatched nationalist Chinese, seizing Beijing by the middle of August. They then turned their military ire toward Shanghai.

ABOVE

A Japanese armoured train car follows troops forward into China. Railroads were a favourite target of Chinese nationalist and Communist saboteurs fighting against Japanese rule.

RIGHT

The dedication ceremony of the Naval Flag of the Rising Sun, held in Hibiya Park, Tokyo, in 1934.

BELOW

A pilot from the American Volunteer Group, which assisted the Chinese Air Force from 1941. The inset patch shown here was sewn on the back of the jacket and instructed any Chinese person to safeguard the pilot after a crash or parachute landing.

This important trading port had long been a centre of nationalist Chinese support and had taken part in many boycotts against Japanese goods. The vengeful Japanese besieged Shanghai, and, although this led to a bitter, seven-week struggle, the city capitulated. Japanese forces were now free to march up the Yangtze River into the heart of nationalist China.

The American president, Franklin D. Roosevelt, was shocked by the developments and wanted to move quickly to help the Chinese. An American neutrality law stated that, once a war had broken out, the United States had to place an arms embargo on all belligerent nations. Roosevelt realised that China, weaker than Japan, would be dependant on American military aid to continue the war. For this reason, he chose to ignore the conflict in China – since war had not actually been declared – and continued to allow the Chinese to purchase arms from the United States on credit. US isolationist forces were perturbed, but could do nothing; Roosevelt had followed the letter of the law. However, when Roosevelt seemed to threaten Japan with an economic embargo in an October speech, isolationists felt he had gone too far. Desperate to avoid a war with

Japan, they protested vehemently against the president's statements. At this point, Roosevelt realised that he could take few positive actions against Japanese aggression in the Far East.

Japanese victories and atrocities

The Japanese military had been convinced that the fall of Shanghai would force China to capitulate. However, this time Chiang Kai-shek and his followers had decided to continue the struggle against Japan, no matter what the cost, and they put up spirited resistance. Chiang realised that, although his forces were numerous, they could not stand up to the disciplined Japanese in pitched battle. Thus he chose a strategy of fight and retreat, hoping to enmesh his enemy in a war of attrition. Surprised that the Chinese continued to resist, the Japanese decided to drive on the nationalist Chinese capital at Nanking. If it fell, surely the Chinese would end their pointless resistance? Accordingly, Japanese forces slowly drove up the Yangtze River, taking heavy casualties every step of the way. In December 1937, after intense fighting, the Japanese conquered Nanking. During the conflict, the full extent of their racial animus toward the Chinese had become apparent. Here, in the heart of nationalist Chinese power, they showed their enemies no mercy. For an entire month, Japanese troops ran riot over the city in an orgy of rape, looting and murder. One Japanese soldier recalled, 'The Chinese were too many for a platoon to kill with our rifles, so we borrowed two heavy machine guns and six light machine guns.' He and his platoon used the weapons to gun down 500 Chinese civilians in cold blood. When order was finally restored, one-third of the city had been destroyed. Some 200,000 men, women and children had been butchered in an atrocity so horrible that even the Nazis complained. The 'Rape of Nanking' disgusted the entire world, but still the appeasers in Europe and the isolationists in America did nothing.

Later on in December, the Western democracies were provided with ample provocation for action. British and American vessels had long enjoyed the right to ply the waters of the Yangtze River because of favourable agreements with the Chinese. However, now the Japanese controlled the river, and they decided to make that fact clear. In the middle of that month, they seized a British gunboat and, in an even more provocative move, Japanese aircraft attacked and sank the US gunboat *Panay*. Although both London and Washington lodged protests, the protest from the United States was noticeably weak. There was good evidence that the Japanese attack on the *Panay* had been premeditated, but the Japanese claimed that the incidents were innocent mistakes and agreed to formally apologise and pay an indemnity for the loss of the vessel. Their intentions, however, were obvious;

BELOW
A Japanese Type 89A medium tank in the early 1930s. Although design began in 1929, issue of this tank did not start until 1934. The principal result of earlier field trials, some of which took place in Manchuria in winter, was the adoption of air-cooled diesel engines as standard for Japanese tanks.

ABOVE

Chinese Communist forces crossing Chiachin Mountain on the 'Long March'. Having only narrowly avoided defeat at the hands of the nationalists, the Communists trekked 9650km (6000 miles) through unforgiving terrain to keep their hopes of revolution alive.

they had sent out the message to the world that Japan now controlled China.

Even in the face of such a clear threat, Britain and the United States chose to avoid a clash with Japan. Just as in Europe, a series of aggressive actions was either ignored or appeased by the Western democracies. This weak response would embolden the Japanese to ever greater military adventures as they were absolutely certain that the West would not intervene. Furthermore, true warriors would not tolerate such affronts. If the West ever did choose to fight, Japan thought it would have little to fear from such cowards.

Having seized much of what they wanted in China, the Japanese now sought a negotiated peace. Ironically, Nazi Germany proposed to act as the intermediary for the peace talks. It quickly became apparent at the talks that the Japanese terms called for an almost complete Chinese surrender. Chiang

Kai-shek, unwilling to accept this, fled with his army and government to Chunking in the remote interior of China. Here he hoped to wait out the Japanese in a continued war of attrition and plead for international aid.

Unhappy that their peace overtures had been rebuffed, the Japanese went on the offensive once again. As a result, by the end of 1938, they had seized all of the major Chinese seaports and their advances had placed most of north China and the port cities on the east coast under Japanese rule. However, the vast interior of China and its massive population remained beyond their control; they simply did not have enough men or material to conquer the country as a whole. Thus Japan could not win the war in China, and was also unwilling to end it through negotiation, so the war there continued. From time to time, the nationalist army and the Communists launched attacks on the Japanese invaders, but often they fought among themselves. The intermittent fighting dragged on, with only few major battles. During this period the Chinese people suffered greatly from Japanese repression, internal turmoil and near-constant famine. However, the Japanese found the rather subdued nature of the continued war in China acceptable, although it involved nearly 1.6 million troops. They had now set their sights on expansion in other parts of Asia.

The expansionists in the Japanese cabinet were certain that, if Japan were to reach its glorious potential, military action needed to be taken – but where? Once again the Kwantung Army, fuming over a border dispute, took matters into its own hands and in July 1939 began an undeclared conflict with the Soviet Union. The conflict in Mongolia lasted for over a month and was decided by the Soviet's use of massed armour, a weapon which was lacking from the Japanese arsenal. In the fighting, the Japanese 23rd Division was totally destroyed and Japanese forces suffered an overall casualty rate of an astounding 73 per cent. In disgrace, the Kwantung Army broke off the conflict and both sides settled for a negotiated peace. Though some within the Japanese military would long for revenge against the Soviet Union, most began again to look elsewhere for future Japanese expansion.

US–Japanese relations deteriorate

The continuing conflict in China set the United States and Japan on a road to war. Roosevelt was determined to keep aid flowing to China, mainly through French Indo-China and Burma, while the Japanese were determined to interdict the trade routes. In addition, the United States seriously began to consider using economic embargoes against Japan as a method of controlling its aggression. At this time, a debate raged in the United States as to the effect that sanctions might have on Japan. Many argued that an embargo – especially on oil – would send a forceful message and serve to curb Japanese aggression. Others warned that an embargo would only strengthen the hand of the militants in Japan, who could press for a military solution for Japan's economic problems. Japan had to take the threat of embargoes seriously, for the island nation relied on the United States for much of its raw materials, especially iron and oil. As a warning to Japan, in July 1939 Roosevelt informed the Japanese that the United States would unilaterally end the Japanese-American commercial treaty. It was the first step toward economic sanctions. However, a few months later, events in Europe would dramatically change the face of the diplomatic world in the Far East.

During the spring of 1940, the German 'blitzkrieg' knifed through western Europe, crushing the Netherlands and France, both important colonial powers in the Pacific. In addition, although unconquered, Britain was sorely pressed by defeats on the battlefield and aerial assault. These events gave the militants in the Japanese Government a wonderful opportunity; with events unfolding in the West, these European powers could do little to defend their valuable possessions in the Pacific. Seizure of European colonial possessions in the Far East – most notably the

The Nakajima Ki-27 entered service over northern China in March 1938, and became master of the skies until confronted by the faster Soviet Polikarpov I-16 fighters. At the beginning of World War II, the Ki-27s took part in the invasion of Burma, Malaya, the Dutch East Indies and the Philippines. The type proved useful for training once replaced by more modern types. The craft shown here is from the 3rd Chutai, 64th Sentai, based at Chiangmai in Thailand in March 1942.

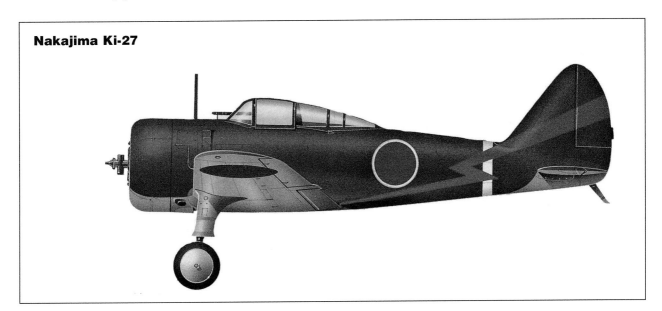

Nakajima Ki-27

Japanese reinforcements disembark from a troop train in China in 1937. Though the army bragged that it would conquer China in a month, the Chinese fought on in a dogged war of attrition, which proved to be a serious drain on Japanese resources.

Dutch East Indies and French Indo-China – would help end Japanese reliance on imports from the United States and shut valuable trade routes to the nationalist Chinese. Even the militants realised that such moves would probably lead to war with the United States. Tempting though this was to some, there were still enough moderates in the Japanese cabinet wanting to avoid it. The military chose to move slowly.

The Japanese contented themselves with demanding trade concessions from the Dutch East Indies and insisting that French Indo-China sever its trade with the nationalist Chinese. To Roosevelt, these moves seemed to presage Japanese aggression in South East Asia and so, to counter them, he announced restrictions on the sale of iron and oil to Japan. Those that believed that US economic action could control Japan's appetite for expansion were in for a rude awakening. Japan was unperturbed by these restrictions, and kept the pressure on the weakened European colonies.

In September, they forced the Vichy French Government to allow construction of Japanese military bases in northern Indo-China. Washington responded decisively by placing an embargo on the export of all iron and steel to Japan.

However, in September 1940, the Japanese ratcheted up the diplomatic pressure. Convinced that Italy and Germany were going to dominate a new world order, Japan hurried to sign the Tripartite Pact with the Axis powers. It provided that, if one of the nations was attacked by a nation not presently at war, it would receive all possible, 'political, economic and military' aid from the other two. Of the major world powers, only the Soviet Union and the United States were not already at war. Since Germany maintained a non-aggression pact with the Soviet Union, it was obvious that the Tripartite Pact was aimed at the United States. Some of the moderate Japanese military leaders, including the Commander of the Combined Fleet, Admiral Isoroku Yamamoto, believed that it was a flawed pact, for it would provoke the United States to war. Powerful as he was, Yamamoto dared not stand against it; he knew this would only get him killed by the militarists.

While far from a declaration of war, the Tripartite Pact served as something of a wake-up call for the United States. It was now obvious that the nation had to start planning for war with Japan. The threat of war in the Pacific – when combined with the dire situation in Europe and the Tripartite Pact – called for a coherent American strategy. As early as 1939, a joint army-navy board had formulated the Rainbow plans to provide for various contingencies. In November 1940, Roosevelt met with Chief of Naval Operations, Admiral Harold Stark, who proposed that in case of war the United States should devote most of its energies to defeating Germany, while maintaining a defensive attitude in the Pacific. This plan, known as Plan Dog, soon received the approval of Army Chief of Staff, General George C. Marshall. Adopted into American wartime strategy, Plan Dog soon became the basis of secret discussions between the United States and Britain regarding the coming of war in Europe. American strategy was now set: it would be 'Europe first'.

In South East Asia, the Japanese continued their aggressive actions. In July 1941 they demanded from the Vichy French the right to build military bases in southern Indo-China, a move that would effectively make the area a Japanese colony. After appealing to both Germany and the United States for aid, the French were forced to comply. Roosevelt felt the continued litany of Japanese military expansion to be extremely provocative. In his view, a Japanese military base in South East Asia would be used to launch even more aggressive actions throughout the region. On 26 July, the beleaguered president made a fateful move: he froze all Japanese funds and assets in the United States and cut off all oil exports to Japan. Britain and the Netherlands soon followed suit.

Japan imported over 88 per cent of its oil, the vast majority of that coming from the United States, Britain and the Dutch East Indies. A total American oil embargo not only would affect the day-to-day lives of the civilian population but, more importantly, also threatened to bring the Japanese war machine to a quick and grinding halt. Incensed, Japanese militants decried it as 'a declaration of economic war' and those in the cabinet who had always believed that Japan should seize economic resources throughout the Far East now had their hand strengthened. All their oil import problems would be solved by a quick takeover of the Dutch East Indies. War loomed.

BELOW
In Shanghai, Japanese security forces blockade the international section of the city. As war against the West loomed, Japan took ever more aggressive action against foreign nationals in Shanghai.

CHAPTER TWO

DAY OF INFAMY

Admiral Isoroku Yamamoto decided to launch a surprise attack on Pearl Harbor designed to destroy US power in the Pacific in one titanic blow.

In July 1941, in response to Japanese encroachments on the Dutch East Indies and French Indo-China, the United States froze all Japanese assets and placed an embargo on the sale of oil to Japan. When added to a previous US embargo on iron and steel, it threatened to place severe restrictions on the Japanese military, which relied on imported US oil and steel for its survival. It was the first real punitive action the West had taken against a litany of Japanese aggression, including the invasion of China and the 'Rape of Nanking'. Before 1941, the isolationist United States had been unwilling to do anything which might provoke Japan to war; however, with dramatic events unfolding in Europe – including the fall of France – President Roosevelt was finally willing to take the risk. It is well known that Roosevelt was a firm supporter of Britain and that he feared the consequences of a German take-over in Europe. Accordingly, by early 1941, the United States and Britain had undertaken a series of talks regarding US entry into the conflict. However, it was in the Far East that the threads of the global crisis which threatened to draw in the United States finally came together.

There is no doubt that Roosevelt hoped to avoid war in the Pacific, but he had decided that a firm hand would stem Japan's desire to dominate the region. Denying critical raw materials to Japan would help bring her to the bargaining table and aid the cause of the country's moderates. However, Roosevelt did not confine himself to purely economic actions. He recalled to active duty General Douglas MacArthur to lead the US Armed Forces, Far East command, with the task of preparing the Philippines for defence against a Japanese invasion. MacArthur – who had been serving as the military advisor to the Philippine Government – now commanded the Philippine Army and all American units in the islands. Pleased with his new command, he boasted that, given time, he would be able to repel any Japanese attack.

To the brink of war

In August 1941 the United States went even further, sending a lend-lease mission to China. Their desire to supply the nationalist Chinese with military aid against Japan was now clear. In addition, the American armed forces allowed some pilots and ground personnel to resign in order to join the American Volunteer Group in China. Commanded by Colonel Claire Chennault, the group – dubbed the 'Flying Tigers' – used obsolete P-40 Tomahawk fighters to help Chinese nationalist forces in their outmatched struggle with the Japanese Air Force. To Roosevelt and most Americans, such moves – along with

OPPOSITE
A stunned US serviceman surveys the damage wrought by the Japanese attack on the airbase at Wheeler Field near Pearl Harbor. The aircraft there, which were lined up in neat rows, made perfect targets for the Japanese raiders.

ABOVE

A Japanese mini-submarine of the type that attempted to attack Pearl Harbor. Though none of the submarines entered the anchorage, the US destroyer Ward *caught sight of one and warned US authorities – but the warning came too late.*

RIGHT

Early in the morning of 7 December 1941 Japanese pilots ready their aircraft for take-off and the fateful attack on Pearl Harbor. Though the incoming raiders were detected by radar they were mistaken for friendly aircraft and Pearl Harbor remained unaware of the approaching threat.

the economic embargo – were warranted responses to Japan's constant aggression in the Pacific.

The Japanese interpreted their actions in a different way. Even the moderates in the Japanese cabinet saw them as yet more evidence that the USA was meddling in their effort to create the greater East Asian co-prosperity sphere – a Japanese euphemism for their growing empire. The most recent US moves, especially the oil embargo, seemed designed to humiliate the proud Japanese military; this no warrior could ignore. With only a limited supply of oil reserves to hand, the Japanese had to consider their options rather quickly before their war machine in China sputtered to a halt. Cabinet members were now faced with three choices. Japan could give way to American pressure and abandon its ambitions in the Far East, including China. However, this would involve an admission of defeat, something anathema to the Japanese militants. The second option involved reaching a compromise with the United

States through negotiation. Such a solution meant that Japan would be forced to rein in some of its foreign designs in order to resume trade with the United States. The final option, long supported by the most militant Japanese expansionists, involved the seizure of European colonial possessions throughout the Far East by military force. Following this, Japan would be self-sufficient in many natural resources, including oil, and would no longer be reliant on American trade. However, most realised that military action against European possessions would result in war with America and leave Japanese forces vulnerable to American air assault from the Philippines. Thus it appeared that the third option would, at the very least, require an attack upon American holdings in the Philippines.

The Japanese military favoured war with the United States, but the Japanese Premier, Fumimaro Konoye, wanted continued negotiations with the Americans. Konoye remained a firm supporter of expansion in

ABOVE
The USS Phoenix, *moored far from battleship row and spared the worst of the attack, is silhouetted against a backdrop of destruction after the first wave of Japanese attacks on 7 December 1941.*

Taken by surprise, few of the powerful ships in Pearl Harbor were able to respond to the brutal Japanese attack. Here firemen work feverishly to extinguish the blazing wrecks of US ships in the aftermath of the first wave of Japanese attacks.

Struck by two torpedoes, the California lists heavily after the first wave of attacks. Ready for an impending inspection, the California had several of its water-tight doors open when the Japanese struck.

Asia, but believed that a war with the United States would be detrimental to Japan's overall goals. After receiving limited approval from the military about conducting negotiations, Konoye made several proposals to the United States through the Ambassador in Washington, Kishisaburo Nomura. Nomura worked hard for a compromise with the United States, for he also wanted to avoid war. However, he was often kept in the dark regarding Japan's true positions on many issues, often being used as a decoy. In Washington, for the USA

the negotiations were handled by Secretary of State Cordell Hull. He was also genuine in his desire to compromise, but quickly discovered that the two sides were very far apart in their negotiating stance.

As we now know, the militarists in the Japanese cabinet granted Konoye only a limited window of opportunity for negotiations, a window far too narrow for any real success. On 3 September, they informed Konoye that he had until 15 October to bring the United States to heel or 'we shall immediately decide

ABOVE

The second wave of Japanese attackers focused on the Pennsylvania *(seen in the background of this picture), which was in dry dock. Many of the bombs missed their target, however, and wrecked the destroyers* Downes *(left) and* Cassin *(right).*

HMS Prince of Wales

At the end of 1941, Britain was on the defensive in the Far East, relying on its 'fortress' of Singapore, but two capital ships, HMS Repulse and HMS Prince of Wales, were sent to the area. They arrived in Singapore on 2 December, only to be sunk eight days later by Japanese torpedo-bombers.

US sailors speed past the smouldering wreckage of the West Virginia and the Pennsylvania after the close of the Japanese attacks on Pearl Harbor.

to open hostilities against the United States, Great Britain and the Netherlands'. Konoye rushed to meet the demanding agenda, offering to remove Japanese troops from Indo-China at the conclusion of the Japanese war in China. Although he refused to go further at this point, Konoye suggested that he and Roosevelt hold a summit conference in the Pacific to debate a more far-reaching compromise settlement. The American President was interested in

the possibility at first, but both Hull and the Secretary of War, Henry Stimson, persuaded him that the differences between the nations were too great to be affected by personal diplomacy. In addition, Stimson believed that Roosevelt's presence at such a meeting would be construed by the Japanese as a sign of weakness and would help to encourage its militarists. Thus, the United States declined the meeting in a communication on 2

October, and put forward the request that the Japanese consider withdrawing their troops from China.

Realising that his diplomatic initiative had failed, Konoye resigned as Premier on the deadline set by the military, 15 October. He was replaced in power by General Hideki Tojo, who was a leading proponent of war. Nicknamed 'the Razor', Tojo was intelligent and hard-working. He had served as a brigade commander and later as chief of staff in the Kwantung Army. Thought to be too bold and headstrong by some, he was to preside over Japan's assault in the Pacific. Before he could move, however, Emperor Hirohito intervened. Although he was supposed to be above politics, in a quite unusual move – some historians believe it vindicates the Emperor of guilt for the conflict – he requested that his government step up its efforts to seek a negotiated settlement with the United States. Obediently, Tojo agreed but, apart from a

significant backdown by the United States on several important issues, the decision for war had already been made.

Negotiations fail

In new diplomatic proposals, the Japanese offered to interpret the Tripartite Pact with Germany only defensively and even brought up for negotiation the position of Japanese forces in China. However, although the proposals were important, they were also vague, meaning that negotiations would take time. This was time the Japanese did not have. Their oil reserves were running dangerously low; settlement or war had to come very soon.

In Washington, special envoy Saburo Kurusu joined Nomura and Hull in the talks. Roosevelt and Hull were querulous of the new Japanese proposals but they chose to continue negotiations. This was partly for military reasons. Both the army Chief of Staff General George C. Marshall and Admiral

ABOVE

Though the Japanese attack had been quite successful at Pearl Harbor, it left the job only half done. Several battleships, as seen here, had sustained heavy damage but were salvageable. The US Pacific Fleet had not been totally destroyed.

A US naval aviator, of the rank of lieutenant, from the USS Enterprise *in December 1941. The carrier was on patrol south of Hawaii when the Japanese attack began, but a scouting party of 18 aircraft later stumbled across the second wave of the Japanese attack. Only half of the 18 US aircraft survived to land safely at Pearl Harbor.*

Stark had warned Roosevelt that, in the case of war, American forces – especially those in the Philippines – were inadequate. Continuing with the negotiations, it was hoped, would give them time to redress the situation. Hull offered a hard-line proposal, informing Nomura that Japanese forces would have to leave both Indo-China and China before America would renew trade with Japan. Tojo saw this proposal as clear provocation. On 25 November, a Japanese task force left port, bound for Pearl Harbor. The force could be recalled if an unforeseen diplomatic breakthrough took place before noon on 1 December, after which time, as one Japanese Admiral stated, 'the situation would be placed in the lap of the gods'.

Negotiations in Washington continued until the very day that Pearl Harbor was attacked. Nomura and Kurusu, though, were unaware of the impending attack and negotiated in good faith, not realising they were there as decoys. The American negotiators were not entirely in the dark regarding Japanese intentions. By the autumn of 1941, their cryptanalysts had broken the Japanese diplomatic code and were reading messages written to Nomura, often before even he was aware of their content. The code-breaking effort was dubbed 'Magic', and it gave the United States an edge on

information. However, it did have serious weaknesses. Unlike the Ultra code-breakers in Europe, Magic was unable to read Japanese military codes, information that would have been much more revealing to US planners. Additionally, since the Japanese cabinet had decided to leave Nomura in the dark about its decision for war and the location of the coming attack, the code-breakers had only tantalising hints of what was to come. US negotiators had to be content with the knowledge that Japan was negotiating in bad faith and had already made the decision for war. Roosevelt knew from reading a decript that 29 November was the deadline for successful negotiations, after which, 'things are automatically going to happen'. Some historians argue that this and other information gleaned from various decripts should have warned Roosevelt that an attack on American holdings in the Pacific was imminent. They conclude that Roosevelt was so desperate to enter the European conflict on Britain's side that he was willing to court an attack in the Far East.

Forces and plans

The United States had long recognised war in the Far East as a possibility and had contingency plans at the ready. The main plan for war with Japan, dubbed Plan Orange, had been in existence since shortly after World War I. It foresaw a major problem for American strategy: the Philippines. An American possession since the Spanish-American war, this island chain was poorly defended and lay more than 8045km (5000 miles) from the nearest US base in Hawaii. War planners had calculated that Japan could transport over 300,000 soldiers to the Philippines within one month, while a US relief force would take up to three months to cross the Pacific Ocean, thus the islands would be lost to Japan. The Philippines was also reckoned to be the most likely place for a Japanese attack upon the outbreak of war. Unwilling to surrender an American mandate to a foreign threat, Plan Orange called for US troops to hold out in the area around Manila until American seapower had arrived in a

cross-ocean rescue effort. At the very best, it was optimistic.

With the advent of the Rainbow Plans and Plan Dog, Plan Orange declined in its relative importance. The United States had decided to stand on the defensive in the Far East in order to concentrate on the defeat of Germany. To this end, part of the US Pacific Fleet moved to take part in the ongoing Battle of the Atlantic. The weakened fleet, based in the main at Pearl Harbor in Hawaii, numbered three aircraft carriers, eight battleships, seven heavy cruisers and numerous smaller craft. Great Britain was involved in heavy fighting in Europe and so also stood on the defensive in the Far East, relying on the prowess of its great fortress at Singapore. In all, nearly 89,000 troops and 150 obsolete aircraft stood ready in defence, and Britain sent two capital

FAR LEFT
After the Japanese attack (from the left) the West Virginia *and the* Tennessee *have taken heavy damage while the* Arizona *burns in the foreground – in the attack one of her powder magazines exploded, ripping the ship apart and killing 1500 men.*

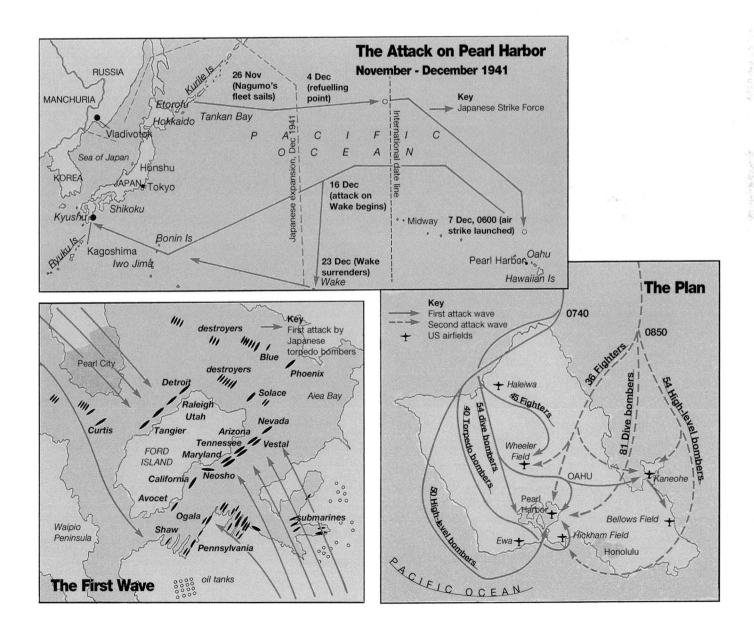

ships, the *Prince of Wales* and the *Repulse*, to the area. Australia – which had felt threatened by Japanese expansionism and had long called for more of an active stance – had little in the way of naval power to add to the Allied mix, and, renowned for their bravery in combat, her armed forces were divided, having already committed three divisions to the war in North Africa. Thus Allied naval power almost matched that of the Japanese, but was divided into three widely separated commands. The Philippines and Singapore would have to hold out against the expected attacks if the Allies were to stand a chance.

The flamboyant General Douglas Mac-Arthur led the all-important force in the Philippines. With one American and 10 Filipino divisions under his command, totalling nearly 200,000 men, he believed that he could repel any Japanese invasion on the beaches, rather than relying on the defence of Manila. He had, however, vastly over-

estimated the capabilities of his Filipino soldiers, who had received little training. Their training programmes got under way in the autumn of 1941, but when the invasion came in December many of the Filipino soldiers did not know how to fire their weapons. One American officer remembers that the Filipino soldiers had learned only two things during their short training periods: 'one, when an officer appeared, to yell attention in a loud voice, jump up and salute, the other to demand 3 meals per day'. It was with this half-trained army and one American division that MacArthur proposed to defeat the battle-hardened Japanese Army in the Philippines.

American planners in Washington were only too happy to believe MacArthur's projections for the defence of the Philippines; otherwise, given the strategic reality of Plan Dog, the islands would simply be sacrificed to Japanese aggression. The United States also began a massive infusion of modern equipment

BELOW

One of the few ships to raise steam during the initial Japanese attacks, the Nevada *churns through the water of Pearl Harbor doing her best to defend other ships in the anchorage and to make her way to sea.*

LEFT
*Carnage at Pearl Harbor.
This aerial photograph
shows (from right to left) the*
Oklahoma *(capsized), the*
Maryland, *the* West Virginia
*(resting on the bottom of the
harbor), the* Tennessee *and
the* Arizona.

into the area: everything from 105mm (4.1in) howitzers to radar was earmarked for shipment to MacArthur's forces. Most importantly, the USA decided to send in some 300 B-17 'flying fortress' bombers. Operating at high altitude, it was hoped that these bombers would lay waste to any Japanese invasion and then launch attacks on Japanese forces elsewhere in the Far East. MacArthur estimated that his forces would be trained and re-equipped, ready to withstand a Japanese invasion, by April 1942. Even so, when the Japanese attack came in December, only 35 of the 300 new bombers had arrived.

Japan's military plan called for a quick seizure of the Philippines, Malaya, Hong Kong and Borneo, followed by a move on the Dutch East Indies. It had the warm support of most in the military leadership, but the Commander of the Combined Fleet, Yamamoto, disagreed. Having studied English at Harvard and travelled extensively in the United States, the Admiral realised the latent power of Japan's enemy. He told all who would listen that Japan lacked both the manpower and the resources to win a war against the USA. He also believed that seizure of far-flung possessions in the Pacific would put his beloved fleet at great risk. If given the opportunity, the United States would mass its fleet and move east in an effort to destroy the Japanese Combined Fleet, which would then have to disperse itself in a vain effort to defend all of its colonial possessions. Yamamoto remarked: 'If in the face of such odds we decide to go to war – or rather are forced to do so by the trend of events – I can see little hope of success in any ordinary strategy.'

In an effort to avoid a disastrous all-out war, Yamamoto proposed to launch a surprise attack against the American Pacific Fleet at Pearl Harbor. He hoped that, after striking this crippling blow, Japan would have over six months of peace to establish its empire in the Pacific without any US interference. In addition, he hoped that, combined with the construction of a defensive ring around his country, this shattering blow would convince the United States that a war against Japan was not worth fighting. In his view, it was Japan's only hope, albeit a rather slim one. Realising that the militarists in the Japanese Government had already opted for war – a war they would lose – he thought that his plan would at least give his nation a fighting chance.

Yamamoto had been toying with the idea of a surprise attack on Pearl Harbor for some time and aired his idea in Japanese naval circles in early 1941. Many objected, claiming that the scheme was far too great a gamble,

but Yamamoto persevered. By the end of September 1941, he had prepared a plan for the Naval General Staff that called for a surprise attack on Pearl Harbor led by a force of six aircraft carriers. Although they were intrigued, staff members knew that it suffered from two great weaknesses. Firstly, the massive flotilla would have to steam some 5631km (3500 miles) without detection, a feat they believed to be impossible. Secondly, Japan possessed no torpedo that would function effectively in the shallow water of Pearl Harbor. Yamamoto's plan seemed doomed.

To minimise the chance of discovery, Yamamoto chose a route for his fleet that wound far north of any normal shipping route. Beginning in the Kurile Islands, the fleet would proceed far to the north of Midway and descend on Hawaii from the north. In October 1941 a Japanese liner *Taiyo Maru* made a practice run along the route without sighting another ship of any kind. In addition, Japanese scientists developed a new torpedo-stabilising device that would allow a torpedo dropped from a plane to function well in the 12m (40ft) deep water of Pearl Harbor. Finally, the navy worked to convert 40cm (16in) armour-piercing naval shells into bombs for use by both high level and dive

BELOW

The scene at Pearl Harbor from the hills outside the base where many of the officers lived. It was near this spot where Admiral Kimmel, Commander of the US Pacific Fleet, watched the Oklahoma *capsize. This photograph shows the* Arizona *on fire and sinking after the raid.*

bombers. In a very short time, Yamamoto had overcome the worst fears of his critics.

Even so, many in the naval staff, including the Chief of the Naval General Staff, Admiral Osami Nagano, still balked at the risky plan. The Naval War College therefore conducted war games for the Pearl Harbor attack. One ended in disaster when the Japanese fleet was discovered at sea, and the other ended in partial success. In a typical Japanese act of military defiance, Yamamoto threatened to resign his post unless his plan was approved, regardless of the wargame outcome. Reluctantly, Nagano agreed and the plan to attack Pearl Harbor became a rather last-minute addition to Japan's wartime strategy against the United States.

A day which will live in infamy

As November turned to December, the Japanese strike force, under the command of Admiral Chuichi Nagumo, made its way across the north Pacific. The powerful armada, consisting of six aircraft carriers with a complement of 360 planes, was escorted by two battleships, three cruisers and eight destroyers. Luck was with the Japanese, for they encountered little in the way of rough weather – which made

for easy refuelling – and they came into contact with only one merchant vessel that did not report their presence. As the fleet bore down on Pearl Harbor, intelligence indicated that all of the battleships and most of the cruisers of the US fleet were present in the harbour, but there were no aircraft carriers. The Japanese suspected that the United States possessed four aircraft carrier task forces, whereas in reality she had only three based around the carriers *Enterprise*, *Lexington* and *Saratoga*. When Nagumo learned this information he was worried that the US carriers might be lurking close by to surprise the Japanese fleet at sea. Yamamoto, however, had been clear in his orders: the attack was so important that it had to go in, no matter what. He was even willing to lose three of the six carriers to enemy action, meaning that Nagumo should fight his way in, if need be. Thus Nagumo continued his advance toward Pearl Harbor. As it turned out, he need not have worried; the *Enterprise* and *Lexington* were both on patrol south of Hawaii, and *Saratoga* was in for repairs. Nothing therefore stood between the Japanese and success.

Before dawn on 7 December, only 320km (200 miles) from their unsuspecting target,

ABOVE

A panoramic view of the second wave of Japanese attacks on Pearl Harbor. As evidenced by the anti-aircraft fire, American forces were much better prepared for the second assault and greeted the attackers with a hail of fire.

the Japanese aircrews were ready and at breakfast. At dawn, 183 aircraft – including 49 bombers, 51 dive bombers, 40 torpedo planes and 43 fighters – rumbled into the sky, led by Commander Mitsuno Fuchida. The pilot could not believe his luck, for his attacking aircraft went undetected and unmolested during their approach towards the American fleet. Once at Pearl Harbor, Fuchida was astounded to see the American battleships and cruisers anchored closely together in rows two deep off of Ford Island, making them wonderful targets. He hoped to launch his torpedo bombers first, but the excitement was too much and several Japanese planes of all types rushed toward their targets. Fuchida ordered an all-out attack and every plane moved in to play its role in history. At 0753 hours, Fuchida radioed back to Nagumo the code words 'Tora, Tora, Tora', the signal that the attack had begun.

In Pearl Harbor the American Pacific Fleet awoke on Sunday morning oblivious to the approaching danger. They had been there since May 1940 as something of a warning to the Japanese against aggression in the Pacific. Many within the US Navy felt that the location was too exposed and that the fleet should be located on the west coast, but their arguments had fallen on deaf ears. Although in naval circles it had been suggested that the Japanese might open a conflict with a surprise attack on Pearl Harbor, no additional precautions had been taken to protect the fleet. Some historians wonder whether this lack of protection was part of a grand conspiracy to force the United States into World War II. There is no doubt that Roosevelt was keen to enter the conflict on Britain's side, but had been rebuffed in his efforts by isolationists in the government and the population. Even though Magic's code-breaking intercepts of diplomatic traffic reported that Japan was headed toward war, none were sure where it would start. Most speculated that the focal point of the attack, if it came, would be the Philippines. In addition, cryptanalysts had recently broken part of the Japanese naval code, but had only picked up bits and pieces of interesting information, none of which pointed precisely towards an attack on Pearl Harbor. Thus, although circumstantial evidence exists, it is a historical injustice to suggest that Roosevelt sacrificed the lives of the brave men at Pearl Harbor in an effort to force his country into war.

Believing Pearl Harbor to be safe from attack, the commander of the Pacific Fleet, Admiral Husband Kimmel, and the commander of the US army forces in Hawaii, General Walter Short, had done little to ready the installation for attack. The US fleet was moored very closely together in pairs off Ford Island and did not have net protection against torpedo attack. It was believed that such protection would hinder the fleet if it had to move quickly. On land, anti-aircraft gunners had not been issued live ammunition, and the hundreds of military aircraft based at the principal air fields in the area – including Wheeler and Hickam fields – were parked closely together as protection against sabotage. The neat rows of aircraft made wonderful targets, and would have required nearly four hours to be ready for take-off.

Surprise and disaster

On the morning of 7 December, the only air patrols being flown out of Pearl were searching to the west. However, in August a radar system had been set up to detect any possible attack, albeit running on a part-time basis with rather inexperienced officers. It was supposed to be shut down by 0700 hours, but the station at Opana had not closed on time and, at 0702 hours, detected the Japanese attack aircraft while they were still 209km (130 miles) distant. The radar operator warned his superior in Oahu, but was told that his radar had only detected an expected incoming flight of B-17s, and 'not to worry about it'. At 0653 hours, word had come in from the destroyer *Ward* – which was patrolling the entrance to Pearl Harbor – that it had encountered and attacked a submarine. A lone navy lieutenant had received the message and, at 0700 hours, informed his superiors, who decided to wait on further information from the *Ward*. However, this information would never come, for the Japanese attack force was at hand. There were two chances for American forces at Pearl Harbor to ready themselves against the Japanese attack, and both had been wasted. The greatest US base in the Pacific was unprepared, and both Kimmel and Short would pay for their mistakes by losing their careers.

In the skies above Pearl Harbor, the Japanese attack aircraft separated into two groups. Dive bombers and fighters went off to attack the nearby American air bases, while torpedo planes, dive bombers and

high-level bombers began their attack run against the American warships. Aboard the battleship *West Virginia* an ensign, Roland Brooks, mistook the first Japanese bombs for an explosion in the boiler room, sending fire teams to investigate. Aboard the *Nevada*, the band was making ready for the raising of the colours and, at 0800 hours, broke into the 'Star Spangled Banner' just as the first wave of torpedo planes began their low-level attacks. After completing its attack, one Japanese aircraft sprayed the band with machine-gun

*Expecting a third assault,
US servicemen at an anti-
aircraft position scan the
skies for incoming Japanese
aircraft. Admiral Nagumo
made a critical error by not
ordering the third attack –
leaving Pearl Harbor at best
a flawed victory.*

fire. The band broke for cover – and the attack on Pearl Harbor had begun.

It was on the outer rank of battleships moored on Battleship Row off Ford Island that the Japanese found their best hunting. Almost instantly, torpedoes began to slam into the American vessels. Six struck the *West Virginia*, five the *Oklahoma*, and the *Arizona* and *California* took two hits each. Confusion reigned throughout the US Pacific Fleet. At first, many sailors believed the commotion to be an all-too realistic drill, only awakening to the real situation as the torpedoes and

bombs began to explode all around them. On many vessels, important officers – including four battleship captains – were ashore enjoying their weekend, which only added to the monumental confusion caused by the abrupt attack. Aboard the stricken ships, junior officers struggled to gain control of the situation and mount a defence. As men reached their battle stations, anti-aircraft and small-arms fire rose to meet the attackers. However, since the ships had only been on a 'Number 3 condition of readiness', this meant that only one anti-aircraft battery in each sector was ready to take action. Thus the attackers were able to continue their assault on the Pacific Fleet almost unmolested.

As Japanese torpedoes slammed into the *West Virginia*, water flooded in and threatened to capsize the stricken ship. Only the quick thinking of Lieutenant Commander J.S. Harper saved the day. Even though communications throughout the vessel had been lost, he directed counter-flooding to keep it on an even keel. To order counter-flooding was an extremely difficult decision to make, for Harper realised that it would trap and drown several of his comrades below decks. However, he had little choice, and after he had given the order, the *West Virginia* slowly settled onto the shallow bottom of Pearl Harbor, with the vast majority of the crew surviving. The *California*, too, was in desperate trouble, having been holed below the water line, struck by two torpedoes. Furthermore, as the ship had been expecting an inspection, several of her watertight doors stood wide open, and sea water was surging through them and into the ship.

A flawed Japanese victory

Aboard the *Oklahoma* five torpedoes struck in such rapid succession that they made counter-flooding impossible. The stricken ship soon took on a pronounced list and began to capsize. An observer on Ford Island saw the huge vessel roll over, 'slowly and stately ... as if she were tired and wanted to rest'. High above the scene on a hill at Makalapa, where many of the senior officers lived, Admiral Kimmel rushed out of his house to watch the grim demise of his fleet. He looked on in amazement as the vessel started rolling over. A shocked wife of one of his fellow officers stated, 'Looks like they've got the *Oklahoma*', and Kimmel could only answer, 'Yes, I can see they have.' The massive ship continued to roll until its superstructure jammed in the mud on the floor of Pearl Harbor, leaving her bottom-up only eight minutes after the first torpedo had struck home. Those aboard the ship either drowned or managed to keep alive in air pockets on the overturned vessel until rescue teams arrived. Those who had been on deck simply walked with the slow turn and wound up on the bottom of the vessel as additional Japanese planes rushed in to launch strafing attacks. Over 400 men perished on the *Oklahoma*, and the survivors were leaping into the oil-soaked water when an even worse disaster hit the American fleet.

The *Arizona*, hit by only two torpedoes and faring well, took a direct hit from a dive bomber on the forecastle. The bomb penetrated into, and detonated, the forward powder magazines and the resulting explosion ignited into a huge ball of fire and smoke that rose over 152m (500ft) into the air. The explosion was so powerful that it blew men off of the nearby *Nevada* and buffeted the plane of Commander Fuchida circling overhead. The vast conflagration quickly transformed the *Arizona* into a blazing hulk, and the ship disappeared beneath the waters. There were survivors, including Major Allen Shapley, a Marine who had been blown off the ship by the explosion and had swum to safety through the oil-soaked, burning water. However, over 80 per cent of the *Arizona*'s crew of 1500 men died, making it one of the greatest single disasters to have occurred in American naval history.

While the attack raged at Pearl Harbor, other Japanese aircraft bombed and strafed the nearby American airfields. At Kaneohe Bay nearly all of the navy Catilina Flying Boats were destroyed in a two-wave attack. More importantly, though, Japanese bombers and fighters struck the Army Air Corps fields – Bellows, Wheeler and Hickam – where the fighter planes tasked with protecting the Pacific Fleet were stationed. Once again, anti-aircraft fire was minimal, meaning that the Japanese could destroy row upon row of American fighters at their leisure. Considerable attention, too, was given to the hangar areas where many of the US troops were taking shelter.

Stumbling into the carnage came the expected B-17 flight that had so confused the radar operators earlier. Having been given no prior warning, many of the B-17 pilots mistook the Japanese fighters as a welcoming committee. However, even had they been forewarned, the pilots could have done nothing; they were low on fuel and their planes were unarmed. Regardless of the situation, they had to land. Separating into small groups of ones and twos, the aircraft made their way to fields all over Hawaii, one even landing on a golf course, with the result that most of the B-17s reached the ground safely. It was one of the few American successes of that morning. One Japanese pilot,

BELOW
A Japanese lieutenant in the typical garb of a naval aviator in 1941. These highly trained pilots and their superior aircraft gave the Japanese a significant edge over the Allies in the first phase of the Pacific War.

US servicemen who have just survived the Japanese attack get their first look at the damage to their airfield. Few of the 380 aircraft in the area had made it into the air to combat the Japanese – and 310 aircraft were destroyed or damaged on the ground.

Lieutenant Yoshio Shiga, was amazed to see the resilience of the big American bombers. After watching a B-17 land amid an attack by a swarm of Zero fighters at Hickam, he made a mental note that these bombers would prove worthy adversaries in the future.

At 0830 hours a short lull in the fighting ensued as the first wave of Japanese planes began to run low on fuel and had to return to their carriers. Having achieved great surprise, Fuchida's force had suffered only minimal losses, totalling five torpedo planes, one dive bomber and three fighters. The surprised defenders of Pearl Harbor began to regroup and prepare for a renewed Japanese assault. They did not have long to wait, for at 0900 hours a second wave – 80 dive bombers, 54 high-level bombers and 36 fighters – began their assault on Pearl Harbor. This time the Japanese pilots did not go unopposed, facing a pitifully few US fighters that had struggled off the ground during the brief respite. Though their numbers were possibly only 14, the US pilots held their own amid

the tumult, with two pilots, Lieutenants Welch and Taylor, accounting for five enemy kills. In addition, anti-aircraft fire was much stronger during the second wave of Japanese attacks, claiming the loss of six Japanese fighters and 14 dive bombers. However, once again, a flight of American aircraft stumbled into Pearl Harbor; this time it was a scouting party of 18 aircraft from the distant *Enterprise*. As they made their way in to land, the planes were met with a hail of anti-aircraft fire. Only just over half of the aircraft arrived safely.

The second wave of Japanese attackers again hit the American airfields, but this time focused most of their strength on any undamaged ships in Pearl Harbor. The battleship *Pennsylvania*, which was in dry dock, became the favourite target of attack. With this mighty ship were the destroyers *Downes* and *Cassin*. Although the *Pennsylvania* suffered only minor damage, nearly every bomb that missed her seemed to hit *Downes* and *Cassin*, and in the end both were destroyed. Nearby, to the west, the destroyer *Shaw* occupied a floating dry dock. Shortly after 0930 hours, a direct hit ignited her powder magazine, resulting in an incredible explosion. Guns and bodies flew everywhere and an observer over 0.8km (0.5 miles) away on Ford Island was nearly struck by the debris. By 1000 hours the last of the Japanese attackers circled the harbour to leave. The attack was over.

At Pearl Harbor, six battleships had been sunk, and a total of 18 ships were damaged. This was indeed a severe blow to the strength of the US Pacific Fleet. A total of 3600 had been killed or wounded during the attack. The scene at the nearby airfields was even worse, for of the 380 aircraft that were present in the area 180 had been destroyed and a further 130 damaged. All across the area, men and women gathered to tend to the wounded and to rescue men from the oily, burning waters of Pearl Harbor and from the hulls of overturned ships.

After the second attack, Commander Fuchida returned to the Japanese carrier *Akagi* to report on the fighting. He told Admiral Nagumo that four battleships had been sunk and four were damaged, and that considerable damage had been done to the American airfields. He added that anti-aircraft fire during the second wave of attacks had been considerable, then went on to suggest that the next wave of attacks should target oil tanks, repair facilities and arsenals. He was supported in this by Commander Minoru Genda, one of the operational planners of the mission. All across the great fleet, the pilots signified their desire to return and complete the destruction of the American fleet. Nagumo then posed an important question to Fuchida: would the American fleet be out

BELOW
The remnants of Hangar Number 3 and a barracks at Wheeler Field. Many men rushed to shelter in these buildings – only to become casualties as the Japanese attackers focused much of their second-wave attack on such support structures.

BELOW
The Aichi D3A 'Val' dive bomber. Designed for carrier duties in 1936, this accurate bomber was one of the main Japanese weapons at Pearl Harbor. Though the 'Val' quickly became obsolescent, aircraft of this type sank more Allied naval vessels than any other Axis aircraft.

of action for at least six months? Fuchida answered in the affirmative, but went on to add that additional attacks should go in as soon as possible.

Nagumo was of another mind. He had never fully supported the risky attack on Pearl Harbor, but in his opinion it had succeeded. Now was the time to withdraw. For him, the purpose of the attack was to weaken the US Pacific Fleet to the point where it could not intervene in the coming Japanese military expansion in the Far East. Fuchida had confirmed that the attack had achieved this;

to Nagumo, that was enough. The possibility that the missing American carriers might turn up out of nowhere to attack the Japanese fleet still haunted him. If they appeared while his planes were being launched – or, even worse, while they were away launching a third attack on Pearl Harbor – the results would be disastrous. He believed it was best to move away with his precious fleet intact, secure in the knowledge that the American battleships would not bother Japanese expansion efforts for many months. Thus, within an hour, the order came for the fleet to turn about

Aichi D3A 'Val'

and make its way back to Japan. Fuchida and others were furious; although they had achieved a great victory, they had left the job only half done.

When news of the Japanese fleet's retirement reached Tokyo, several naval officers begged Yamamoto to order Nagumo back to Hawaii to launch further assaults. At Pearl Harbor, too, the Americans also wondered why the Japanese aircraft did not return to finish the job. Although their fleet teetered on the brink of destruction, the Japanese mission had not been a complete success. Yet still Yamamoto refused to order Nagumo to return. He believed that if Nagumo was forced to return, fearing for his fleet, he would launch a cautious attack that would be more trouble than it was worth. The Japanese fleet continued its homeward journey, confident in what it believed to be a great victory over the Americans.

Ramifications

In Washington D.C., Ambassador Nomura had been busy with last-minute negotiations with Secretary of State Cordell Hull. Specifically Nomura was busy decoding the final portion of a 14-point Japanese response to Hull's latest negotiation stance. At 1300 hours Washington time, Nomura was due to deliver the final part of the message to Hull, a message that stated that negotiations seemed to be at an end. However, a shortage of staff meant that Nomura was late. By the time the meeting took place, Hull already knew that Pearl Harbor had been attacked. He gave Nomura's document a cursory reading and then told him that in all his years of public service he had never seen such 'infamous falsehoods and distortions on a scale so huge that I never imagined until today that any government on this planet was capable of uttering them.' He then motioned Nomura to leave.

Shortly after noon on 8 December, President Roosevelt appeared before a joint session of Congress. In his speech he stated: 'Yesterday, December 7, 1941, a date which will live in infamy, the United States was suddenly and deliberately attacked by naval and

OPPOSITE

Valuable 'flying boats' were among the targets of the first Japanese attack. Fearing the unmatched reconnaissance capabilities of such craft, the Japanese left few unscathed.

BELOW

American air power in the Pacific suffered a tremendous blow at Pearl Harbor. However, the aircraft lost in the attack represented only two days of aircraft production for the industrial giant.

Pearl Harbor represented the beginning of a long, arduous war for the United States. Here, immediately after the Japanese raids, determined sailors busy themselves with the task of rearming clips and belts.

air forces of the Empire of Japan.' He did not ask Congress for a declaration of war, because he felt none was needed; he merely requested that Congress recognise that a state of war had been 'thrust upon the United States' by the Japanese attack on Pearl Harbor. In short order the resolution passed Congress with only one dissenting vote. The United States had now entered World War II.

Roosevelt did not ask Congress for a declaration of war against Germany and Italy. However, only a few days later, on 11 December, Hitler made one of his greatest errors of the war. Although not required to do so by the Tripartite Pact, since Japan had been the aggressor in the confrontation, Germany declared war on the United States, thus freeing Roosevelt to put his 'Europe first' strategy into action.

In Japan Emperor Hirohito announced to the nation that a state of war existed between Japan and the United States and Britain. His announcement contended that the United States, Britain and China had been unable to recognise the peaceful intentions of Japan and had forced Japan to the brink. He went on to say: 'The situation being such as it is, Our Empire for its existence and self defence has no other recourse but to appeal to arms and to crush every obstacle in its path.' Prime Minister Tojo then went on to inform the nation that 'The key to victory lies in a faith in victory ... as long as there remains ... this great spirit of loyalty and patriotism, we have nothing to fear.'

Tojo, though, was mistaken; his nation had much to fear. As Fuchida had believed, although the attack on Pearl Harbor was dramatic, it had not achieved its main goals. In all probability, even without attack on Pearl Harbor, the American Pacific Fleet would not have been able to intervene in Japanese expansion for more than six months, leaving the Japanese free to expand without the need for this clarion call to war. As it was, the attack on Pearl Harbor galvanised the American population like no time before or since. Yamamoto had hoped that America would not be willing to put up with the loss and sacrifice it would take to break through a ring of defences around Japan. The attack on Pearl Harbor, though, provided America with whatever will it might have lacked.

Although the loss of six battleships at Pearl Harbor was difficult to bear, most of the ships were old, and all but two were salvageable. In addition, no heavy cruiser or submarine had been struck in the raid, and none of the critical carriers were there. The lack of Japanese follow-up attacks on the base facilities at Pearl Harbor was also a critical mistake. Destruction of those facilities would have forced the US Pacific Fleet to withdraw to the coast of California, making the war in the Pacific much more difficult. Thus the raid on Pearl Harbor, although traumatic, had actually failed to neutralise the strength of the American fleet or to destroy the American ability to make war. With its carriers intact

and its unrivalled industrial capacity, the United States would soon be able to make up for the losses at Pearl Harbor which, in real terms, represented only two days of factory aircraft production.

In many ways, instead of being a crushing Japanese victory, the attack on Pearl Harbor was a failure that led to Japanese defeat. Yamamoto had known the risks and he also knew that Japan would lose a prolonged conflict with the United States, but he had hoped that the attack on Pearl Harbor would be so devastating and the accompanying Japanese expansion so overawing that the United States would choose not to fight. Such was not the case; America chose to fight on. Yet first the United States and its wartime allies would have to suffer through a period of unremitting Japanese victory while America – on the defensive – put its industrial power into motion.

BELOW

The burial of American dead at Kaneohe Naval Air Station. Yamamoto had hoped that his victory would convince the United States that a war was not worth fighting. Instead, sights like these galvanized the American population as never before.

CHAPTER THREE

JAPANESE JUGGERNAUT

After the triumph at Pearl Harbor, Japanese forces won a stunning string of victories throughout the Pacific – easily overcoming the vaunted Allied forces in Singapore and the Philippines.

While Admiral Yamamoto knew that the Japanese victory over the Americans at Pearl Harbor was flawed, the military leadership of Japan had chosen the course for war. They now decided to press their advantage with all due speed. The Japanese plan of action called for nearly simultaneous major advances into Malaya and the Philippines. Subsidiary moves would seize Hong Kong, as well as lesser Allied island possessions in the Pacific. Finally, Japanese forces would move into the Dutch East Indies. Such an assortment of offensive actions would sorely press Japanese military, naval and logistic power, but speed was of the essence. Their advance had to be complete before the stunned Americans could react and bring any major force to bear in the Pacific. Even though the American fleet was nearly crippled, force levels in the Southern Campaign were roughly equal. The Allies maintained single divisions in Burma and Hong Kong, two divisions in the Dutch East Indies, three divisions in Malaya and four divisions in the Philippines, making a total of 11. Against this force, the Japanese – who had to leave the bulk of their forces in China – sent the Southern Army with a strength of only 11 divisions, under the command of General Hiseichi Terauchi. Despite equal numbers, the Allies were at a disadvantage. Their forces had to remain in place for defensive purposes; they could never present a united front to the Japanese. Terauchi's forces, however, could rely upon surprise and mobility to force Allied units into weak positions. In addition, the Japanese enjoyed overwhelming edges in naval and air power in the area. Even so, they would be required to advance on a strict time schedule, having to fight and win several battles in which they were outnumbered in order to achieve victory during that window of opportunity.

Initial Japanese victories

The first Japanese moves in the Southern Campaign occurred on 8 January when, prior to their invasion of Malaya, their forces carried out an amphibious landing on the Kra Isthmus in Siam. The landing resulted in only nine fatalities and caught the British by surprise; they had planned to move defensive forces into Siam. The Japanese were concerned; although the initial operation had gone well, Force Z, led by the powerful British ships *Prince of Wales* and *Repulse*, was on a sortie in the area. The presence of such powerful vessels, a battleship and a battle cruiser respectively, with their escort of three destroyers, threatened any new landing operations. There were few Japanese capital ships in the area to respond to Force Z, and, if the *Prince of Wales* and *Repulse*

OPPOSITE
Thousands of Allied prisoners await their fate. Their Japanese captors, who abhorred the idea of surrender, routinely treated their prisoners with a great deal of barbarity.

The Japanese cruiser Mogami *on trials in the Bungo Straits in 1935. The dominance of their fleet gave the Japanese a crucial edge during their unbroken string of victories in 1942.*

attacked fully loaded Japanese troop ships, the results would be disastrous. Some in the Japanese Navy were perplexed, but once again Admiral Yamamoto had the answer. After a Japanese submarine had spotted the British ships off Indo-China, Yamamoto – a prime advocate of naval air power – ordered land-based aircraft in the area to destroy them. On the morning of 10 December, 84 bombers and torpedo planes duly located and attacked Force Z. The British ships put up a hail of anti-aircraft fire but the one-sided battle was over in less than an hour. The *Repulse* was struck by 10 torpedoes and suffered a direct hit from a 250kg (550lb) bomb, sinking within minutes. A total of seven torpedoes and two 500kg (1100lb) bombs slammed into the *Prince of Wales*, which took nearly an hour to sink. The threat to future Japanese landings had been dealt with and British naval power in the Pacific destroyed. The age-old argument over whether aircraft could sink battleships was answered emphatically; the war in the Pacific would be won in the air.

The American Far East Air Force was a formidable weapon of war, numbering some 277 planes, including 35 heavy bombers and 100 modern fighters. However, it was located mainly at Clark Field outside Manila. As it was within the range of land-based Japanese bombers, this location remains highly controversial. It was expected that the Philippines would be attacked upon the

outbreak of war with Japan, and the fact that the planes were not removed from harm's way is inexcusable. In the early morning of 8 December, these American forces in the Philippines received word of the attack on Pearl Harbor. General Lewis Brereton, commander of MacArthur's air forces, quickly requested that he be allowed to launch an air strike against Japanese forces in Taiwan, but approval for his bombing mission did not come until nearly noon. His bombers were warming their engines when 54 Japanese bombers and 36 Zero fighters appeared overhead. Like they had at Pearl Harbor, Japanese pilots found the American planes grouped closely together, forming a wonderful target. At a cost of only seven aircraft, the Japanese wiped out over half of the American air strength in the Philippines in a matter of minutes. It was a disaster for the Americans, a disaster that MacArthur and Brereton should have avoided. However, for the Japanese, the victory assured air supremacy, which would prove to be a critical advantage during the battle to take the Philippines, for when the Japanese landings finally came American air power could do nothing.

In the Pacific, Vice Admiral Inouye and the 4th Fleet were tasked with the seizure of Guam and Wake Islands. While Guam fell nearly without a shot, Wake was a different matter. Located nearly 1600km (1000 miles) east of Midway Island, it was an important defensive outpost and the site of newly constructed US defences. In addition, Admiral Kimmel had made plans to send aircraft carrier task forces to the island's aid in the event of an attack.

Japanese aircraft from Kwajalein Atoll struck Wake shortly after the first attacks at Pearl Harbor. Though the damage was significant, the 450 US marines in their defensive works were not overawed, as the Japanese invasion force would soon learn. When they reached Wake on 11 December – supported by three light cruisers and six destroyers – the marines, manning 127mm (5in) shore guns and anti-aircraft batteries, waited until the fleet approached to within 4572m (15,000ft) before opening fire. The results were devastating: two destroyers were sunk and all of the Japanese cruisers were heavily damaged. As the invasion fleet turned to flee, the four surviving American planes on Wake attacked, severely damaging a troop transport.

Hoping to relieve the Wake Island defenders and ambush a portion of the Japanese fleet, Kimmel had ordered the *Saratoga* to the scene; but he had also fallen from favour in the wake of the Pearl Harbor disaster and consequently had been removed from command. Unbelievably, this move took place before the new commander of the Pacific Fleet, Admiral Chester Nimitz, had even reached Pearl Harbor, and the relief attempt at Wake Island was now under the direction of Vice Admiral William Pye, with only temporary command.

In this power vacuum, the *Saratoga* made its way toward Wake Island. Had the carrier moved more quickly, it could have destroyed the Japanese invasion fleet and possibly saved the island's defenders. However, Pye was unwilling to take risks in his interim position, and all three American carrier groups remained just out of reach of the island. A new, more powerful Japanese invasion fleet approached, this time including the carriers *Soryu* and *Hiryu*

BELOW

Japanese troops mop up the last resistance in Kuala Lumpur. Their lightning-quick advance through Malaya placed the British fortress of Singapore at great risk.

on their way home from Pearl Harbor. Even so, the combined might of the American carriers could have won the day, but still they stood back from the coming fight. Although the Marines resisted valiantly, Wake Island fell on 23 December. The Japanese now dominated the central Pacific and the route between the United States and the Philippines had been severed.

British defeat in Malaya

In the Far East, the island of Singapore was the crown jewel of British imperial possessions. Its capital, Singapore – an important port, connected to Malaya only by a causeway – was defended by three divisions, including British, Australian and Indian troops. The island bristled with coastal defences, but these powerful guns were meant to protect Singapore against an invasion from the sea, and would be of little use in defending the port against a land-based assault from the north. While Britain hoped that the 'Gibraltar of the east' would be able to hold out against a concerted Japanese attack, American planners believed the port to be far too vulnerable to a land assault, and that its garrison was inadequate. To protect Singapore, the British had not prepared northern Malaya for a defensive stand, but rather had long planned to move their forces forward into Siam. Little did they know that the Japanese would pre-empt this move with their own invasion.

The Japanese attack on Siam took place on 8 December. It was audacious, relying initially on only one division. In fact, during the entire campaign, the Japanese were outnumbered on the ground by 2 to 1, but made up for this by speed of movement and

BELOW

Japanese troops storm into Kuala Lumpur during the campaign in Malaya. During their advance the Japanese often used bicycles to speed down jungle trails and stay one step ahead of defending Allied forces.

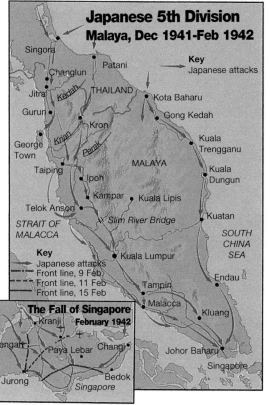

Japanese 5th Division
Malaya, Dec 1941-Feb 1942

Key
→ Japanese attacks

Singora
Changlun
Patani
Jitra — Kedah
THAILAND
Gurun
Kota Baharu
Kron
Gong Kedah
George Town — Krian — Perak
Kuala Trengganu
Taiping
MALAYA
Kuala Dungun
Ipoh
Kampar
Kuala Lipis
Telok Anson
STRAIT OF MALACCA
Slim River Bridge
Kuatan
SOUTH CHINA SEA

Key
Japanese attacks
Front line, 9 Feb
Front line, 11 Feb
Front line, 15 Feb

Kuala Lumpur
Tampin
Endau
Malacca
Kluang
Johor Baharu

The Fall of Singapore
February 1942
Kranji
Tengah
Paya Lebar
Changi
Jurong
Bedok
Singapore

command of the air and sea. After landing, Japanese forces of the 25th Army began twin offensives southward toward Jitra and Patani. British forces in the area – mainly the 11th Indian Division – found themselves extremely vulnerable in the face of the rapid Japanese advance. However, their presence was seen as essential, since the British were loathe to cede the important agricultural area of northern Malaya to Japanese control, and furthermore Japanese possession of airfields in the area put Singapore at even greater risk. As a result, at the end of a long and tenuous supply line, British forces in northern Malaya were left in exposed positions to face the brunt of the Japanese attack.

These British forces had hoped that the dense jungle terrain would help their defence. However, the lightly equipped Japanese infantry soon proved to be adept at jungle fighting. With relative ease, their infantry moved down even the smallest jungle trail on bicycles they had brought with them. Shocked by the speed of the Japanese

ABOVE

Malay soldiers took part in the defence of Malaya alongside British, Indian and Australian troops. Here, a Malay soldier is on the alert in typical swamp country. British forces hoped that the unforgiving jungle terrain would aid in their defensive efforts – but the Japanese proved masters of jungle warfare.

advance, British forces in sketchy defences near Betong found their flanks turned and were forced to retreat. Similarly, on 14 and 15 December the 11th Indian Division faced the Japanese 5th Division in battle near Jitra. Although the Indian unit consisted of recent recruits and newly minted British officers, these were poorly trained in jungle warfare. Lacking unit cohesion, they were unable to stem the onslaught of one of the most professional armies in the world. Like the forces near Betong, they were surprised by the speed of the Japanese advance and were often in danger of envelopment. The 11th Indian Division quickly began to crumble. Only with the greatest difficulty and after the loss of two brigades did it break free and manage to begin a fighting retreat to the south. For the British, these battles on the Malay frontier had been disastrous, resulting in twin defeats

as the Japanese routinely outmanoeuvred their stunned opponent. After retreating behind the Perak River, they waited, hoping to make a stand there.

Once behind the river obstacle, the British forces aimed to wage a fighting retreat down the peninsula, slowly falling back to prepared defensive positions and thus transforming the war in Malaya into one of attrition that the Japanese could ill afford. However, they found that the jungle terrain worked against them; they were spread far too thinly to guard every road, track and river path. After launching probing attacks, the Japanese located the clearest route to British and Indian positions, then advanced around them, sometimes even reaching the next proposed defensive line before the Allied troops. In addition, the Japanese had brought their assault boats which, given

due to constant retreat, the 11th Indian suffered a disastrous defeat. Japanese forces, again threatening to outflank it, completely annihilated two of its brigades in a brutal battle along the Slim River.

The drive to Singapore

Desperate to defend their 'Gibraltar of the East', the British sent two additional divisions to reinforce the garrison at Singapore, but this force did not arrive until 3 January. By this point, the string of defeats in Malaya had made the situation of the British forces in Singapore increasingly untenable. The disaster on the Slim River and the threats of continued amphibious landings forced them to pull back to positions in central Johore, the Malay province immediately north of the now vulnerable Singapore. Japanese forces rushed to take advantage of their Slim River victory. On 14 January they entered Johore, only to run headlong into the strong defences of the 8th Australian Division at Gemas. Expecting to face a less resolute foe, they were met with a surprise. Fully trained and spoiling for a battle, the Australians fought with grim tenacity and inflicted a defeat on the Japanese 5th Infantry Division, which had seen constant action since it had landed in Malaya. Had all of the Allied divisions in Malaya been of this quality, Singapore's defence might have been quite different.

Despite their tenacity at Gemas, the Australians quickly found themselves flanked. An entire Japanese battalion had landed behind them on the coast, and the Japanese Imperial Guards Division had broken through a British defensive line farther west. Once again, Japanese mobility and initiative had turned a defeat into a victory, while another Allied unit found itself executing a fighting withdrawal in danger of destruction. However, due to the actions of a brave rearguard in a defensive stand near Pelandok, which involved savage, sometimes hand-to-hand fighting, the 8th Australian Division managed to avoid encirclement and make its way to the south.

By 15 January the Japanese had driven south over 643km (400 miles) in a campaign of almost bewildering speed, rather like the Germans' Blitzkrieg in Europe. Now only 160km (100 miles) from Singapore itself, the Japanese 25th Army redoubled its efforts. In 10 days of heavy fighting, they drove the Allied forces ever southward. With Japanese advancing all around them and landings taking

Japanese naval and air superiority, launched amphibious landings behind British defensive positions almost at will. Thus British forces found themselves routinely outflanked both by land and by sea, and the result was a slow, fighting withdrawal, with brave rearguards struggling to thwart Japanese envelopment of the defenders.

The hardest pressed of the British units was the beleaguered 11th Indian Division, which routinely had to fight desperate rearguard actions as it tried to cover the main road through Malaya. The commanding general in the area, British General A.E. Percival, sent the 9th Indian Division – which had seen comparatively little action defending eastern Malaya – to reinforce the 11th Indian Division, but, making a critical error, issued his orders far too late. On 7 January, exhausted, low on supplies and suffering from low morale

place behind them, all British, Indian and Australian troops were forced to evacuate Malaya by 31 January and take refuge in the city of Singapore. The last troops marched across the causeway accompanied by the droning of the pipers of the 2nd Argyll and Sutherland Highlanders. The 'Gibraltar of the East' would have to stand on its own.

While the British were falling back towards Singapore, two disasters struck their Far Eastern empire. After a spirited defence by a force of British regulars and Canadian militia, Hong Kong fell to Japanese rule on Christmas Day. In a chaos reminiscent of the 'Rape of Nanking', the victorious Japanese troops ran amok. Entering an infirmary at St Stephen's College, Japanese soldiers systematically bayoneted the wounded to death in their beds. Any doctors or nurses who attempted to interfere received similar treatment. After the carnage, the soldiers destroyed the furniture and used it as a makeshift funeral pyre upon which to burn the corpses. The terrified

nurses were all herded into a room and were kept imprisoned there while Japanese soldiers spent two days repeatedly raping them to the extent that their victims could not remember how many times they had been raped.

The second disaster for the British was that Japanese forces invaded British Borneo. For the Japanese, this island offered much-needed oil reserves. After three amphibious landings had surrounded the small British garrison there, on 21 January they landed a force at Balikpapan and seized the oilfield refineries of the city intact. One of the Allies' last remaining naval forces – four destroyers under the command of American Rear Admiral W.A. Glassford – was located nearby, off the island of Timor. In an attempt to ward off the Japanese, Glassford took his tiny force to strike at the vulnerable Japanese transports off Balikpapan and, on the night of 24 January, the ships launched the first American naval battle of World War II. Sneaking undetected into the midst

of the Japanese transports, the destroyers sunk four Japanese transports, using both torpedoes and their 127mm (5in) guns, before withdrawing with no casualties. Yet it was only a small victory amid catastrophic defeat; all resistance on Borneo had faltered by the end of January.

The price of surrender

In Singapore the Allied force, now numbering some 45 battalions, made ready to withstand an attack from the 31 battalions of the Japanese 25th Army. The British command under Percival was supposed to be able to resist for an almost indefinite length of time, especially given its considerable edge in manpower, but once again the Japanese held a critical edge in air and naval power, as well as retaining the initiative. The northern shore of Singapore Island, only 1.6km (1 mile) distant from the mainland, was a vulnerable stretch of 48km (30 miles). Percival expected a Japanese attack at any point along the coast,

and was forced to spread his defending forces thinly at a ratio of one battalion per mile. The remainder of the force was held in a central, mobile reserve which was meant to rush to the scene of a Japanese invasion. On 8 February the Japanese launched the bulk of their forces across the Johore Strait, striking a defensive force of only six Australian battalions. Facing these superior numbers, the Australians fought valiantly, but had to fall back. Even the intervention of the central reserve force was not enough to force the Japanese invaders back into the sea. Yet again, an inferior Japanese force had used speed and audacity to gain a local superiority in numbers and win a crushing victory.

Allied forces, now squarely on the defensive, fought rearguard actions as they fell back into Singapore itself. On 15 February the British command team faced an unexpected disaster: the Japanese seized the reservoirs that supplied water to Singapore. With no fresh water for such a massive city, Percival now

BELOW

After the loss of the critical municipal water supply, on the evening of 15 February 1942 General Percival (carrying the Union Jack) trudges toward Japanese lines to surrender his force at Singapore. In the greatest disaster in British military history, 130,000 soldiers surrendered to a Japanese army less than half that size. The 'Gibraltar of the East' had fallen.

had to consider the possibility of a fantastically high civilian death toll. Realising that the end was at hand, and unwilling to be the cause of an urban catastrophe, Percival decided to surrender. On the evening of 15 February he trudged toward the Japanese lines carrying a Union Jack, accompanied by one of his officers carrying a white flag of truce. The Japanese, who considered surrender to be the greatest disgrace imaginable, were shocked to see Percival nearing their lines. In what has been called the greatest disaster ever in British military history, Percival surrendered his force of 130,000 to a Japanese Army that was only half the size.

The 'Gibraltar of the East' had fallen virtually without a fight. Disgraced forever, Percival and his forces entered captivity under the Japanese. True to form, Japanese soldiers ran riot over a defeated enemy, with the commanding officer of the Imperial Guards Division actively encouraging deplorable behaviour in his troops. The British, Indian and Australian prisoners-of-war were herded into makeshift prison camps where they lived under horrific conditions until their fates were decided by their captors. Many of the Indian troops found a way out of the bestial prison system by joining the Indian National Army in order to fight alongside the Japanese against British rule of their homeland. General Tojo, who was now a virtual dictator in his country, quickly decided upon the fate of the remaining prisoners-of-war: they would be put to work.

The Japanese had decided to construct a railroad through Siam into Burma to connect their newly won empire. It was a nearly impossible task, for the railroad had to cross steaming jungles, high mountains and raging rivers, but the Allied prisoners-of-war would be used as forced labour. Hated, beaten, malnourished and stricken by disease, the prisoners moved from camp to camp along the line of the railroad, working at backbreaking tasks. Amazingly, they completed the railroad, but at a horrendous cost. Over 16,000 Allied prisoners-of-war and 60,000 native forced labourers died during its construction. The once-proud army of Singapore had been destroyed in one of the worst war crimes of World War II.

ABOVE
In this photograph from the Japanese propaganda magazine Freedom, *published in Shanghai, Japanese lieutenant Matsuda announces the fall of Singapore to stunned British prisoners at an internment camp near Hong Kong.*

A US Marine of the 1st Defense Battalion, which numbered 450 men and was tasked with defending Wake Island. The first Japanese amphibious assault on the island – on 8 December 1941 – was beaten off, but two weeks later, when the Japanese returned with 1000 troops, they soon had the small Marine detachment surrounded. With no hope of relief, the defenders were forced to surrender.

ABDA

As Japanese forces ran riot through Malaya, Borneo and later the Philippines, it quickly became obvious that the wealth of natural resources held by the Dutch East Indies would be among their targets. Except for the invasion of Borneo on 16 December, the Japanese had not made any moves into the islands of the East Indies, as they were waiting for their lines of communication to be secured by victories further north. In addition, their military command realised that British and American forces in Singapore and the Philippines presented the greatest threat; the Dutch forces in the East Indies could be mopped up later.

The threat to the East Indies was especially troubling to Australia, which was virtually defenceless, having sent the bulk of its army to help in the war in Europe. As a result, the Allied forces in the East Indies, scattered over a wide area of the bewildering island chain, scrambled to attain some kind of command unity and ABDA (American-British-Dutch-Australian) Command was created. On 10 January.1942, General Archibald Wavell arrived on Java to take control of his forces, but it was already too late.

On paper it seemed that ABDA could marshal an imposing force, including Australian home defence forces and the Dutch East Indies Army. Although large in numbers, these forces had received little in the way of training and often consisted of indifferent Dutch native troops. They had little air support and, in addition, were never joined

in an effective way, but were littered about the East Indies in a vain attempt to defend everything. The ABDA naval force, however, was more formidable. It consisted of 11 cruisers, 27 destroyers and 40 submarines: the surviving elements of the British, Dutch, Australian and American Asiatic fleets. Against this rather ragtag force, the Japanese planned to use only two divisions of their best troops, aided by speed, surprise and massive naval and air support. Their plan called for a two-pronged assault through the island chain, aimed at the isolation of Java. The Japanese carrier fleet, still basking in the

glory of Pearl Harbor, was stationed south of the invasion forces to shield against any major enemy attack.

The East Indies fall

On 11 January the Japanese opened their offensive by striking the Celebes. However, although the amphibious landings at Menado went well, they botched their first paratroop drop of the war. Jumping from too great a height, the 334 Japanese paratroopers were scattered all over the island, serving only to confuse their own advancing troops. Despite this setback, the tiny Dutch garrison of 1500 men was quickly overwhelmed and the airfields of the northern Celebes were now ready for Japanese use. Their forces followed with amphibious landings at three further locations on the island, soon crushing the remainder of the rather weak Dutch resistance before moving further east and attacking the islands of Ambon and Timor in order to sever the lines of communication between the East Indies and Australia. However, there they were met with a struggle. ABDA forces on these islands were leavened with Australian and American units that fought a spirited, if doomed, defence. The Australians particularly

ABOVE

A new colonial ruler takes control. In a show of martial strength, Japanese troops march near the Battery Road in Singapore, not far away from the Raffles Hotel – once a bastion of British rule.

fought with a dogged determination, realising that the Japanese offensive might be aimed at the eventual occupation of their homeland.

Australia's fear of invasion was to become all too real. Realising that Australia's northernmost port, Port Darwin, served as a supply base for ADBA operations as well as a naval base, the Japanese navy ordered Nagumo's carriers to deal with the threat. Accordingly, at 1000 hours on 19 February, 188 Japanese aircraft swooped down on Port Darwin. Four of the carriers that had taken part in the attack on Pearl Harbor formed the nucleus of the strike force. Once again, the raiders concentrated their initial fire on naval vessels in the harbour, sinking eight before moving on to the destruction of the military facilities around the harbour. Unlike at Pearl Harbor, they also struck the town itself, setting it ablaze and forcing the population to flee. The raiders had managed to destroy Port Darwin as a functional naval base and had lost only two aircraft.

Even though Australian forces fought grimly on in both Ambon and Timor, both had fallen by the end of February. The

Japanese pincers were now closing on Java. In late February, the Japanese made plans to land the 48th Division on the island to administer the *coup de grâce* to the Dutch East Indies. However, on 24 February American patrol planes caught sight of the Japanese invasion fleet near the island of Bawean in the Java Sea. It was protected by four cruisers and 14 destroyers, and was under the command of Admiral Takeo Takagi. Under the command of Admiral Karel Doorman, an ABDA naval force – five cruisers and 12 destroyers – sallied forth from its base at Surabaya to meet this fleet at sea in an effort to stop the amphibious landing in its tracks. After nearly three days of searching, it sighted its target. Thus the Battle of the Java Sea began with an hour-long gunnery duel at long range. Initially both sides proved less than accurate in their gunnery efforts, until an armour-piercing shell struck and severely damaged the British cruiser *Exeter*. Forced to guard the stricken ship, Doorman turned his fleet away to break off the engagement, and the Japanese destroyers quickly responded with a torpedo attack that sank one of the

BELOW

In a historic and tense meeting at 1900 hours on 15 February, a stern-faced General Yamashita dictates surrender terms to the defeated British General Percival at Singapore.

Dutch destroyers, but Doorman made good his escape.

Although he had to send most of his own destroyer force back to port for refuelling, Doorman chose to renew the attack on the Japanese fleet at night, hoping to break through to the vulnerable troop transports. Shortly after 2230 hours his force, now numbering only four cruisers and one destroyer, stumbled onto the Japanese fleet once again. The Japanese, who had given considerable emphasis to training in night-fighting techniques, were not at all surprised. Launching a punishing torpedo barrage from 7315m (24,000ft), they made quick work of the battle, sinking the Dutch cruisers *De Ruyter* and *Java* and killing Doorman. The other cruisers, the USS *Houston* and

the HMAS *Perth*, both escaped, but Takagi hunted down the stricken ships with a ruthless efficiency, catching them the next night. *Houston* and *Perth* fought against the superior Japanese fleet for hours until their ammunition was spent and they had to resort to firing illumination rounds at the enemy. They gave as good as they got, sinking or damaging six Japanese ships, before they were finally destroyed. The Battle of the Java Sea had ended, and with it any ABDA hopes for victory. ABDA naval forces had been destroyed and their sacrifice had delayed the invasion of Java by only a single day. Having been beaten at sea, the result on land was inevitable. The 48th Division landed on Java on 1 March and faced only light resistance. Although some Dutch regulars fought with

ABOVE

In August 1945, after the defeat of Japan, a victorious General MacArthur embraces General Percival (left) who had surrendered at Singapore and General Wainwright (right) who surrendered to the Japanese upon the fall of Corregidor in the Philippines. Both men clearly show the signs of their long captivity.

spirit, their native soldiers had seen enough. Never satisfied with Dutch rule, much of the population of the East Indies saw the Japanese as liberators, and would later prove to be enthusiastic collaborators in Japanese rule. Realising that all was lost, Dutch forces at Batavia (now Jakarta) surrendered on 2 March and, on 12 March, all Allied forces in the area surrendered. ABDA was now no more. Only two pockets of resistance remained in South East Asia: Burma and the Philippines.

The fall of Burma

The British colony of Burma occupied a strategically important place in South East Asia, standing between the advancing Japanese forces and the most important British colony of all: India. It also served as the main supply route to Chiang Kai-shek's forces in China. This supply route began at Rangoon, Burma's capital and main port, and extended by rail to Lashio, some 965km (600 miles) north. From there, supplies followed the Burma Road to China. Having been claimed as a British colony only in 1886, Burma still chafed at British rule and several leading Burmese dissidents had even gone to Japan for training in how to resist their British overlords. As a result, a high level of tension existed in much of the colony and the single division raised from the native population was of dubious value. In January 1941 the British theatre commander, General Wavell, ordered the 17th Indian Division into the colony to stiffen defences there. Other Allied forces were there as well, for the Chinese 66th Army guarded the Burma Road in the north, and an additional two Chinese divisions, under the command of General 'Vinegar Joe' Stilwell, protected the China-Burma border. In the air, the Allies could only rely on the strength of one British squadron and one squadron of the 'Flying Tigers'. However, British forces in the area did not expect the Japanese to attack Burma until the invasion of Malaya had run its course. Believing that they had time to prepare, the 17th Division moved to the Salween River to ready their defensive lines, but the Japanese 15th Army, under the command of General Shojira Iida, had no intentions of waiting. On 16 January the force, numbering two well-trained divisions, began their invasion with 300 aircraft in support.

The Allied air forces, especially the 'Flying Tigers', fought hard in the defence of Rangoon, but were soon overwhelmed, giving the Japanese air supremacy throughout the region. Using speed and enveloping movements, the Japanese overthrew the Allied positions on the Salween River by early February, forcing the 17th Division to retreat to the Sittang River in defence of Rangoon itself. During the retreat, Japanese troops struck the 17th Division in the flank and attacked the only bridge over the Sittang. In something of a panic, the British commander at the bridge blew it up, hoping to hold the Japanese at bay. This was a terrible mistake; the 17th Division was still on the wrong side of the river. Fighting its way through the attempted envelopment, its men were faced with disaster when they reached the shattered bridge; it had been their only escape route. Desperate men threw down their weapons and swam across the torrent. Although 3300 reached the other side and safety, many of their weapons had been lost and the unit was now thoroughly demoralised.

It was into this dire situation that the British sent General Harold Alexander to command the tottering Allied forces. Arriving in Rangoon on 5 March, Alexander soon realised that the city was doomed, for the Japanese were already encircling it from the north and had nearly blocked all routes out of it. Making good their escape, Allied forces – now reinforced by an armoured brigade – left Rangoon on the last available open road and headed north to Prome. On reaching Rangoon, the Japanese stopped briefly to be joined by the fresh 18th and 56th Divisions and 100 additional aircraft, before the reinvigorated 15th Army pursued the retreating Allies into the Irrawaddy River valley. Alexander had hoped to hold firm south of Mandalay, where his force was soon joined by a Chinese division, but his plans collapsed in the face of Japanese advances on both of his flanks. On 24 March, after sharp defeats at Prome and Toungoo, the Allies were forced to retreat yet again. Adding to the growing debacle were mounting Japanese victories over Chinese forces in the north. By April, the Japanese stood ready to assault Mandalay.

Demoralised, running out of supplies and fatigued, the Allied forces could only decide to part ways and abandon Burma. The nationalist Chinese chose to exit to the north via the Burma Road, while other Chinese followed Stilwell up the Irrawaddy and through the

mountains to safety. Alexander and the British forces marched north-west to Kalewa, hoping to help guard the now-endangered eastern frontier of India. However, the British route of retreat wound through the nearly trackless jungle. Accompanied by thousands of Burmese civilians, the British force slowly made its way toward India and safety, constantly harried by the advancing Japanese and only days ahead of the monsoon rains. During this epic retreat, many of the native forces deserted and thousands more died in the jungle heat. On 17 May, the survivors reached Imphal. Of the 30,000 British troops who had begun the campaign, only 17,000 remained. Burma had fallen and the Japanese now stood at the doorstep to India.

The fall of the Philippines

Perhaps the most critical campaign in the Japanese southern advance took place in the Philippines. Here, it was hoped that strong American forces under the command of the brash MacArthur would be able to stand against Japanese invasion for months, giving the United States time to marshal its forces.

It was assumed that MacArthur's army would be a perpetual thorn in the Japanese side. One American reporter summed up the popular belief that 'If the Japs come down here they will be playing in the big leagues for the first time in their lives'. However, the American forces in the Philippines looked strong on paper, but in reality were quite weak. A total of 16,000 US combat troops were augmented by a huge army of Filipinos, but the latter were poorly trained and equipped and simply not ready to take part in battle. Making matters worse, MacArthur had lost the bulk of his air forces due to a Japanese attack on 8 December, only 10 hours after the attack on Pearl Harbor. In contrast, the Japanese invasion force, commanded by General Masaharu Homma, consisted of two crack divisions, the 16th and the 48th – veterans of the fighting in China – supported by three massive fleets totalling two aircraft carriers, two battleships, 13 cruisers and 31 destroyers. The aircraft of the carriers were supplemented by land-based aircraft operating out of Taiwan.

After staging preliminary landings, the main Japanese force struck on 22 December

ABOVE

A rare photograph depicting Japanese invasion forces nearing the beach at Lingayen Gulf in the Philippines. MacArthur mistakenly attempted to defeat the Japanese invasion on the beaches, leading to disaster at Bataan.

Japanese troops make ready to accept the surrender of Filipino forces approaching under a flag of truce. MacArthur placed far too much reliance on his under-trained and poorly supplied Filipino soldiers.

at Lingayen Gulf on the main Philippine island of Luzon. MacArthur, believing in the strength of his army, eschewed the old scheme, Plan Orange. This had called for a retreat to the rugged Bataan Peninsula near the capital city of Manila, where, relying on stockpiled supplies, MacArthur's force could stand on prepared defensive positions and hold out while waiting for help to arrive. By December, MacArthur thought that the strength of his army was such that he could hold all of Luzon against Japanese invasion. Consequently, his new plan called for meeting and defeating the invading Japanese on the beaches, and the supplies for the defending forces were relocated accordingly.

On the day of the invasion, MacArthur's mistake became immediately apparent. Two half-trained, ill-equipped and over-extended Filipino divisions met Homma's battle-hardened veterans on the beaches of Lingayen Gulf and, on their first day of combat, faced a fearsome combination of concentrated Japanese infantry, naval and air assaults. As they began to crumble against the onslaught, General Jonathan Wainwright, commanding

the forces in northern Luzon, threw his best unit – the highly trained Philippine Scouts – into the fray in an effort to stabilise the deteriorating situation. In a gallant stand, 450 Philippine Scouts without anti-tank weapons held up a Japanese armoured column for two hours, allowing the other Filipino units to escape to the south.

MacArthur soon realised his mistake as the Filipinos fled from the Japanese attack. 'Viewing the broken, fleeing North Luzon Force [MacArthur] realised that his cherished plan of defeating an attempt to advance toward Manila from the north was not now possible.' Belatedly, he returned to the idea of mounting a stand on the Bataan Peninsula. However, his forces would now have to fight their way back there, a distance of some 240km (150 miles), through rugged terrain. Making matters worse, the American and Filipino soldiers had abandoned the majority of their much-needed supplies during their flight to the south. The situation became even more tenuous when a second Japanese force of 7000 men landed at Lamon Bay south of Manila and began their own advance upon the Philippine capital. However, all was not lost for the main American force. At this point in the campaign, General Homma made a critical mistake which enabled them to escape. His orders had called for a quick seizure of Manila, where he expected them to make their last stand. Not suspecting that the Americans were actually headed for Bataan, Homma did not press his advantage in that direction. Despite this, he succeeded in capturing Manila on 2 January.

The American and Filipino forces anchored their defensive line on Mount Natib. Their supplies were already low; the situation could only steadily worsen. The defenders were on half-rations of only 2000 calories a day. There was no fresh meat or fruit and only enough rice to last 20 days. In an effort to find food, the cavalry shot and ate its horses and then hunted down and killed water buffaloes. Making matters worse, medical supplies of all kinds were in short supply. As a result of malnutrition and the tropical conditions, diseases including malaria, scurvy, beriberi and dysentery soon swept through the forces. By March, 500 people per day were being admitted to hospital for malaria alone. Wainwright would later write: 'Our perpetual hunger, the steaming heat by day and night, the terrible malaria and the moans of the wounded were terribly hard on the men.' Even though a few intrepid submarine commanders were able to run the blockade, the dominance of the Japanese Navy made certain that few supplies would reach the beleaguered defenders of Bataan. MacArthur pleaded with Washington for help, but he received none. Mounting a relief expedition would take time and would involve placing the remainder of the American fleet at risk, a risk that Roosevelt was not prepared to take. The defenders of the Philippines were on their own.

Disaster on Bataan

In early January, Homma's forces struck the American lines near Mount Natib. Initially the Japanese assaults were rebuffed at heavy cost by murderous artillery fire. However, a Japanese battalion did what the Americans thought impossible and infiltrated through rough terrain of Mount Natib itself, appearing behind the American lines. In danger of being cut off, American and Filipino soldiers retreated south, having to leave much of their artillery behind, but by 26 January, they once again held

firm on the Bagac-Orion line. There were now 83,000 defenders and 26,000 civilian refugees crowded into an area of only 16 square km (10 square miles). Both sides settled down along the Bagac-Orion line. Although the defender's position had weakened considerably, the Japanese too had suffered heavy losses and were gripped by supply shortages and disease. Only the Japanese, however, could expect to receive additional supplies and reinforcement; Bataan would fall in only a matter of time.

Although MacArthur had made several critical mistakes in his defence of the Philippines, and was disliked by his men – who referred to him as 'Dugout Doug' for his propensity to stay far behind the lines – MacArthur became a hero in the United States. Amid unrelenting worldwide defeat, only the defence of Bataan stood out as a bright spot. Newspapers ran constant headlines lauding the American stand at Bataan and the glorious general who commanded the gallant defenders. In the midst of defeat – largely of his own making – MacArthur became America's first hero of the war, receiving the Congressional Medal of Honor and a $500,000 payment from the president of the Philippines. Although the fall of the Philippines was now inevitable, Roosevelt decided that the hero was too valuable to sacrifice. On 12 March, on Roosevelt's orders, MacArthur left the Philippines by ship, promising to those left behind in Bataan: 'I shall return.' These words would serve to stir American imagination later in the war, but in March 1942 they held very little weight with the weary troops, who realised that their commander had fled.

Command of the American and Filipino forces on Bataan now fell to Wainwright, who knew that the end was near, but was determined to fight to the last. After defeating several Japanese amphibious landings to their south, the defenders once again settled down to wait for the coming cataclysm. General Homma, although unhappy with the slow pace of the war in the Philippines, was satisfied to wait for the arrival of reinforcements before launching any new offensive. At the beginning of April, due to

BELOW
A Subedar-Major of the 20th Burma Rifles. Considerable tension exisited in Burma between the Burmese people and the British colonials. Many native soldiers, if they had not already deserted, died in the jungle on their long retreat back to Imphal after the fall of Burma.

the victories elsewhere in South East Asia, two fresh divisions finally arrived and, on 3 April, the Japanese launched a final, all-out push to destroy the defenders of Bataan.

From the safety of Australia and now quite out of touch, MacArthur ordered a massive counter-attack. His troops could not obey the fantastic order. Rations on Bataan were down to 1000 calories a day, 'barely sufficient to sustain life without physical activity'. Nearly 80 per cent of the front line troops were suffering from malaria, 75 per cent had dysentery and 35 per cent had beriberi. The front totally collapsed. Having moved his headquarters to the heavily defended island of Corregidor in Manila Bay, Wainwright realised that surrender was the only option for the men on Bataan, sending them the message 'God help you all over there.' Early in the morning of 9 April, the remaining

American and Filipino forces on Luzon surrendered. Now only the fortified island of Corregidor remained between the Japanese and total victory.

Corregidor bristled with gun batteries designed to repel sea attacks. In addition, many of the rocky island's defenders could take refuge in a tunnel system that was impervious to Japanese artillery fire. The troops on the island were at a distinct disadvantage; they were low on all types of supplies, especially water, and the ragtag, disease-ridden group of defenders had little ammunition. Determined to bring the Southern Campaign to an end, Homma ringed Corregidor with over 100 artillery pieces and launched a devastating barrage that continued for over three weeks. On 4 May alone, nearly 16,000 shells struck the island prior to the Japanese assault.

BELOW

A bevy of Japanese soldiers escorts a lone American prisoner in the Philippines. At first the Japanese haul of prisoners was small – but as the fighting on Bataan intensified they would soon find themselves inundated with captives.

LEFT
US forces on Bataan were dangerously low on all types of supplies – in part due to a Japanese blockade. Some ships did try to run the gauntlet, but most failed, like this vessel sunk off Corregidor Island.

BELOW
The agonizing Allied retreat on the Bataan Peninsula claimed hundreds of lives.

Manning the few intact shore batteries, US Marines took a heavy toll on the attackers as they approached; however, the Japanese were soon able to get both their infantry and their tanks ashore.

The end was at hand. At 1000 hours General Wainwright sent a last message to Washington, 'Please say to the nation that my troops and I have accomplished all that is humanly possible and that we have upheld the best traditions of the Unites States and its Army ... With profound regret and with continued pride in my gallant troops I go to meet the Japanese commander.' And Corregidor surrendered.

The 'Bataan Death March'

The victorious Japanese now marched their new prisoners into captivity. They had not expected to take so many, nor that they would be in such bad condition. They had planned to employ a phased march and hoped to have supplies on hand for 40,000 prisoners but they had bungled. Little transportation and almost no supplies – especially medical supplies – were available when the 'Bataan Death March' began. While some Japanese officers and men treated their captives with respect, many disdained the Americans and Filipinos and engaged in acts of savage barbarity. Those who could not keep pace with the march, or who accepted water or food from well-meaning civilians, were routinely killed, often being hacked to death with samurai swords. Thus the Americans and Filipinos, defeated, sick and starving, had to march many miles to a distant prison camp. One American prisoner, Second Lieutenant Kermit Lay, remembers the nightmare journey:

In our group there was a cavalry captain from Kansas City named Miller who I had known before the war in Manila and who I used to hang around with. When he was captured he still was wearing Cavalry boots. During the March the boots got so heavy that they began to rub huge

BELOW

Ashen-faced and stricken with disease, American soldiers pictured during the infamous Bataan Death March to the distant Cabanatuan Prison Camp. Note that the prisoners' hands are tied behind their backs.

*blisters on his feet. He also had dysentery and was
real sick. A former MP company commander and
I tried to hold him up. We were on either side of
him, but it was hard going on us and we began to
fall further and further back. Finally, one of the
men at the rear of our column, who kept watching
for guards, yelled to us that a Jap was coming. By
now we were dragging Miller. When the guard
got to us he rammed his bayonet right through
Captain Miller. Naturally we dropped him and
ran up and got in the middle of the column. Now
some people think there was one Death March.
There were many Death Marches.*

With the fall of the Philippines, the
Japanese victory in their Southern Campaign
was complete. Utilising air and sea supremacy,
speed and concentration of force, the
Japanese had achieved an incredible series of
victories. The outmatched American, British,
Australian and Dutch forces in the area had
never been able to combine their forces in an
effective way, and so had been overly reliant
on native forces which were of questionable
loyalty. In the two places where the Allies
should have held longest – Singapore and
the Philippines – critical command errors
had helped lead to disaster, a military disaster
that, in both cases, ended in human tragedy.
The old colonial possessions of Europe
had been conquered, ABDA seemed like a
distant memory and beleaguered Australia
stood as the last Western outpost in the
Pacific. As Yamamoto had planned, Japan
had succeeded in seizing vital resources and
in flinging up a defensive barrier around
the home islands. He now hoped that this
barrier would be sufficient to convince the
United States that the war was not worth
fighting. It was up to the Allies to decide
whether or not to embark upon the long
road back to the Philippines, Singapore
and victory.

ABOVE

*The last American and
Filipino defenders surrender
outside their stronghold
on Corregidor Island. The
Japanese Southern Campaign
had been a total success.*

CHAPTER FOUR

THE TURNING POINT

Between April and June 1942 the Allies and the Japanese clashed in a series of carrier battles climaxing in a pivotal struggle at Midway.

In an unchecked string of victories – from Pearl Harbor to the fall of Burma and the Philippines – Japan had won a far-flung empire that was almost self-sufficient in natural resources. In addition, their defensive ring around the home islands seemed to be well nigh impregnable. Flushed with success, Japanese militarists, including Premier General Tojo and the influential victor of Pearl Harbor, Yamamoto, pressed for even greater naval and military exploits. The question was – where should Japan now focus its energies? Many in the army urged war with the Soviet Union or an invasion of India. More naval-minded men favoured actions against the British in Ceylon, the Australians at Port Moresby or the Americans at Midway.

Even before the final path of war had been decided, Japanese forces began a move southwards towards Australia. In January 1942 Japanese forces had captured New Britain and begun converting Rabaul into a major naval and air base. The new facility, together with the giant Japanese base at Truk, formed the centre of Japanese power in the south Pacific. The bases were, however, uncomfortably close to Australia and Allied bases in New Guinea. Although the military ruled out an attempt to conquer Australia, it did support an effort to seize the remainder of New Guinea, aimed at crushing any Allied counter-attack.

Accordingly, on 8 March 1942, Japanese troops landed at the villages of Lae and Salamaua on eastern New Guinea's Papuan peninsula. Under the command of Admiral Shigeyoshi Inouye, they were the leading edge of an invasion force that was directed to oust the few remaining Australian defenders from the island.

War plans

The overall strategic debate had still not been decided. In March and April 1942, the main Japanese strike force, consisting of five carriers under the command of Admiral Nagumo, steamed into the Indian Ocean and wrought havoc among the British merchant shipping there, sinking nearly 100,0000 tonnes of shipping in the Bay of Bengal alone, before launching attacks on the British naval bases at Colombo and Trincomalee in Ceylon. After an abortive effort to engage the Japanese in a night action, the outmatched British fleet of two carriers fled to the safety of East Africa, leaving the Japanese in control of much of the Indian Ocean. However, this victory meant little; few losses had been inflicted upon the British. Convinced that the true threat to Japanese dominance would come from US forces in the Pacific, Yamamoto longed to finish the job he had started at Pearl Harbor: the destruction of the US fleet. He doubted

OPPOSITE

Increasingly carriers came to dominate the Pacific War. This picture (taken from the deck of the carrier Ranger*) shows the mighty US carrier* Lexington *in 1938 – later to be lost in the Battle of the Coral Sea.*

OPPOSITE TOP
A flight of Douglas Dauntless dive bombers moves to attack in 1942. The accurate Dauntless was one of the most effective weapons in the American carrier fleet.

OPPOSITE BOTTOM
Admiral Ernest King, Commander in Chief of US naval forces and architect of the naval war against Japan.

BELOW
The British aircraft carrier Hermes *on fire and sinking after a clash with the Japanese fleet in the Bay of Bengal in February 1942.*

whether operations against Ceylon or New Guinea would lure the fleet into open battle; thus, while his naval forces were fighting in the Indian Ocean and off New Guinea, he was busy laying plans for a climactic battle against the Americans at Midway Island.

While the Japanese planned their next move, Allied forces in the Pacific began building up to their own offensives. The Allies installed a divided command structure: the Pacific War would fall under the purview of the United States, while Britain would control the war in South East Asia. The Australians, understandably, were perturbed to find that a war for their national survival would fall under the control of a foreign nation. To placate them, the United States created the Pacific War Council, which included representatives from Australia, Britain, Canada, China, the Netherlands and New Zealand, but, even though this group would often offer its advice regarding the course of the war in the Pacific, the United States retained almost total control.

Forced to fight a war in two theatres in opposite hemispheres, the United States was quickly beset by supply problems. Theatre commanders and the armed services quarrelled almost endlessly over the limited supply of men and material. Such inter-service rivalry is not uncommon, and it came to play a major role in the war in the Pacific. Although the Americans had committed to a 'Europe first' strategy, the disastrous defeats in the Pacific initially made this impossible. Nearly cut off from Australia and far behind the Japanese in military and naval might, the United States began 1942 by sending nearly 80,000 men to shore up Allied defences in the south-west Pacific – nearly four times as many men sent to Europe in the same period – hoping to subdue Canberra's fears of Japanese invasion and the resulting Australian threat to remove forces from Europe for defensive purposes. With this matter solved, the American army and the navy engaged in a bitter argument over who would lead the war against Japan. Since it involved blending ground and sea campaigns, neither service trusted the other to carry out the task. General George C. Marshall and Admiral Ernest King, the heads of the army and navy respectively, decided

on a compromise solution, dividing the Pacific Theatre into two. General Douglas MacArthur received command of the South West Area of the Pacific Theatre, consisting of Australia, the Philippines, the Solomon Islands and the Dutch East Indies. The remainder, designated the Central Pacific Area, was placed under the command of Admiral Chester W. Nimitz, the commander of the Pacific Fleet. During the war against Japan the relationship between the two men would often become strained as both vied for supplies and dominance.

Inferior US forces

Nimitz's and MacArthur's forces stood at a distinct disadvantage to the Japanese. The Pacific Fleet, now divided into carrier task forces, contained only four carriers, less than half the strength of the Japanese fleet. In addition, Japanese planes and pilots proved superior to American planes in every way. Their pilots were veterans; the Americans were relative novices. Their plane, the Zero, was agile and deadly, and Japanese carrier-based torpedo and dive bombers were formidable weapons of war; the standard US navy fighter, the Gruman Wildcat, could not stand up to the Zero, and the US torpedo

plane, the Douglas Devastator, was so slow as to be almost useless, carrying torpedoes of faulty design. The best weapon in the American arsenal was the accurate and deadly Douglas Dauntless dive bomber, but the Americans were still learning the art of carrier warfare and initially placed far too much emphasis on torpedo attacks against naval foes, using their dive bombers almost as an afterthought.

Although his forces were quite limited, under orders from the Commander in Chief of the US Fleet Admiral Ernest King, Nimitz ordered several hit-and-run raids against Japanese targets. On 10 March, one raid launched from the carriers *Yorktown* and *Lexington* struck Japanese forces at Lae and Salamaua in New Guinea. The raid was a success – even though American torpedoes were inadequate – sinking four ships and damaging nine others. Frightened by the attack, Admiral Inouye slowed his operations against New Guinea. He was convinced that he needed aircraft carriers, but he would have to wait for his support; the vessels were bound for operations in the Indian Ocean. Thus the move on New Guinea was postponed while the Japanese sorted out their planning. Ultimately, Yamamoto came to favour an initial offensive in New Guinea followed by an assault on Midway to bring the American fleet to battle. The naval staff in Tokyo and the military questioned the value of a battle at Midway, so far from any source of supply, but events would help Yamamoto get his way, setting the course for the pivotal battle of the Pacific War.

BELOW

The famous Mitsubishi A6M, popularly known as the 'Zero', with its astonishing manoeuvrability and good endurance, was greatly feared by all Allied pilots in the Pacific in the early stages of the war. The Battle of Midway represented the Zero's zenith; thereafter the agile Japanese fighter found itself ever more outclassed by the American planes Hellcat and Lightning.

Mitsubishi A6M 'Zeke'

The Doolittle raid

Almost immediately after Pearl Harbor, military planners in Washington were considering a bombing raid against Japan. Colonel James Doolittle's risky scheme would launch B-25 bombers from an aircraft carrier within 804km (500 miles) of Japan. The planes would proceed to bomb Tokyo and then land on friendly airfields in China. Marshall and Nimitz knew the raid had little military value but hoped it would serve as a morale boost during this time of crisis.

After a short training period, the army pilots and their 16 medium-range bombers left San Francisco aboard the carrier *Hornet*. However, north of Midway, the US force encountered Japanese picket boats and, unwilling to risk a confrontation with

Japanese carriers, the commander, Admiral William Halsey, ordered that the bombers be launched immediately. This was a real gamble; they were still 1045km (650 miles) from their targets in Japan and were in danger of running out of fuel before they could reach friendly territory in China. However, Doolittle pressed on and surprise was complete when, on 18 April, the American bombers appeared in the sky over Tokyo, carried out their mission and flew on almost unmolested to China. The crews of 15 of the 16 planes crash-landed or bailed out in China as their aircraft ran out of fuel, and one went on to land in the Soviet Union. Eight men from the Doolittle raid fell into the hands of the Japanese, three of whom were executed by firing squad. Incensed at the other raiders'

ABOVE

The B-25 bomber of Colonel James Doolittle takes off from the flight deck of the carrier Hornet *bound for the bombing raid on Tokyo on 18 April 1942. The raid caused little damage, but set Japan on course for defeat at Midway.*

ABOVE

The American aircraft carriers Lexington, Ranger, Yorktown *and* Enterprise. *In the end America's industrial might outstripped Japan in the production of these critical vessels, tipping the balance of the Pacific War.*

escape, Japanese forces in China went on a rampage, killing anyone they thought might have helped or harboured them.

The Doolittle Raid achieved its goal, boosting sagging morale in the United States. Although the raiders had done little real damage, destroying 90 buildings and killing 50 civilians, American citizens felt a certain measure of revenge for Pearl Harbor. In Japan, the reaction to the raid was much more important. Both Tojo and Yamamoto were embarrassed it had taken place and that the life of the Emperor had been put at risk. It could not happen again: Japan had to extend its defences farther out into the Pacific and destroy the American fleet. To achieve these twin goals, Midway would have to be taken.

Yamamoto remained firm in his belief that operations against New Guinea should proceed in order to protect the vital southern flank. However, these operations would be moved forward and would be stripped of much of their naval support as the main fleet made ready for the showdown at Midway.

Operation MO

In April 1942, during preparations for the advance on Midway, Admiral Inouye prepared to launch Operation MO, the seizure of Port Moresby. He was on a strict timetable, for several of the ships dedicated to MO would be required for the attack on Midway. Inouye had received fewer carriers than he had hoped – the *Shoho*, the *Zuikaku* and the *Shokaku* – for Yamamoto had husbanded the others for the upcoming clash with the US Pacific Fleet, believing three carriers to be more than enough for Inouye's needs. Japanese intelligence indicated that three US carriers had taken part in the raid on Tokyo and were back in Hawaii, and that a submarine had sunk the US carrier *Lexington*, thus few, if any, US naval forces would be in the Coral Sea during Operation MO.

Inouye divided his powerful force into three main groups: one group, including the light carrier *Shoho* and various cruisers and destroyers, was dedicated to the landings at Port Moresby; and a second, much smaller group, to the seizure of the island of Tulagi. Concerned with defence, Inouye placed most of his naval strength, including *Zuikaku* and *Shokaku*, in a strike force to cover the entire operation and to destroy any emerging US naval threat. The plan called for the seizure of Tulagi on 3 May, after which the strike force would steam into the Coral Sea to protect the Port Moresby landings.

US cryptanalysts had long been trying to decipher the Japanese naval codes, but without success. However, in the wake of the Doolittle Raid, nearly every Japanese ship took to sea in a vain effort to hunt down the attacking US carrier force. The resulting flurry of Japanese radio traffic gave US code-breakers a wealth of information and, led by the efforts of Commander Joseph Rochefort at Pearl Harbor, they quickly succeeded in deciphering much of the basic JN 25 Japanese naval code. The introduction date for a new Japanese code had been postponed from April until June 1942 because it took so long for the new code books to reach the fringes of the far-flung Japanese Empire, which meant that by mid-April American cryptanalysts were able to inform Nimitz that the Japanese had sent carriers to Inouye and intended to take Port Moresby.

Nimitz had but two weeks to react. After consultation with his staff, and with Admiral King, he decided to attempt to block the coming Japanese move on Port Moresby. He directed the carrier *Lexington* from Hawaii to join the *Yorktown* in the Coral Sea. In addition Halsey's task force, returning from the raid on Tokyo, would be sent to the area. It was a great gamble, for now all of his carriers were away from Hawaii, leaving that area vulnerable to Japanese attack, but Nimitz felt confident in his decision, as intelligence indicated that a Japanese attack on Midway and Hawaii was not imminent. He also realised that the battle would be joined before Halsey could reach the Coral Sea, leaving the US force at a disadvantage, but this was a risk he was prepared to take.

On 1 May the *Lexington* and the *Yorktown* joined to form Combined Task Force 17 under the overall command of Admiral Frank Fletcher. Soon afterwards, partly due to the heroic efforts of Australian shore-watch teams, Fletcher learned of the first Japanese landings at Tulagi. On 4 May, aircraft from the *Yorktown* launched a surprise raid on the Japanese landing force there and, although the attack was rather uncoordinated, succeeded in sinking four ships and driving the Japanese

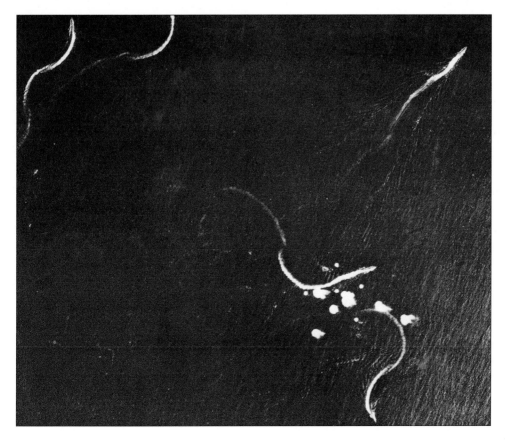

LEFT
Japanese ships zigzag wildly in an effort to avoid American bomb attacks during the Battle of the Coral Sea. Though their tactics were often poor, American pilots exhibited great bravery in the battle.

force back to Rabaul. Now aware there was at least one US carrier in the area to oppose Operation MO, Admiral Inouye nevertheless felt that he had the advantage, and ordered his strike force, under the command of Admiral Takao Takagi, to dispose of the American threat.

The Battle of the Coral Sea

On 6 May Combined Task Force 17 steamed into the Coral Sea where it hoped to ambush the Japanese invasion force off the narrow Jombard Passage. It was joined by a force of three cruisers and two destroyers under the command of Australian Admiral J.G. Crace. To the north-east, Takagi began to prepare for battle. Both forces knew that the enemy was in the area, but neither knew precisely where. At dawn the next morning, Fletcher detailed Crace's force to stand off the Jombard Passage to monitor the approach of enemy vessels while the carriers moved off to make ready for the ambush. Both Japanese and American forces sent up reconnaissance planes in a frenzied effort to locate enemy aircraft carriers.

The Japanese were the first to make contact. Just after dawn, a Japanese scout plane radioed that it had sighted an American carrier and a cruiser. Takagi ordered the attack and a full flight of strike aircraft flew away from *Shokaku* and *Zuikaku*. However, the attacking aircraft were chagrined to learn that the US ships were in fact the *Neosho* and the *Sims*, an oiler and a destroyer which had been detached from the main fleet for safety. Enraged, the Japanese pilots made short work of the pair, losing six valuable aircraft in the process.

BELOW

During the Battle of the Coral Sea, Shokaku *was damaged by a strike from the* Yorktown; *although she caught fire she was saved with some difficulty, and had to return to Japan for repairs. The loss of many of her aircraft and aircrew meant that she could not take part in the Battle of Midway.*

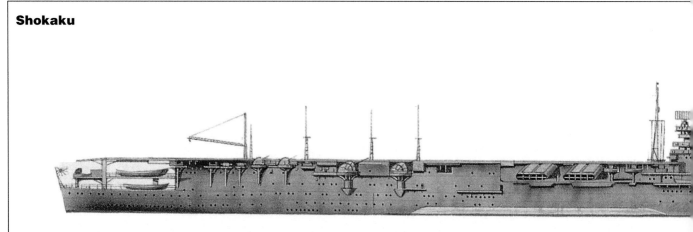

Shokaku

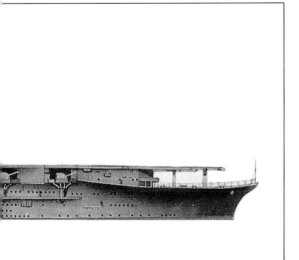

On 7 May, Fletcher met with a similar problem, but his luck was better than his opponent's. Two hours after dawn, an American air patrol caught sight of a small force of Japanese cruisers and gunboats bound for Port Moresby. Due to a signalling error, the sighting was reported as two aircraft carriers. In a hurry to seize the initiative, Fletcher ordered a full strike from both the *Lexington* and the *Yorktown*, and a powerful air armada took off to attack the wrong target. In a stroke of luck, en route the American attack aircraft stumbled across the light carrier *Shoho* guarding the Port Moresby landing forces, and over 90 aircraft diverted to attack the unsuspecting carrier and its escorts. As the commander of the *Shoho* turned into the wind

ABOVE

The US carrier Lexington, *struck by two torpedoes and a bomb, struggles for her life in the Battle of the Coral Sea. At first, damage control was successful and it looked as if the great ship would be able to survive.*

to launch his own aircraft, the carrier slowed, making it an easy target, and torpedoes and bombs slammed into the doomed ship as the American aircraft swept aside the few Japanese Zeros that rose to engage them. Several direct hits soon transformed the *Shoho* into a blazing hulk, and within 40 minutes the Japanese carrier had been sent to the bottom with the loss of nearly 700 crew. The Americans had drawn first blood in the carrier war.

Jubilant pilots returned to the US carriers to report their victory. During the balance of the day, Japanese land-based aircraft struck at Crace's force off the Jombard Passage. Through superior seamanship, Crace was able to avoid severe damage from the Japanese attack, as well as from an attack made by several US B-26 bombers who mistook his force for the Japanese. Both Fletcher and Takagi, realising that enemy carrier forces were near, searched for each other in vain, though they were less

than 320km (200 miles) apart. Due to cloudy conditions, scout aircraft did not locate the opposing fleets until dusk settled, putting an end to air operations. Ironically, the Japanese finally located the *Yorktown* at sundown; several disoriented Japanese pilots made an attempt to land on the carrier.

The next morning, scouts from both fleets discovered each other almost simultaneously, but the Americans were able to launch their strike aircraft first. Flights from both

the *Yorktown* and the *Lexington* attacked *Shokaku*, having lost contact with *Zuikaku* in a rain squall. This attack was destined to be different to the assault on *Shoho*. Defending Japanese Zeros were ready for the incoming American planes and took a terrible toll on the poorly trained American pilots in their inferior aircraft. Coming in two waves, the attackers made significant errors. The torpedo planes dropped their weapons too far from their targets to be effective and the Japanese discovered that their ships could actually outrun the slow American torpedoes. A few of the American dive bombers broke through the Japanese cover to deliver their payloads and damaged *Shokaku* with several hits, but *Shokaku* remained afloat and steamed slowly to the north.

Fighting to a draw

At the same time, a Japanese attack force struck *Yorktown* and *Lexington*. The inexperienced Americans had few fighters in the sky to intercept the Japanese strike, and even these were positioned too low to be of any real use. Torpedo planes and dive bombers raced in to the attack, focusing on the larger, slower *Lexington*. Of 11 torpedoes fired at the mighty carrier, two found their mark and a bomb struck the main deck. In the boiler room damage was severe, with medics trying to help men burned so badly that 'skin [was] literally dripping from their bodies'. The smaller, more nimble *Yorktown* was able to avoid all incoming torpedoes but suffered a direct hit by an 362kg (800lb) bomb that penetrated the ship to the fourth deck.

By the time the Japanese attack ended near midday, both American carriers had been damaged but still remained operational. The *Yorktown* was in relatively good shape and, by 1245 hours, the *Lexington* was able to report that the fires and damage were under control. However, this was not to last. Soon a massive series of explosions shook the huge ship; these were caused by gasoline or fuel vapours that had been ignited by the smouldering fires. The *Lexington* was now beyond repair and the order was given to abandon ship. That evening a US destroyer sent the stricken vessel to the bottom.

The loss of the *Lexington* forced Fletcher to reconsider his plans for action. Now standing at a disadvantage in any continuation of the battle, he decided to withdraw. To the north, Takagi and Inouye were also considering

LEFT
Survivors of the Lexington *reach to pull their lifeboat alongside a rescue ship. Though 216 men died in the battle, 2735 other men and a dog (the captain's cocker spaniel, Wags) went over the side and were rescued without one of them drowning.*

Nakajima B5N 'Kate'

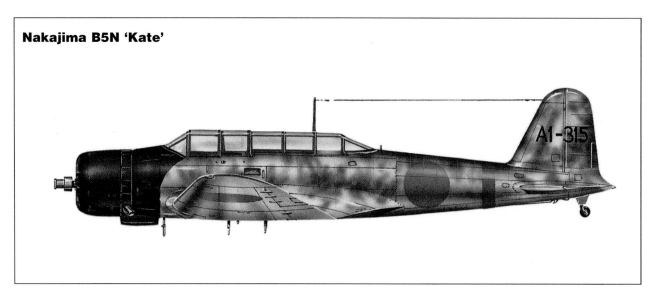

ABOVE

The Nakajima B5N 'Kate' Japanese torpedo bomber – without question the best carrier-borne torpedo bomber in the world. Such aircraft sank the USS Hornet, Lexington *and* Yorktown. *By 1944, though, the feared 'Kate' had become obsolete.*

their options. Inouye decided to postpone the invasion of Port Moresby – for ever, as it would turn out – and Takagi decided to retire to Truk. He had good reason; the *Shokaku* was damaged and his pilots had reported that they had sunk both American carriers. When Yamamoto learned of Takagi's retirement, he was livid, ordering the reluctant admiral back into the battle. It was too late; the American task force had already left the area. The Battle of the Coral Sea was over and had been fought to a tactical draw. The Japanese had lost 77 aircraft, 1074 men and the light carrier *Shoho*. The US had lost 66 aircraft, 543 men and the fleet carrier *Lexington*. The battle, though, was much more of a victory for the United States. The invasion of Port Moresby had been thwarted, and the aura of Japanese invincibility had been shattered, a psychological victory for the United States of immense proportions. Even more importantly, the *Shokaku* and the *Zuikaku* had lost so many aircraft that they would not be ready for the upcoming Midway operation. This would swing the balance in that pivotal battle in favour of the Americans.

Plans and intelligence

Although he was unhappy with the mixed results of the Battle of the Coral Sea, Yamamoto had no reason to fear the results of his showdown with the American Pacific Fleet at Midway. The *Shokaku* and the *Zuikaku* were out of action, but the Japanese believed that they had sunk or disabled both American carriers at the Coral Sea and that the balance of naval air power would remain strongly in their favour. The great admiral's plan was complex, involving virtually

every ship of the Japanese Combined Fleet, totalling 11 battleships, eight carriers, 22 cruisers, 65 destroyers, 21 submarines and over 200 aircraft. Divided into 16 groups, the massive fleet would engage in a bewildering series of feints and diversions, climaxing with the capture of Midway Island. Possession of the island would fling the Japanese cordon of defence out further, halting any new bomber raids on the home islands. More importantly, surprised American forces, reacting to the stunning loss, would rush to the scene from Pearl Harbor. Unable to discern the true aim of the multiple Japanese threats, the American fleet would disperse and meet their doom at the hands of the waiting Japanese carrier strike force. Thus the seizure of Midway would finally offer the complete naval victory that Yamamoto had long sought.

The Japanese attack would begin with an attack on the Alaskan Aleutian islands of Attu and Kiska, utilising a fleet based around the strength of two aircraft carriers. It would, it was hoped, neutralise American air power there and create a diversion from the assault at Midway. The next day, the main carrier strike force – based around four carriers under the command of Admiral Nagumo – would launch air strikes on Midway, then, after softening up the defences, a separate invasion fleet would approach the island from the south-west. Yamamoto himself would command the 'main body' based around the strength of three battleships and a single carrier, which would lurk 480km (300 miles) to the west, positioned between the Midway and Aleutian forces, which were waiting to engage the

American fleet in a traditional battle of surface vessels. Although his forces were dangerously divided, Yamamoto relied upon surprise to keep the Americans off balance. They would be far away in Hawaii while the Combined Fleet was at its most exposed. After the Aleutians and Midway had fallen, the vast fleet could concentrate its forces. With reconnaissance flights undertaken by seaplanes, and a protective screen of submarines based off Hawaii, Yamamoto would know exactly when the US Pacific Fleet left its anchorage, and thus would be able to prepare for the forthcoming battle.

Surprise, however, would not be on the Japanese side at Midway. The delay in conversion to a new code-book meant that

US code-breakers were still able to crack many Japanese naval transmissions. The flood of radio traffic in the run-up to the Midway operation gave American cryptanalysts much to work with. It was clear that the Japanese were preparing for a major operation, but the question was where? Guesses – including Midway, New Guinea and Hawaii itself – ran through the US military establishment. A great many of the code-breakers believed that the focal point, referred to in the Japanese transmissions as AF, would be Midway. However, Nimitz, among others, wondered why the Japanese would dedicate their entire fleet to the seizure of that tiny, seemingly insignificant island. Commander Rochefort, one of the leading code-breakers, hit upon

BELOW

Disaster strikes the Lexington. *After surviving the Japanese attack at the Coral Sea, a violent explosion shook the carrier as one of her gasoline systems ignited. Captain Sherman and other officers were still aboard as this picture was taken. Still the* Lexington *remained afloat, until an American destroyer administered the final blow that sent her to the bottom.*

ABOVE

Airstrips at Midway Island before the Japanese onslaught in June 1942.

a ploy to unmask the identity of AF. Setting a trap for the Japanese, the commander at Midway radioed that the water-distillation plant had broken down and supplies were low. On cue, the next day the Japanese radio transmissions indicated that AF had water-supply problems. Nimitz and King now knew beyond any doubt that the Japanese were preparing to attack Midway. By 24 May Rochefort had divined that the attack on the Aleutians would begin on 3 June and was also able to predict the exact time of the Midway invasion, as well as the composition of the Japanese forces involved.

Realising that surprise was now on their side, King and Nimitz decided to make a stand at Midway using most of the forces at their disposal. The carriers *Hornet* and

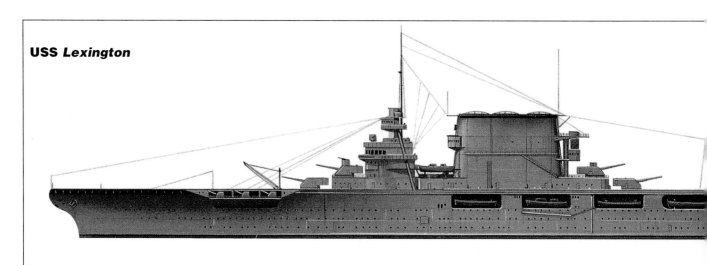

USS Lexington

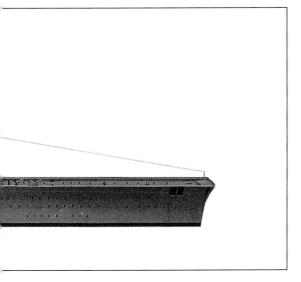

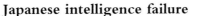

Enterprise were already refuelled and ready for action, although their commander Admiral Halsey was not, having gone down with a severe case of dermatitis. Admiral Raymond Spruance, a relative novice concerning carrier battles, was appointed in his place. Nimitz also appointed Admiral Fletcher to command the carrier forces under Spruance's overall control. The third available US carrier, the *Yorktown*, which had sustained damage at the Battle of the Coral Sea, steamed into port on 22 May and entered dry dock. Nimitz went to inspect the damage, for he needed the carrier in the coming battle. Although engineers estimated as much as 90 days to repair the ship, Nimitz ordered repair crews to have the *Yorktown* ready in three days. Over 1400 workers scrambled over the ship, working around the clock to repair the bomb-damage. Sporting steel plates to patch the holes in her side, still containing the several hundred workers shoring up her structure, *Yorktown* left Pearl Harbor to join forces with *Hornet* and *Enterprise*. The three carriers would hold position nearly 480km (300 miles) north-east of Midway to await the arrival of the Japanese fleet. Together with land-based aircraft from Midway, the US force was now the equal of Nagumo's strike force.

Japanese intelligence failure

By 1 June, the entire Japanese force had formed up and was at sea, steaming towards an American trap. Yamamoto remained quite unaware of the peril awaiting him. The Japanese had planned to carry out an aerial

ABOVE
The captain of the Lexington *gives the order to abandon ship and men desperate for their lives tumble into the Pacific Ocean. Nearby destroyers, though, saved all of the men in the water.*

LEFT
In her short war career the Lexington *had failed to inflict severe damage on the enemy, largely as a result of the inexperience of her air group and because of faulty tactical US Navy doctrine. The loss of a big carrier was a heavy price to pay for the Coral Sea victory.*

reconnaissance of Pearl Harbor, refuelling long-range sea planes at French Frigate Shoals. However, the submarine carrying the fuel found American ships occupying the area and the operation was cancelled. Had it been carried out, Yamamoto would have learned that the US carriers were at sea. Japanese submarines raced toward Pearl Harbor as an early warning system of American fleet action but failed to take up station until the American carriers had already left. Thus Yamamoto remained confident that his complicated operation would succeed and result in the destruction of the US Pacific Fleet.

Midway: the fleets come together

On the morning of 3 June, Japanese carrier-based planes raided the US port at Dutch Harbor in the Aleutian Islands. The raid, although quite successful, failed to confuse the Americans as to the real goal of the Japanese offensive: Midway. Also on the same day, American long-range reconnaissance caught sight of the Japanese invasion fleet. Even though high-flying B-17s from Midway attacked the fleet, they did little damage. Yamamoto and Nagumo now knew their force had been discovered, but still had no idea that any American carriers were near. On the morning of 4 June, Nagumo made ready to attack Midway as planned, as a precaution ordering several reconnaissance planes to be launched from his cruisers. The cruiser *Tone* had problems with its launch catapult, delaying its plane's take-off, which proved to be critical, for this plane was to search to the east in the direction of the American carriers.

Just after dawn, the Japanese launched half of their available aircraft in an attack on Midway Island, holding the other half in reserve in case any American naval units were in the area. Soon afterwards, an American scout plane discovered the Japanese carriers and radioed their location to its own waiting carriers and to the land-based planes of Midway. Spruance rushed to bring his massed task force to within striking distance of the unsuspecting Japanese fleet. Midway was prepared: every plane that could fly had taken to the skies, either to protect the island or to attack the Japanese carriers.

Shortly before 0700 hours, the Japanese planes struck. American fighter pilots fought determinedly in the defensive but took heavy losses to the superior Japanese Zeros.

Under heavy anti-aircraft fire, and amid the confusing aerial battle, the Japanese raiders accomplished little, failing to destroy the American airfield. The commander of the Japanese air strike, Commander Tomonaga, radioed back to Nagumo that a second strike was necessary to neutralise the island for the arrival of the invasion fleet.

RIGHT

Survivors of a stricken US carrier clamber out of the water to safety. At Midway US carriers proved much less vulnerable than their Japanese counterparts, allowing sailors safely to abandon ship.

Hard decisions for the Japanese

The danger posed by American forces on Midway became apparent when, shortly after 0700 hours, land-based planes struck Nagumo's carrier force. Numbering only 10 aircraft, the attack force achieved little – the slow American torpedo planes proved again to be vulnerable and all but three were lost to the Japanese defenders – but it was enough to convince Nagumo to launch a second wave. He had 93 aircraft on hand, but they were armed with torpedoes and armour-piercing bombs for an attack on the American fleet. However, with no American ships in the area, at 0715 hours Nagumo took the planes below decks to be re-armed with high-explosive bombs for an attack on Midway. Within 15 minutes, a disturbing

ABOVE

Bombs fall in Makushin Bay at Dutch Harbor on 3 June 1942. The Japanese attack on the Aleutian Islands was supposed to divert American strength from Midway but failed due to the growing edge in US intelligence.

report came in from the *Tone*'s scout plane: it had sighted American ships in the area, but no carriers. Alarm broke out immediately on Nagumo's flagship, *Akagi*. If American carriers were near, it could mean disaster for his fleet. Although already halfway through, re-arming the attack aircraft was halted as Nagumo waited for more information. At the same time, a second wave of attack planes arrived from Midway, serving to confuse the situation even further.

First into the attack was a wave of 16 dive bombers under the command of Major Lofton Henderson. His Marines, without fighter escort and inexperienced at dive-bombing techniques, attacked at a shallow angle, making them easy targets for the defending Japanese Zeros. A total of half of the Marine planes were shot down,

including Henderson's, without registering a single hit on the Japanese fleet. Two more attacks followed, delivered by high-level bombers and torpedo planes, but once again the Japanese fleet escaped without damage. During the mêlée, the *Tone*'s plane informed Nagumo that the American force included at least one carrier. Nagumo was now caught in a tactical dilemma: half of his attack aircraft were armed for an attack on Midway, but half were armed for an attack against the American fleet. Making matters worse, the first wave of Japanese attack aircraft were only minutes away from returning to their carriers, low on fuel. If he launched an assault on the American ships, he would have to watch his returning aircraft crash into the sea as they ran out of fuel, but if he allowed those planes to land on their carriers he ran the risk of being attacked by American aircraft while his carriers were jammed with planes in states of refuelling and re-armament. Against the advice of the commanders of the *Hiryu* and *Soryu*, who wanted to launch an attack on the US fleet, Nagumo chose to land the planes. Thus the aircraft for the second strike, many of which had already been taken up on deck, had to be taken below for re-armament once again. In the rush to re-arm, bombs from the aircraft were not properly stowed in the magazines and were simply pushed to one side.

Nearly 240km (150 miles) away, the American carrier commanders had decided on a very risky course of action. Spruance initially had planned to launch an attack on the Japanese fleet at 0900 hours from a distance of 160km (100 miles), which would leave his short-ranged planes with plenty of fuel to return to their carriers. However, it soon became apparent that if the attack was launched earlier it stood a chance of catching the Japanese carriers while they were at their most vulnerable: during the landing of their Midway strike aircraft. Seizing the opportunity, Spruance ordered the launch after 0700 hours at the very limit of his planes' range. It took some time for the attackers to form up, but by 0745 hours they were on their way. Bringing up the rear of the American fleet, Admiral Fletcher, aboard the *Yorktown*, was the last to launch his strike force, holding half of his planes in reserve. In total, some 155 aircraft sped toward the Japanese carrier force.

The zenith of the Zero

When the American attack aircraft began to arrive at the last estimated Japanese position, they found nothing. Dive bombers and fighters from the *Hornet* failed to locate the Japanese and had to return home empty-handed; however, most of the attack aircraft sighted the Japanese carriers and pressed home the attack with abandon. They could hardly believe their luck, for the Japanese carriers were packed with aircraft, and fuel lines and munitions lay everywhere. Fifteen torpedo planes from the *Hornet* were the first to strike but, taking a terrible beating from swarming Japanese Zeros and from relentless anti-aircraft fire, all 15 were destroyed. Not a single torpedo found its mark.

Running low on fuel and with only minimal fighter cover, two more torpedo squadrons from the *Enterprise* and *Yorktown* flew in to renew the assault but all of the Zeros were now alert to the threat. Brushing aside a small defensive force of six US fighters, they wrought havoc among the outmatched torpedo planes, while the Japanese carriers escaped unscathed.

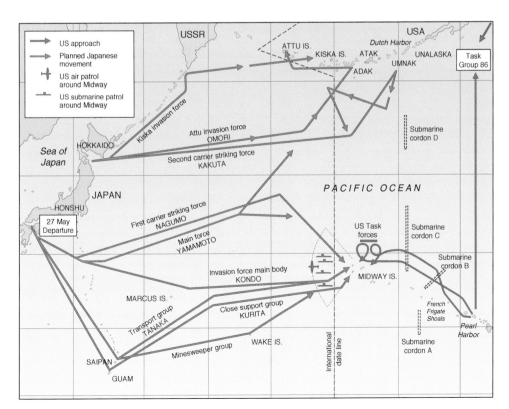

RIGHT
The Japanese carrier Akagi *before the war. She sank at Midway after attack by Dauntlesses from the* USS *Enterprise.*

BELOW
A Japanese naval rating from the Combined Fleet, May 1942. He is wearing the white rig which was uniform for clean work, such as office duties.

Aboard the *Akagi*, Nagumo watched the destruction of the American force with delight. US pilots, although demonstrating an unbelievable bravery, were tactically unsound and their machines were poor. It seemed that he would have time to re-arm his aircraft and launch a devastating attack on the now located and vulnerable American carrier fleet. He would have his victory.

Dive bombers deal a fatal blow

The torpedo-plane attack had been quite costly for the Americans, who had lost 41 aircraft and 80 airmen, had not registered a single hit on a Japanese ship, and had attracted the attention of the defending Japanese Zeros. However, the Japanese fighters could not defend against the sudden appearance of US dive bombers. A total of 37 planes from the *Enterprise*, led by Lieutenant Clarence McClusky, had followed a lone Japanese destroyer, hoping that it would lead them to the carriers. Just as the Zeros foiled the last of the torpedo attacks, McClusky finally sighted his targets.

One torpedo-plane pilot remembers the scene: 'I saw this glint in the sun and it just looked like a beautiful silver waterfall; these dive bombers coming down.' Nagumo's decision to land the Midway strike planes was catastrophically wrong: the Japanese carriers had no fighter cover and were still strewn with planes, fuel and munitions. American dive bombers made the Japanese pay by launching a textbook strike.

Almost immediately, two bombs struck Nagumo's flagship, the *Akagi*, igniting pools of fuel and detonating vast stores of torpedoes and bombs which were scattered among the aircraft parked on the flight deck. The flagship was soon awash in a torrent of flame. Commander Fuchida, who led the attack on Pearl Harbor, was aboard the *Akagi* and remembers the attack:

The terrifying scream of the dive bombers reached me first, followed by the crashing of a direct hit. There was a blinding flash and then a second explosion much louder than the first. I was shaken by a weird blast of warm air … I got up and looked at the sky. The enemy planes were already gone from sight … I was horrified at the destruction that had been wrought in a matter of seconds. There was a huge hole in the flight deck just behind the midship elevator. The elevator itself, twisted like molten glass, was drooping into the hangar. Deck plates reeled in grotesque configurations. Planes stood tail up belching livid flames and jet-black smoke. Reluctant tears streamed down my cheeks as I watched the fires spread, and I was terrified at the prospect of induced explosions, which would surely doom the ship.

Nearby, the *Kaga* was struck by four bombs, one of which exploded near the island bridge, killing the captain and most of the command crew. Another bomb penetrated deep into the ship's interior, detonating stores of bombs and torpedoes. Wracked by explosions and engulfed in flames, its fire-fighting equipment destroyed, the *Kaga* slowly began to sink.

Dive bombers from the *Yorktown* now arrived on the scene, launching a punishing attack on the *Soryu*. Two direct hits lifted the elevator out of the ship and flung it against the bridge. A third bomb detonated in the hangar, setting fire to fuel and detonating munitions. Soon a blazing wreck, *Soryu* had to be abandoned.

Both the *Soryu* and the *Kaga* were lost, and the *Akagi* limped on until evening when it, too, was abandoned.

In an attack that had lasted only six minutes, the American dive bombers had destroyed the heart of the Japanese fleet. Yamamoto was shocked to learn of the fate

ABOVE

Plane inspectors, wearing their distinctive green jerseys and green caps with a black stripe, check the landing gear of a Dauntless on the flight deck of a carrier.

that had befallen Nagumo's carriers. He immediately sent out the call for the far-flung Japanese fleet to gather in an attempt to seize victory from the jaws of defeat. Nagumo had one operational carrier remaining, the undamaged *Hiryu*, which had become separated from the other carriers during the wild mêlée. He ordered an immediate attack on the American carriers.

The Japanese strike back

In two waves, the *Hiryu* launched all of its available aircraft against the *Yorktown*. Fletcher's ship, still carrying scars from the Battle of the Coral Sea, used radar to detect the incoming attack, launched its fighters in defence and made ready for the inevitable. Just before noon, the Japanese 'Val' dive bombers came in on an attack run, defended by a flight of Zeros. This time, the American fighter pilots acquitted themselves well, destroying three Zeros and six bombers before they could reach the *Yorktown*. Three bombs struck the carrier, one falling into the smokestack and another penetrating to the fourth deck before exploding. Similar bomb damage had destroyed the Japanese carriers, but Fletcher's fire teams were able to extinguish the flames and the *Yorktown* remained operational. However, shortly after 1400 hours, Japanese Zeros and 'Kate' torpedo planes returned to finish the job. Once again, the attackers suffered heavy losses, but four 'Kate' pilots made their way through the hail of fire to deliver their deadly torpedoes only 457m (1500ft) from the *Yorktown*. Two torpedoes struck the carrier and the steel patches that covered the damage from her previous battle

gave way. By 1500 hours, the American captain made the difficult decision to abandon his vessel. The Japanese had salvaged some of their pride, but at a high cost; many veteran Japanese pilots had been lost in the attack, and the Americans had finally located the elusive *Hiryu*.

At 1445 hours, an American scout plane caught sight of the last remaining Japanese carrier, and the *Enterprise* quickly launched a flight of 24 dive bombers, led by the young American, Lieutenant Wilmer Gallagher.

BELOW

Although slow and unmanoeuvrable when compared with the Zero, the Grumman F4F was the best that the US Navy could field in the early days of the war. Flown by brave pilots, the Wildcat held its own until more modern aircraft entered service.

Grumman F4F Wildcat

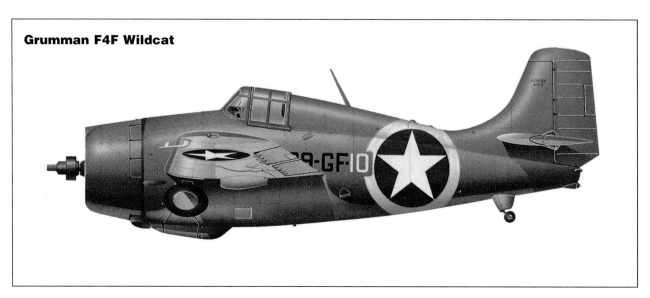

Having taken part in the sinking of the *Kaga*, Gallagher was elated at the chance to destroy another Japanese carrier. At 1703 hours, as the crew of the *Hiryu* sat down to eat, the alarm rang out: 'Enemy dive bombers directly overhead!' There was no time to react before the Dauntless dive bombers came screaming down. Four bombs tore into the ship, one ripping out the forward elevator and another tearing into the hangars below. In minutes the attack was over, and all but three of the attackers made their way safely back to the *Enterprise*. Once again, American bombs set off secondary explosions in the magazines of a Japanese carrier, and the *Hiryu* steamed on, a floating torch that set alight the evening skies. Late in the night she was abandoned, and the Japanese defeat was complete.

Parting shots

Desperate to save some portion of his beloved plan, Yamamoto came rushing to the scene with his battleships and cruisers, hoping to catch the American carriers in an uneven night battle but, realising the danger of a night confrontation, Spruance had decided to retire towards the east. Cheated of his last chance at victory, Yamamoto was forced to cancel the Midway Operation. After months of unchecked victories, he and his staff were

now facing defeat. Some on his staff asked 'How are we going to apologise to His Majesty for this defeat?' Ever the professional, Yamamoto replied 'I am the only one who must apologise to His Majesty.' The defeat was his alone.

The losses were not yet over for either side. During the night, the US submarine *Tambor* located the Japanese cruiser squadron. Although the American submarine was not able to get off a shot before it was sighted, it caused massive confusion in the Japanese ranks. All the cruisers immediately began evasive action – except for the *Mogami*, which had failed to receive the order and ploughed headlong into the *Mikuma*. Both vessels were badly damaged and, at reduced speed, had to limp after the remainder of the retreating fleet. Scouts from the American carriers, having swung back to the west under the safety of daylight, discovered the stricken Japanese cruisers the next morning, and eager dive bombers from the *Enterprise* roared in against them, sending the *Mikuma* to the bottom in a mass of flames. Severely damaged, the *Mogami* managed to struggle on to Truk, but then remained out of the war for an entire year.

Also that morning the Americans were stunned to find that the abandoned *Yorktown*

ABOVE

The Japanese carrier Hiryu, *which survived the initial American attacks at Midway. Aircraft from the* Hiryu *disabled the* Yorktown *before the* Hiryu *too was sent to the bottom by American dive bombers.*

Admiral Chester Nimitz, Commander of the US Pacific Fleet and architect of the victory at Midway and the 'island-hopping' campaign against Japan.

was still afloat, drifting aimlessly at sea. Apparently, the order to abandon ship had been given prematurely, a controversy that surrounds the American victory at Midway to this day. Destroyers arrived on the scene quickly and tried to take the badly listing ship under tow, while a volunteer crew went aboard in an attempt to battle the damage and to use counter-flooding. By evening, the ship had been righted and it seemed that a fleet of tugs would be able to tow her back to Pearl Harbor for repairs. However, it was not to be. Nearly at the same moment, Japanese submarine I-168 fired a salvo of torpedoes, destroying an American destroyer and sinking the *Yorktown*. The career of the great ship that the Japanese twice thought they had sunk was finally at an end.

Conclusion

The defeat at Midway was catastrophic for the Japanese. They had lost four carriers and one cruiser, the heart of their naval dominance. Of greater importance, they lost 322 aircraft, along with their veteran crews. The proficiency of these highly trained pilots had once given the Japanese an important edge, but now Japan's pilot training programme was poor and the advantage in the air war slowly began to shift towards the Americans, who used their most accomplished pilots as instructors. The Japanese defeat at Midway was all the more shocking, since Yamamoto and Nagumo had entered the battle with all of the advantages. Overconfidence, brought on by a series of easy victories, had led the Japanese down the road to disaster. Believing that the Americans would react as expected, Yamamoto had dispersed his naval might, leading to an equal struggle at Midway. Nagumo had been careless in his tactical use of air power, secure in his belief that the Americans were not skilled enough to seize any opportunity afforded by his mistakes. That both men realised the scale of their defeat at Midway was obvious. Japanese reports after the Battle of Midway claimed that Yamamoto had 'secured supreme power in the Pacific'. The navy worked furiously to cover up the loss of the precious carriers. Survivors of the *Akagi, Soryu, Kaga* and *Hiryu* were posted to outlying bases in the Pacific where their stories could not be told. Wounded from the battle were placed in quarantine, unable to receive visits from their families.

While the Japanese pondered their mistakes, US forces revelled in their first victory of the war. They had made many mistakes in the battle that led to near disaster. However, the fortunate timing of the dive-bomber attacks served to hide the errors from most, while Nimitz and his subordinates would learn from these mistakes to become masters of carrier warfare. At Midway, American intelligence operations had provided an inexperienced carrier force with an opportunity and, with almost reckless abandon, Nimitz had seized upon it, winning a victory that changed the war in the Pacific. On a more fundamental level, it was the brave flyers who had won the victory. Without the sacrifice of the torpedo planes, the dive bombers would have never been able to penetrate Japanese defences.

When Admiral King heard about the scale of the victory at Midway, he realised he had been witness to history. He later wrote: 'The Battle of Midway was the first decisive defeat suffered by the Japanese Navy in 350 years. Furthermore it put an end to the long period of Japanese offensive action, and restored the balance of naval power in the Pacific.' The war was about to enter a new phase.

BELOW
Crew members aboard the Yorktown *at Midway as the ship begins to list alarmingly. The seemingly needless loss of the mighty vessel tempered the American victory at Midway somewhat – but the battle stands as the turning point of the Pacific War.*

CHAPTER FIVE

THE ALLIES STRIKE BACK

After victory at Midway, the Allies counter-attacked in New Guinea and altered the balance of the war in a life-or-death struggle on the remote island of Guadalcanal.

After the stunning victory at Midway, Allied forces prepared to take the offensive in the Pacific Theatre. MacArthur, who desired more supplies for the war and craved control over the campaign against Japan, suggested the Allies make ready for both a land and a sea attack on the Japanese base at Rabaul, hinting that this might take only two weeks. Marshall and King agreed that Rabaul should be the focal point of the coming Allied offensive, but disagreed with MacArthur about the plan's specifics. It was to be divided into three 'tasks'. Task I, to be commanded by Nimitz, involved seizing the island of Tulagi in the southern Solomon Islands, an important Japanese base. Task II, a simultaneous drive through New Guinea and up the Solomons, would be divided between MacArthur and Nimitz. Finally, task III would involve the seizure of Rabaul itself.

Almost immediately, problems developed. Nimitz detailed a rather reluctant Admiral Robert Ghormley to command the Tulagi assault – dubbed Operation Watchtower – but the Japanese were now building a base on nearby Guadalcanal island. This would now have to join the planned list of objectives. The landings would fall to the 1st Marine Division, but the commander, General Alexander Vandegrift, did not know

where Guadalcanal was. Using old National Geographic reports, he readied for an operation so poorly planned and supplied that it became known as 'Operation Shoestring'. In Australia, MacArthur planned for an assault on New Guinea, dubbed Operation Providence and based around the construction of an airfield at Buna. However, on 22 July, he was stunned to learn that the Japanese had landed at Buna and were driving to Port Moresby.

Still smarting from the reverse at Midway, the powerful Japanese Combined Fleet hoped to seize all of New Guinea, thus protecting the vital bases of Rabaul and Truk and hampering the Allied supply lines to Australia. Once through the formidable Owen Stanley Mountains, General Harukichi Hyakutake proposed to seize Port Moresby in a decisive land victory, compensating for what had been lost at sea.

The Kokoda Trail

At Buna, by 25 July, nearly 16,000 men of General Tomitary Horii's crack South Seas Detachment were making ready to attack Port Moresby, planning to advance through some of the most rugged terrain in the world – rainforests, high mountains and raging rivers – along the single transportation route in the area, the rugged Kokoda Trail, across the

OPPOSITE
The Allies won victory at Guadalcanal through a series of hard-fought sea battles in the Solomon Islands. Here US Task Force 18 steams into battle through the Solomons.

RIGHT

A Beaufighter of No. 30 Squadron flies over a valley in the Owen Stanley Mountains of New Guinea in 1942.

OPPOSITE

Amid a torrent, Australian engineers struggle to construct a bridge along the Kokoda Trail. The steep terrain made supply efforts on the trail a nightmare.

Papuan peninsula. The Australian commander, Lieutenant Colonel William Owen, believed that the Japanese would not advance over the Owen Stanley Mountains, even though there were few Australian or Papuan forces in the area to block their way.

Outnumbered and surprised, nevertheless the Australians resisted valiantly, forcing the Japanese to fight hard for each step along the jungle trail. The Japanese advance towards Port Moresby was one of the most remote and harrowing of the entire war. Amid the steaming rainforest, on nearly vertical terrain, the battle conditions were miserable. Both sides encountered severe supply problems; disease, including malaria and typhus, was rampant. Each time the Australians halted in defensive positions along the trail, the Japanese would fan out into the trackless jungle and, using machetes to hack their way through the foliage, threaten to envelop them. Finally, the Australians, leavened with meagre reinforcements from the 7th Australian Division, held firm on a pass at the highest part of the Kokoka Trail known as 'The Gap'. If Horii's troops broke through, Port Moresby would be almost defenceless.

Allied victory

In Australia, MacArthur worried that the Allies in New Guinea were heading for another inglorious defeat. Matters were made worse when the Australian Government began to pressurise the British to allow Australian forces to return from North Africa, and MacArthur learned that the Japanese would make a separate landing at Milne Bay in an effort to isolate Port Moresby. He rushed reinforcements to the scene, including the battle-hardened 18th Australian Infantry Brigade, so that, when the Japanese made their landing on 25 August, the Australians were ready.

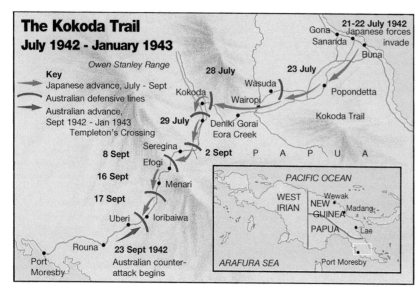

The Kokoda Trail
July 1942 - January 1943

Owen Stanley Range

Key
→ Japanese advance, July - Sept
⤿ Australian defensive lines
→ Australian advance, Sept 1942 - Jan 1943

Templeton's Crossing

21-22 July 1942
Gona — Japanese forces
Sananda — invade
Buna

28 July
23 July
Wasuda
Kokoda
Wairopi
Popondetta

Kokoda Trail

29 July Deniki Gorai
Eora Creek

Seregina **2 Sept** P A P U A
8 Sept
Efogi
16 Sept
Menari
17 Sept

PACIFIC OCEAN

Uberi Ioribaiwa

WEST IRIAN
NEW GUINEA
Wewak
Madang
PAPUA
Lae

Rouna **23 Sept 1942**
Port Moresby Australian counter-attack begins

ARAFURA SEA Port Moresby

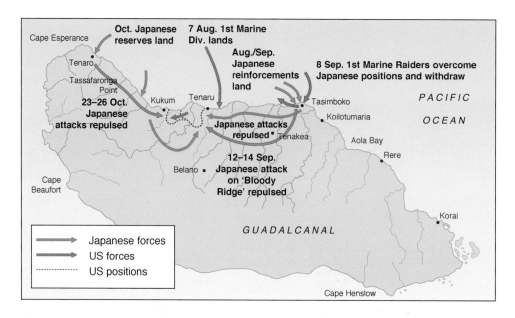

A force of nearly 2000 infantry and a few tanks attacked the Australian positions under a tropical downpour. With tanks bogged down in the mud, and outnumbered by 10 to one, the Japanese flung themselves at the Australian lines in mass suicide charges. In a three-day battle, the Australians held firm before driving the defeated Japanese into the sea; only 600 Japanese soldiers survived to board their transports. Australian forces had won the first victory on land against the Japanese and foiled the effort to isolate Port Moresby.

With the threat from Milne Bay neutralised, MacArthur could now concentrate his forces against the Japanese along the Kokoda Trail. Horii's forces had broken through 'The Gap' on 5 September, but the long struggle was beginning to tell. Supplies were running dangerously low and the Japanese neared starvation, while in Port Moresby the Australians were strengthening their forces for a counter-attack. After the defeat at Milne Bay, with no hope of reinforcement, Horii realised that he would never take Port

BELOW

Australian infantry prepare for battle at Port Moresby. Their victory against the Japanese was the first Allied land victory of the Pacific War and finally secured Australia from invasion.

Moresby and his men would perish in the jungle. Fighting to the north at Guadalcanal had done much to deflect Japanese attention from New Guinea, and the effort to take Port Moresby was a dangerous diversion of resources. Accordingly, on 17 September, the order for retreat finally came. Withdrawing through the jungle, few Japanese survived the second crossing of the Owen Stanley Mountains. Due to the tenacity and staunch resistance of Australian forces – and the unforgiving jungle environment – the Allies had scored their first Pacific victory and Australia was finally safe from invasion.

Guadalcanal: landings and first blood

While the fighting in New Guinea ebbed and flowed, one of the most important battles of the Pacific War unfolded on the island of Guadalcanal. Having decided to seize the island as part of an advance on the Japanese base at Rabaul, by mid-July the Allied invasion force of 26 ships was

gathering. So important was the operation to Nimitz that the Pacific Fleet devoted three of its four carriers to it. They were joined by several capital ships, including the first of a new class of fast battleships, the *North Carolina*, designed to work with carrier forces. Finally, several Australian cruisers, under the command of Admiral Sir Victor Crutchley, rounded out the fleet. Tactical command of the operation went to Admiral Fletcher, the victor of Midway. Admiral Turner commanded the amphibious assault force, while General Vandegrift commanded the 1st Marine Division. During planning, Fletcher contended that his carriers could only remain in the area under the threat of Japanese air attack for two days. Turner and Vandegrift objected strenuously; it would take four days to get the Marines and their gear ashore. However, Fletcher won the argument and, after only one practice landing, which was later called 'a complete bust', the Marines set out for the first amphibious assault of the Pacific War.

ABOVE
An Australian Militia officer poses with a Japanese tank knocked out in the fighting at Milne Bay. Few Japanese men survived the suicide charges against the entrenched Australians.

ABOVE

Fires erupt from Japanese strongholds on the tiny island of Tulagi after the American bombing raid that heralded the beginning of Operation Watchtower.

At midnight on 6 August, the invasion force neared Tulagi and Guadalcanal. The Japanese, whose intelligence service had failed them yet again, were caught totally off guard. As the force neared Tulagi, a radio operator there signalled Rabaul: 'Large force of ships unknown number or types entering sound, what can they be?' The identity of the ships soon became apparent as they launched a thunderous barrage on the island and the Marines began to make their way ashore. On Tulagi, the landings went off without a hitch and the Marines had seized the only town on the island by late morning. However, the Japanese force had moved into the hills to mount a last-ditch defence. In a bitter three-day battle, the Japanese soldiers held true to their code of Bushido, resisting to nearly the last man. Colonel Edson, leader of the 2nd Raider Battalion, remembered: 'Even after we got control, machine-gun nests in dugouts held up our advance for several hours. It was impossible to approach the Nip dugouts except from one direction. You had to crawl up on the cliffs and drop dynamite inside while you were under fire all the time.' Running low on supplies, the Japanese held out in caves, refusing to surrender; only 23 were taken alive.

On Guadalcanal, Vandegrift's Marines faced no resistance as they came ashore. The only Japanese on the island were the unarmed construction crews building an airfield, who now fled into the jungle for cover, leaving behind their supplies, heavy equipment and a nearly completed airfield that the Marines quickly dubbed 'Henderson Field' after the valiant dive-bomber pilot of Midway. However, despite this gain, the Marines knew their position was precarious and worked feverishly to mount a defensive perimeter around Henderson Field even as construction crews completed the runway. Although unsure of the magnitude of the Marine operation, a furious Yamamoto ordered his forces in the area to counter-attack. Under Admiral Gunichi Mikawa, commander of the Eighth Fleet, a force of seven cruisers and one destroyer steamed towards Guadalcanal down the narrow passage between Santa Isabel and New Georgia known as 'the Slot'.

Meanwhile, Admiral Fletcher, whose carriers had been occupied in defending Henderson Field against Japanese air attack, made the decision to remove his carriers from the area. Turner's transports were now vulnerable, and so he also decided to remove them next day. Unknown to him, Mikawa's force was nearing Guadalcanal under the protective cover of darkness. Skilled at night combat, the Japanese ships stealthily moved to within point-blank range of an Allied covering force of five cruisers and five destroyers off the coast of Savo Island. By the time the Allied destroyer *Patterson* caught sight of the Japanese force, it was too late. At 0130 hours on 9 August the night sky in the Solomons erupted

in flares and gunfire as the Japanese launched the Battle of Savo Island. Within minutes, Japanese gunfire had destroyed the Australian cruiser *Canberra*. Receiving only minimal fire from the stunned Allied force, Mikawa's ships went on to win a stunning victory, sinking a total of four Allied cruisers in what would become known as 'Ironbottom Sound'. Only one Japanese ship, Mikawa's flagship *Chokai*, received any significant damage. The way to the destruction of the US transports now lay open. However, not realising that the American carriers had withdrawn and left him in control of the waters around Guadalcanal, Mikawa feared an attack at dawn and lost his nerve, ordering his force to steam back to Rabaul. Thus US Marines remained on Guadalcanal, but the worst American naval defeat since 1812 had important repercussions.

BELOW
A rare photograph depicting Japanese defensive works near the Kokumbona River on Guadalcanal. Here the Japanese began their practice of creating intricate defences and resisting to the last.

The next day, long before the job of offloading had been completed, Turner's transports left the area. The 6000 Marines stationed on Tulagi and the 10,000 on Guadalcanal now had less than a month's rations, no barbed wire or landmines and no heavy weapons. One Marine general remarked: 'We have seized a strategic position. Can the Marines hold it? There is considerable room for doubt.'

Guadalcanal in doubt

Preoccupied with operations in New Guinea, and believing that the Guadalcanal operation was only a Marine raid, the Japanese ordered General Hyakutake to retake the island. Vastly underestimating American strength, Hyakutake sent a force of only 1500 men, under the command of Colonel Kiyono Ichiki, to do the job. On 18 August this unit was landed on Guadalcanal by several destroyers and began to make its way through the dense jungle towards Henderson Field. Shortly after midnight on 20 August the Japanese infantry surged forward into Marine defensive positions near the Ilu River but, fully prepared to meet the attack, the Marines responded with a hail of fire, decimating Ichiki's small force.

Although they attacked again and again, the Japanese failed to dent the Marines' defences. The next day, with a few light tanks, the Marines moved out to destroy the rest of the attacking force. They found Ichiki on the beach with his remaining soldiers, and the tanks ran riot, their treads running over the Japanese 'like meat grinders'. Ichiki committed suicide before they could reach

BELOW

At the Battle of Santa Cruz on 26 October 1942, the South Dakota *claimed to have shot down 26 Japanese aircraft. At Gudalcanal she was less successful, having inadvertently blown the ring main and crippled her entire electricity supply. With no radar, fire control, lighting or navigation aids, she blundered towards the Japanese. She was hit by a number of shells, but survived to participate in all major amphibious operations during the remainder of the war.*

USS South Dakota

him; the Americans had won their first victory on Guadalcanal.

Realising the importance of the American effort on Guadalcanal, the Japanese massed their forces to destroy the enemy. Both sides resorted to supplying and reinforcing their troops on the island at night, using quick destroyers. Japanese destroyers made almost nightly runs, dubbed the 'Tokyo Express', often diverting to shell the Marine positions, while the American effort at re-supply was made somewhat easier by Henderson Field and its fighter aircraft, known as the 'Cactus Airforce'. On 23 August, the Japanese attempted a sizeable reinforcement of their troops on Guadalcanal, resulting in a major naval battle.

ABOVE
Led by native guides, a raider battalion of US Marines leaves the defences around Henderson Field to attack the Japanese in their jungle strongholds on Guadalcanal.

Yamamoto hoped that a major operation near Guadalcanal would draw the American carriers into a battle that would finally give Japan its climactic victory at sea, so he detailed three carriers to cover the troop convoy as it neared Guadalcanal. When American intelligence discovered this, Admiral Fletcher responded by sending the carriers *Enterprise* and *Saratoga* to intercept them and, on 24 August, the carrier forces met in the Battle of the Solomon Islands. Learning the location of the Japanese forces, Fletcher launched his attack aircraft, finding and destroying the light carrier *Ryujo*. The two remaining Japanese carriers, *Shokaku* and *Zuikaku*, responded by launching their bombers and torpedo planes at the US fleet, the planes concentrating their attacks on the *Enterprise* and scoring three hits, but though the 'Big E' was battered she survived to limp

home for repairs. By now, both fleets were bloodied and began to retire. The Japanese had yet again failed to destroy the American carriers in pitched battle, and had also failed in their efforts to reinforce Guadalcanal.

The battle for Guadalcanal degenerated into one of attrition. American air power – centred around the Cactus Airforce – ruled the day, but the Tokyo Express ruled the night. On land, both sides were subject to bombardments and chronically short of supplies; the Japanese even had to eat roots and moss. The hot, humid conditions made life miserable and disease was ever-present. By mid-August, it seemed that the Tokyo Express was winning the supply battle, having landed nearly 6000 men on the island under the command of General Kiyotake Kawaguchi. The audacious general decided to attack the Americans even before he had

BELOW

A US Marine front-line defensive trench on a ridge near Henderson Field on Guadalcanal. These defences repulsed numerous Japanese charges during the attritional struggle on the island.

A camouflaged Japanese supply dump cleverly concealed beneath piles of brush and debris. The dump was captured in the Bonegi River area of Guadalcanal by the US Marines.

A Samoan Petty Officer 3rd Class, wearing a lava-lava, from the USS Saratoga during the Solomons campaign in 1943.

become familiar with the Henderson Field defences. Convinced that Japanese warrior spirit would carry the day, he began trekking through the jungle with few supplies, certain that his troops would soon be feasting on captured American food.

On the night of 13 September, the Japanese launched a frontal assault on a Marine ridge position some 9144m (10,000yds) from Henderson Field. Commanded by Colonel Edson, the Marines fought ferociously in defence of 'Bloody Ridge'. The Japanese poured forwards in human waves amid 'a hellish bedlam of howls', forcing the Marines ever backwards to the very edge of the ridge. However, at dawn, as US machine-gun ammunition was running low, the Japanese assault broke, and fighters of the Cactus Airforce roared in and drove the Japanese infantry into full retreat through the jungle. Nearly one-half of the Japanese attackers lay dead around the Marine positions; the second Japanese attempt to retake Guadalcanal had failed.

Determined to exact revenge, the Japanese redoubled their efforts to reinforce the island via the Tokyo Express. However, the Marines on Guadalcanal also received their first significant reinforcement with the arrival of the 7th Marine Regiment, although the US carrier *Wasp* was lost to a subMarine attack in the effort. Still the Americans feared that the Japanese were building up on Guadalcanal at a faster rate and mounting another effort to strike at Henderson Field. In response, Admiral Turner prepared to land the 164th Regiment, part of the American Division, on Guadalcanal. On 11 October an American force of four cruisers and three destroyers, commanded by Admiral Norman Scott, entered Ironbottom Sound and took up positions off Savo Island to guard the troop landings. On the same night, the Japanese planned a major run of the Tokyo Express, covered by a force of three cruisers and two destroyers under the command of Admiral Aritomo Goto. The two forces would meet in the night Battle of Cape Esperance.

Using surprise and advanced radar, Scott and his ships prepared to strike at the Japanese fleet. The cruiser *Helena* was the first to open fire, catching the Japanese totally unaware. When Goto's flagship, the *Aoba*, was struck with a salvo near the bridge, he believed his own ships were firing at him. Mortally wounded, he died muttering 'stupid bastards'. Confusion also struck the American fleet, with Scott believing he was attacking his own destroyer force. After a lull in the battle, the American ships again opened fire, this time

ABOVE

Ground crew load a 226kg (500lb) bomb aboard a T5F Avenger at Henderson Field on Guadalcanal. The exploits of the 'Cactus Airforce' gave the US Marines a critical edge in the brutal struggle.

sinking a destroyer and fatally damaging the cruiser *Furataka*. The surviving Japanese ships, covered by a salvo of torpedoes, beat a quick retreat up the Slot and within 20 minutes the Battle of Cape Esperance was over. The Japanese lost one cruiser and had a destroyer sunk, with another cruiser badly damaged. The Americans had won their first night battle against Japanese surface vessels of the war, and the US effort to reinforce Guadalcanal was a success.

The tide begins to turn

Once again, in the wake of defeat the Japanese decided to redouble their efforts to retake Guadalcanal. Japanese military and naval leaders now saw retaking the island as a matter of national pride. The Tokyo Express worked overtime to ferry in troops – including General Hyakutake – and supplies under the cover of darkness. Yamamoto diverted four battleships, five carriers, 10 cruisers and 29 destroyers to crush the Marines at Henderson Field and to ambush any US naval forces that tried to intervene. On 12 October two

Japanese battleships, the *Kongo* and *Haruna*, pummelled Henderson Field with over 900 shells, destroying several aircraft and wrecking the runway. One American remembered the experience: 'It is almost beyond belief that we are still here, still alive, still waiting and still ready ... This is the worst experience I've ever been through in my life.' The pounding continued almost nightly and General Vandegrift despaired over the fate of his men. Supplies, especially aviation fuel, were running critically low, in part due to the long supply lines from the USA to Guadalcanal, but also due to the nearly continuous fighting on and around the island. At this point, the United States decided to redouble its efforts. President Roosevelt instructed his military staff to 'make sure that every possible weapon gets through ... to hold Guadalcanal'. Nimitz replaced Ghormley with Admiral Halsey who, learning that he was to control Operation Watchtower, quipped: 'Jesus Christ and General Jackson! This is the hottest potato they ever handed me.'

Within days, Halsey was to discover the true difficulties of his task, for General

Hyakutake had planned a three-pronged offensive on the Marine positions for 22 October, having amassed 20,000 troops and 100 artillery pieces on Guadalcanal. However, his force became entangled in the thick jungle, necessitating a postponement. In the confusion, on 23 October one unit under the command of General Sumiyoshi went forward alone into the attack, only to be destroyed by concentrated Marine fire. The Marines now prepared to face continued attacks; Hyakutake's carefully laid plans were falling apart.

On the night of 24 October the attack came, nearly 3.2km (2 miles) from Bloody Ridge. Here, only the 1st Battalion, 7th Marines, under the command of Colonel Lewis 'Chesty' Puller, stood in defence. Under a tropical downpour, the Japanese repeatedly charged forward in human waves against the Marines' concentrated defensive

fire, only to be mown down. One machine-gunner reported firing 26,000 rounds that night. When morning broke, the Japanese were forced to retreat into the jungle, leaving over 1000 bodies scattered in no-man's-land in front of Puller's positions. The next night, the Japanese came forward again and, in places, reached the American lines, resulting in bitter, hand-to-hand fighting. Once again, the Japanese were beaten back and in the morning had to retreat into the jungle. In total, the Japanese had lost over 3000 men in some of the most harsh fighting of the Pacific War. General Hyakutake was forced to admit defeat and his troops faced a fearful five-day trek through the jungle to their bases. Hyakutake radioed to Rabaul that he had failed because he had underestimated US strength and resolve, going on to request an additional division to complete the task. Guadalcanal was becoming a slaughterhouse.

BELOW
US Marines, weary from the struggle, survey the horrific scene as Japanese dead litter the beach of Guadalcanal. Such sights were all too common after Japanese human-wave assaults on Marine defences.

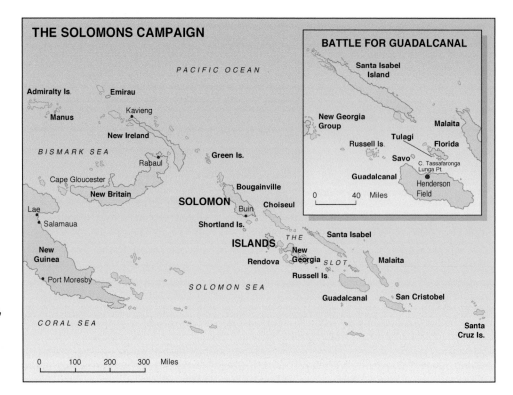

THE SOLOMONS CAMPAIGN

PACIFIC OCEAN

Admiralty Is.
Emirau
Manus
Kavieng
New Ireland
BISMARK SEA
Rabaul
Green Is.
Cape Gloucester
New Britain
Bougainville
SOLOMON
Buin
Choiseul
Lae
Shortland Is.
Salamaua
Santa Isabel
ISLANDS
THE
New Guinea
Rendova
New Georgia
SLOT
Malaita
Port Moresby
Russell Is.
SOLOMON SEA
Guadalcanal
San Cristobel
CORAL SEA
Santa Cruz Is.

0   100   200   300   Miles

BATTLE FOR GUADALCANAL

Santa Isabel
Island
New Georgia
Group
Malaita
Russell Is.
Tulagi
Florida
Savo
C. Tassafaronga
Lunga Pt.
Guadalcanal
Henderson
Field

0   40   Miles

BELOW

Japanese torpedo bombers are greeted with a hail of anti-aircraft fire as they rush to attack the Enterprise *and the* South Dakota *in the Battle of Santa Cruz Island on 26 October 1942.*

Shortly after the clash on land, the American and Japanese fleets met in the Battle of Santa Cruz Island. In the carrier struggle, US aircraft from the *Hornet* and *Enterprise* under the command of Admiral Thomas Kinkaid struck first, damaging the Japanese carriers *Zuiho* and *Shokaku*. However, repeated Japanese counter-attacks sunk the *Hornet* and damaged the *Enterprise*. Therefore the battle resulted in something of a draw, but it left Admiral Halsey with only one damaged carrier and one battleship with which to keep the supply lines open to the beleaguered Marines on Guadalcanal island.

Thus both the Japanese and Americans had suffered critical setbacks in late October, but both were still clinging grimly on to the hope for victory in what was the pivotal struggle of the Pacific War.

Final battles

While both sides continued dangerous supply runs to sustain their forces on Guadalcanal, the Japanese planned one last, great effort to seize victory in the Solomons. Yamamoto and the supreme Japanese command decided to land the entire 38th Division on Guadalcanal in 11 transports, supported by the full strength of

ABOVE
The failure of the Tokyo Express. This Japanese landing barge, packed with troops, never reached its destination on Guadalcanal, being wrecked by fire from Marine half-tracks. The Americans were winning the battle of attrition on Guadalcanal.

ABOVE

In early 1943, having permanently left the defences of Henderson Field, the US Marines pause as they drive through the jungle toward the Japanese bases on Guadalcanal. Starving and defeated, the Japanese were already exiting the 'Island of Death'.

the Combined Fleet. Once again, American intelligence operations caught wind of the massive operation, giving Nimitz and Halsey time to react. Yamamoto's plan called for a massive bombardment to put Henderson Field out of operation for good. Then Tanaka's Tokyo Express would land 38th Division on Guadalcanal, while a carrier force stood by to smash any US effort to intervene. Even as Halsey rushed to gather forces to counter the coming onslaught, coast watchers detected an incoming force of Japanese capital ships. On 12 November, under the command of Admiral Hiroaki Abe, a fleet of two battleships, a cruiser and six destroyers sped down the Slot to deal the death-blow to Henderson Field, thus launching the climactic series of naval battles that would decide the fate of Guadalcanal.

Admiral Turner, who was landing American reinforcements, countered this threat to the Marines by sending a force of five cruisers and eight destroyers under Admiral

Daniel Callaghan to meet Abe in a night battle off Savo Island. Although the radar of the cruiser Helena detected the approaching Japanese force, Callaghan delayed the order to open fire, and the Japanese opened with a devastating barrage. Almost immediately, the cruiser *Atlanta* was disabled and Japanese searchlights snared the *San Francisco*, enabling the battleship *Kirishima* to send round after round into Callaghan's flagship. One of the shells destroyed the bridge and killed Callaghan, momentarily leaving the American fleet leaderless. The American ships concentrated their fire on the massive Japanese battleships, but their shells could do little real harm, and within 20 minutes, the confused and brutal battle came to an end. It was a tactical Japanese victory, for they had sunk three destroyers and two cruisers – one of the cruisers, the *Juneau*, carried the five Sullivan brothers of Iowa, all of whom perished in the fearful struggle – but, although Abe had lost only one destroyer,

THE ALLIES STRIKE BACK / 119

he decided to withdraw to the north. The American sacrifice had saved Henderson Field; the next day the Cactus Airforce discovered the damaged battleship *Hiei* and sent her to the bottom in a hail of bombs and torpedoes.

American victory

Although planes from Henderson Field remained a threat, Tanaka was ordered to proceed to Guadalcanal with his troop transports. On 14 November, American pilots discovered them and their escort of warships and launched a devastating attack. It was a day of horror for the Japanese; four cruisers were either sunk or disabled. Worse still, American aircraft sunk six of the precious troop transports, and thousands of men

perished amid the flames or drowned in the oil-slick waters. Even in this crushing defeat, Yamamoto ordered Tanaka to press onward, sending a battleship and four cruisers to make one last effort to destroy Henderson Field, from which Marine pilots were winning the naval Battle of Guadalcanal.

This time, the Americans were more than ready, with two new battleships – the *South Dakota* and the *Washington* – waiting for the night arrival of the Japanese force among the countless wrecks in Ironbottom Sound. The American destroyer screen took heavy losses and the *South Dakota* suffered from an unexpected electrical failure, but the battle was decisive for the Americans. The *South Dakota* survived over 40 shell impacts while remaining battleworthy, and the *Washington*

BELOW
The tropical conditions on Guadalcanal, reputed to carry the smell of death, provided the US Marines with great obstacles. Here Marines pull their boat up the Matanikan river and through the rapids, taking supplies, previously dropped by planes, to the front line. They encounter another boat headed down river, loaded with wounded.

put on a wondrous display of radar-aided naval gunnery, locking on to the *Kirishima* and pummelling the Japanese battleship with 54 shell hits in under seven minutes, leaving the Japanese ship a blazing hulk. Defeated, the Japanese forces retreated up the Slot, again without damaging Henderson Field. The next day, Tanaka had to try to land his forces in daylight under constant attack by the Cactus Airforce. Of the 38th Division, only 2000 men survived to make it ashore to join their starving comrades on Guadalcanal – the 'Island of Death'.

Weeks of tough fighting remained; however, the Japanese hopes for victory at Guadalcanal were crushed by the loss of the three-day Battle of Guadalcanal. US forces on the island stood at over 35,000; Japanese forces were dwindling and beyond hope. On 9 December, General Vandegrift turned over command on Guadalcanal to General Patch, and the 1st Marine Division left the island after months of savage fighting. By January 1943,

Patch's men were moving out in offensives all over the island against stiff Japanese resistance, while Japanese supreme command decided that it could no longer afford the battle of attrition that was Guadalcanal, and began a stealthy operation to remove their troops, turning down General Hyakutake's request to die like a warrior in a final suicide attack. On 8 February, when Marines and soldiers under Patch's command finally reached the main Japanese bases, they found that they had been abandoned; Tanaka's destroyers had evacuated thousands of soldiers. The astonished Patch radioed Halsey: 'Tokyo Express no longer has terminus on Guadalcanal.'

While the Americans were celebrating their first – and possibly greatest – land victory in the Pacific, the Japanese were left to ponder the realities of true defeat. In the battles around Guadalcanal, the Combined Fleet had lost two battleships, three cruisers, 12 destroyers, 16 transports and hundreds of planes and their trained pilots. In addition,

BELOW

Operating with American forces, New Zealand troops invade the island of Vella Lavella in the Solomon Islands. This move took the Japanese by surprise and helped to seal off their great base at Rabaul.

of the 40,000 Japanese troops sent to Guadalcanal, 23,000 never returned. In many ways it was Guadalcanal, not Midway, that turned the tide of the Pacific War. Tanaka later wrote: 'There is no question that Japan's doom was sealed with the closing struggle for Guadalcanal. Just as it betokened the military character and strength of her opponent, so it presaged Japan's weakness and lack of planning that would spell her military defeat.'

Victories in New Guinea

As events at Guadalcanal neared their climax, Australian forces – with increasing American aid – were forcing the Japanese out of the Papuan peninsula. The Japanese, while retreating down the Kokoda Trail, suffered from a severe supply shortage. A Japanese reporter remembered that the soldiers 'had eaten anything to appease hunger – young shoots of trees, roots of grass, even cakes of

earth. These things had injured their stomachs so badly that when they were brought into the field hospital they could no longer digest any food. Many of them vomited blood and died.' In a case of role reversal, the well-supplied Australians harried the retreating Japanese at every step, fanning out into the jungle to compromise any hastily organised Japanese defensive positions. Though General Horii was killed in the retreat, the tattered remnants of his force reached the base at Gona on 7 November to join the defenders, and the Australians made ready to attack.

The Japanese held firm in strongholds at Buna, Gona and Sanananda. Safe in his headquarters in Port Moresby, MacArthur ordered the 32nd Division's newly arrived troops to reduce Buna, leaving the Australians to deal with Gona and Sanananda. He had no idea what he had asked his men to do. Lacking in heavy weapons, the Allied forces

ABOVE

An amphibious vehicle is used by the US Marines to land supplies after combined American forces landed on New Georgia Island in the Solomons in a surprise attack. In the foreground, Marines begin to organize their supplies.

assaulted through swamps and dense jungle. The Japanese, long prepared for such an attack, had dug networks of invisible and almost impregnable bunkers, and so on 19 November the American infantry under General Edward Harding met a hail of fire and were driven back with heavy losses. Results of the Australian attacks on Gona were the same. Although the Allied forces lacked the requisite weapons, MacArthur ordered them on 'at all costs', and weeks of futile attacks followed which reduced the Australian 7th Division to one-third of its original strength. Realising that the continued victories at Guadalcanal were overshadowing his failed efforts in New Guinea, MacArthur replaced Harding with General Robert Eichelberger, telling him as he left to 'Go out there Bob, and take Buna or don't come back alive.'

After launching an abortive assault on 5 December, Eichelberger wisely postponed any further efforts in Buna until the arrival of reinforcements and tanks. Also reinforced, the Australians were the first to break the deadlock on the Papuan coast, seizing Gona on 9 December after bloody, hand-to-hand fighting with the stubborn defenders. On 19 December, amid the clatter of tank tracks, American and Australian forces began a two-week campaign to drive the Japanese out of Buna. The Japanese, realising that their Papuan forces were doomed, decided to evacuate the force based at Sanananda which, on 22 January, finally fell. At last, MacArthur had his first true victory, but at a high cost. The campaign in Papua had lasted six months and had cost 8500 Allied casualties. He was back to where he had started.

Planning Operation Cartwheel

After the victories at Guadalcanal and New Guinea, the Allies began to prepare for the second phase of their combined offensive: the push towards Rabaul. MacArthur and Nimitz engaged in titanic debates over its control and eventual goal, but both agreed that their force levels were too low for an assault on Rabaul itself. Thus, with the US Joint Chiefs of Staff, they engineered a lesser offensive, dubbed Operation Cartwheel. Forces under the

BELOW

A warrant officer of the 77th Indian Brigade – a Chindit – who participated in operations against the Japanese in Burma in 1943.

command of Admiral Halsey were to advance up the Solomon Islands as far as the island of Bougainville, while MacArthur's land forces moved up the New Guinea coast. This twin offensive would make Rabaul untenable for the Japanese.

As American and Australian troops prepared to advance, the Japanese attempted to shore up their defences. Identifying New Guinea as the focal point of the area, they aimed to bring in the 51st Division as reinforcements. At the end of February, 6000 Japanese soldiers boarded eight transports at Rabaul bound for New Guinea, but on 1 March land-based US aircraft sighted the convoy and B-25 bombers rushed into the attack. The pilots of MacArthur's 5th Air Force had been practising with low-altitude 'skip-bombing' techniques – in which bombs were skipped across the water like stones – and the new attack method proved devastating. Eight Japanese transports were destroyed and fewer than 100 men made their way ashore in New Guinea. The Battle of the Bismarck Sea was a singular success for land-based aircraft against sea power.

The Japanese had lost their fighting edge in the Pacific. Their small economy was unable to keep pace with American ship, aircraft or munitions production. With superiority in numbers, the Allies had

LEFT
The Allies close in on Rabaul. A battalion of paratroops descends from C-47 Dakotas over Nadzab, New Guinea. White parachutes were used for troops; coloured ones for supplies and amunition.

BELOW
American casualties from the fighting on Bougainville disembark from a Landing Craft Tank. The casualties were ferried across Empress Augusta Bay to a hospital on Puruata Island.

introduced several new weapons systems
that offset all early Japanese technological
advantages. In late 1942 and early 1943,
both the twin-engined P-38 Lightning and
the F4U Corsair made their appearance in
the Pacific and both were able to outfight
the vaunted Zero. In addition, US forces
could now rely on a growing number of
specially made landing craft for amphibious
assault duties, ranging from the massive LST
(Landing Ship Tank) – which could carry
over 907kg (2000lb) of cargo – to the smaller,
nimble Amphibious Tractor, which could
crawl out of the surf and onto the beach.

Smarting from the losses off New Guinea,
the Japanese now attempted a massive air
campaign against Allied bases in the Pacific.
Coordinated by Yamamoto, they scraped
together over 300 aircraft, and their 'I-Go'
offensive struck Guadalcanal and American
shipping in early April. Due to the relative
inexperience of the Japanese pilots, it
accomplished little; but, believing the pilots'
exaggerated reports, Yamamoto was sure
he had scored a great victory and decided

to visit outlying airfields to inspire his men
to even greater efforts. However, American
intelligence intercepted messages about his
visit and Nimitz decided to eradicate him. On
18 April, as Yamamoto's plane and its eight
Zero escorts neared Bougainville, they were
set upon by 18 P-38 Lightnings. Striking
from above, the American planes brushed
away the Zero escort and sent Yamamoto's
plane crashing in flames to the jungle below.
The architect of the Japanese war effort
against America was dead.

Advance on Rabaul

At the end of June, Americans and
Australians began the advance on Rabaul
through unopposed landings at Nassau Bay
in New Guinea, thus threatening the major
Japanese base at Salamaua. Almost 644km
(400 miles) away, Halsey's forces began
operations to seize the island of New Georgia
and its strategic Munda airfield. Most of the
American Marines landed nearly 8km (5
miles) from Munda against no opposition,
since the Japanese infantry on the island,

under the command of General Noboru Sasaki, were standing firm in the defence of the airfield. Even so, the men of the American 43rd Division ran into considerable trouble with Japanese rearguards while advancing through the jungle and, when they finally reached Munda, exhausted and poorly supplied, could not dent the stiff Japanese defences there. The battle now bogged down into one of attrition. Once again, an intricate system of Japanese defences greeted any American assault with a deadly hail of fire. General Oscar Griswold launched a new series of assaults on 25 July, after having received reinforcements, including tanks and flame-throwers, and, for 10 days, American forces evicted the Japanese from bunker after bunker with fire and tanks.

Sasaki's men resisted valiantly against overwhelming odds until their leader ordered a withdrawal to nearby Kolombangara Island, where they would fight on in a new series of defences. The struggle for New Georgia took longer and was more costly than Halsey had ever expected. It had taken more than 45,000 troops over a month to evict the 9000 Japanese defenders at the cost of 1136 dead; now Cartwheel was seriously behind schedule. After a Japanese defeat at sea on 6 August, Sasaki abandoned hopes to retake New Georgia, choosing to wait on Kolombangara for the American assault. It never came. Halsey bypassed the island in order to invade Vella Lavella – a move which caught the Japanese by surprise – and succeeded against almost no opposition. Now isolated, Sasaki abandoned Kolombangara and the advance toward Rabaul picked up speed.

Meanwhile, in New Guinea, MacArthur's forces undertook one of their most successful operations of the war against the Japanese bases of Lae and Salamaua. Blending land, sea and air campaigns, MacArthur was able to keep the Japanese constantly guessing and on the defensive. First, massive air strikes destroyed the Japanese air bases in the area, giving command of the skies to the Allies. Then, on 4 September, Australian and American forces hit the beach 32km (20 miles) from Lae. As the Japanese turned

ABOVE
Navy 'Seabees' construct Torokina Airfield on the island of Bougainville. The new installation was the final step in the neutralization of Rabaul.

to face this threat, the 503rd Parachute Regiment made the first combat jump of the Pacific War near Nadzab on the Markham River. The Japanese bases were quickly surrounded and their troops removed on a harrowing inland trek overland to Finschhafen on the Huon Peninsula. After the fall of Lae and Salamaua, MacArthur called for a quick advance on Finschhafen following the Japanese along an overland route, while one battalion of the 9th Australian Division struck Finschhafen from the sea. Unnerved, the Japanese attacked the Australians with over 6000 men, but the defensive lines held and MacArthur's part of the Allied effort to neutralise Rabaul was nearly complete. It was one of the famous commander's greatest successes of the war.

The last part of the Allied effort to neutralize Rabaul involved the seizure of Bougainville and the construction of airstrips there. From these forward air bases, Allied fighters would support land-based bombers in the area, conducting raids on the massive Japanese base at Rabaul and making it untenable. Heavy bombers of the 5th and 13th Air Forces struck Rabaul in preparatory raids and, now aware that Rabaul was the target, the Japanese moved many fighters in for defence. The resulting air battles over Rabaul were indecisive, but managed to divert attention from Bougainville. Through a series of feints and raids, Halsey's landing force achieved surprise when, on 1 November, it landed in Empress Augusta Bay on Bougainville. The 3rd Marine Division met little resistance and soon pushed its perimeter inland to allow the Seabees to construct the vital airstrip.

That night a Japanese force of four cruisers and six destroyers raced southward from Rabaul in an effort to destroy the Marine beachhead. However, the four cruisers and eight destroyers of Admiral M. Stanton Merril's Task Force 39 lay in wait. In the Battle of Empress Augusta Bay, Merril's force sent the Japanese packing and saved the Marines from disaster. Still determined to

BELOW

In September 1943 American bulldozers advance toward Lae in New Guinea. Fleets of bulldozers crushed all in their path and made the way clear for artillery to be brought forward for the assaults on the Japanese bases.

Douglas SBD Dauntless

destroy the Marines, Admiral Mineichi Koga – Yamamoto's successor as commander of the Combined Fleet – ordered eight cruisers and four destroyers south to Rabaul. American intelligence alerted Halsey to the approaching threat, but he had no capital ships in the area. He took a monumental gamble, bringing his carriers *Saratoga* and *Independence* within the range of Japanese land-based aircraft and capital ships in an effort to destroy the gathering Japanese fleet at Rabaul. Though Halsey fully expected to lose both carriers, on 5 November they closed to within striking distance of Rabaul and launched their 96 attack aircraft. Several planes were lost, but most of the Japanese cruisers were damaged and the American carriers escaped unscathed. Realising that the Japanese were about to face another attritional struggle, Admiral Koga moved his cruisers and most of the aircraft to the Japanese base at Truk. With this move, Japan had now accepted defeat in the Solomons Campaign. The battle for Rabaul had been won, and now that the great Japanese base was neutralised Allied forces could shift their attention to other parts of the Pacific.

Fighting in Burma

With the fall of Burma, the vital overland supply route to China – the Burma Road – had been cut, putting the Chinese war against Japan in peril. Supply pilots braved the flight over the Himalayas – known as 'the Hump' – into China, but an Allied counter-offensive into Burma was required. General Archibald Wavell, commander of Allied forces in India, longed to mount a massive combined

offensive to evict the Japanese, but at this early stage in the war there were not enough men or material to support his proposal, and he had to content himself with a limited invasion of Burma. This was known as the Arakan Campaign.

The object of the campaign was to advance down the swampy Mayu Peninsula and capture the port of Akyab. On 21 September 1942 the 14th Indian Army Division crossed into Burma near Chittagong against minimal Japanese resistance. However, after struggling against the jungle conditions and stiffening Japanese resistance, the Allied advance quickly ground to a halt outside Bonbiak. Further attacks by British soldiers along the border and by Stilwell on the Ledo Road made little impact and, with soldiers on the Mayu Peninsula running low on supplies and dying from tropical diseases, Wavell decided to halt the campaign. It had cost the lives of some 2500 Allied soldiers for no gain, and he began to despair of ever launching an effective attack into Burma.

However, General Orde Wingate convinced Wavell to launch one final, rather unorthodox, attack into Burma in spring 1943. Wingate had learned the principles of guerrilla tactics from Jewish insurgents in Palestine and had long ago proposed launching a 'Long Range Penetration' raid into Burma to sever Japanese supply lines there as part of the Arakan Campaign. Not entirely taken by the idea, Wavell had allowed him to train a force of 3000 in the principles of guerrilla warfare and by early 1943, the 77th Indian Brigade, known as the 'Chindits', was

Rabaul ablaze on 2 November 1943. American bombers, supported by fighters from Bougainville, would make the Japanese base at Rabaul untenable, signalling victory for Operation Cartwheel.

ready for operations. Wingate was now able to convince Wavell that, even though the wider Arakan Campaign had stalled, his raid should proceed. On 8 February 1943, the Chindits crossed the Chindwin River into Burma. Trained to live off the land in jungle conditions, using only what they could carry by mule and airdrops for supplies, they caught the Japanese totally by surprise, quickly severing the road and rail links between Mandalay and Myitkyina before melting away into the jungle.

The Japanese waited, believing that the Chindits would soon emerge from the jungle due to lack of supplies. This was not the case; a growing number of Japanese troops were assigned to guarding their now vulnerable supply lines. Had the Chindits remained in the jungle, the outcome of their raid might have been different, but Wingate ordered his men to cross the Irrawaddy River to the south into more open country. This was to be a mistake; they were now out of the range

of airdrops and subject to almost continuous Japanese attack. Now Wingate had no choice but to order his men back across the Irrawaddy and into the jungle, but the Japanese had blocked his path. On 24 March, Wingate ordered his highly-trained fighters to split up and use infiltration tactics to cross the river and make their way back to India. In small groups, without supplies, the Chindits faced a 240km (150-mile) jungle trek. Living on a diet of plants and snakes, only 200 of them survived.

The First Chindit Campaign had been a costly failure. However, the aura of bravado surrounding the raid transformed Wingate into a British national hero and helped to boost British morale. Now Wavell was even more sceptical regarding the efficacy of future campaigns into Burma. Allied leadership, on the other hand, would demand that an assault in Burma be part of a continued coordinated effort to push the Japanese back in the ongoing Pacific War.

CHAPTER SIX

JAPAN ON THE DEFENSIVE

Decisively beaten at Midway and Guadalcanal, the Japanese confronted the Allied counter-offensives in Burma, New Guinea and the Central Pacific.

After scoring an important victory at Midway and displacing enemy units from the Solomon Islands, the United States armed forces in the Pacific theatre initiated more aggressive actions against the Japanese Empire. In Washington, the Joint Chiefs of Staff devised a strategy in which General Douglas A. MacArthur's South-West Area forces would push north through New Guinea. At the same time, Admiral Chester W. Nimitz and his Central Pacific Area fleet would sweep west through the Gilbert and Marshall Islands. Late in 1943, Nimitz and his staff formulated a plan to seize the easternmost of the three chains, the Gilberts. Called Operation Galvanic, the campaign called for Vice-Admiral Raymond A. Spruance to lead his 5th Fleet against Japanese positions within the archipelago in November.

For Operation Galvanic, Spruance had 139 vessels. These included 29 troop transports that were to land members of the V Amphibious Force on islands within the Gilbert chain. Under the command of Major-General Holland M. Smith, V Amphibious Force contained the 2nd Marine and 27th Army Divisions, as well as an Assault Force. The latter group fell under the command of Rear-Admiral Richard K. Turner and consisted of seven battleships armed with 356mm (14in) and 406mm (16in) guns, eight cruisers,

35 destroyers, and eight escort carriers, collectively holding 218 warplanes. It had been devised to pound enemy positions on the islands with shells and air strikes, while the V Amphibious Force descended upon the beaches. Rear-Admiral Turner also enjoyed the use of the 7th United States Army Air Force (USAAF) to help with this task. Meanwhile, Rear-Admiral C.A. Pownall led Task Force 58, which included five battleships and 11 fast carriers possessing 700 aircraft. Pownall's role was to patrol the waters around the Gilberts and prevent any outside Japanese warships from coming to the aid of their beleaguered comrades within the chain.

In September 1943, the Japanese high command in Tokyo set to work formulating a defensive strategy called the New Operational Policy. This plan envisioned a line of defence that ran along New Guinea, Biak Island, the Carolines and the Marianas. Japanese forces east of this line received instructions to hold their positions if attacked and wait for reinforcements if besieged. Within this eastern sector, Rear-Admiral Keiji Shibasaki commanded Japanese defensive positions in the Gilberts and had converted several islands into well-protected fortresses. One such island was Betio, which was within the Tarawa cluster. Betio measured 3.2km (2 miles) long and 0.8km (half a mile) wide and was occupied

OPPOSITE

Members of the 163rd Infantry Regiment, 41st Division emerge from an LST in preparation for an attack on a Japanese garrison at Aitape on the northern coast of New Guinea. The Americans seized the town with little difficulty.

ABOVE

Several Navy Air Group Commanders and Squadron Commanders get together on the flight deck of their carrier before taking off to raid Tarawa in the Gilbert Islands on 18 and 19 September 1943.

by an entrenched 4500-man garrison which possessed heavy machine-guns, mortars and artillery pieces.

On 20 November, an American flotilla of three battleships, four cruisers and nine destroyers opened fire upon Betio. In addition, aircraft from Furafuti arrived to strike the island from the air. However, despite these preparatory actions, the 2nd Marine Division was met with stiff resistance when it landed on three beaches surrounding the island. The divisional commander, Major-General Julian C. Smith, then sent in his reserve regiment, ensuring that superior numbers and armaments would prevail over the fanatical courage of the Japanese defenders. Ultimately, although the American Marines had to use flamethrowers, grenades and explosives, they destroyed the entire garrison on Betio. When the battle ended on 23 November, only 17 Japanese soldiers survived, along with 129 Korean labourers. Out of the 17,000 American Marines who had attacked the island,about 1000 died and a further 2000 suffered injuries.

On 20 November, Major-General Ralph C. Smith landed his 27th Army Division upon

Makin atoll, which lay 160km (100 miles) north of the Tarawa cluster. After three days of fighting, the Americans took the island; they had suffered only 64 dead and 150 wounded. On the same day, south-east of the Tarawa cluster the 68th Marine Regiment's 5th Amphibious Reconnaissance Company seized Abemama atoll without a fight. Meanwhile, Task Force 58 kept Japanese reinforcements away from the Gilberts by pummelling air bases at Nauru island and Mili atoll in the Marshall chain. To the south-west, American warplanes from the *Saratoga* and *Princeton* damaged seven cruisers and two Japanese destroyers which were docked at Rabaul, while 5th USAAF fighters knocked Japanese aircraft out of the skies around New Britain and Bougainville.

During the fighting over the Gilberts, the Japanese did manage to inflict some damage upon the Americans. One submarine damaged the light carrier *Independence* in November; and another destroyed the escort carrier *Liscome Bay* four days afterwards, killing several American sailors in the process. However, the Gilberts had fallen securely into American hands

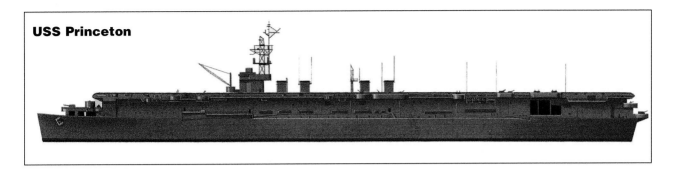

USS Princeton

by the end of the month, enabling the 5th Fleet to turn its attention north-west to the Marshall Islands. By the beginning of 1944, the Americans were ready to attack.

In preparation for this campaign, Admiral Spruance added more vessels to Turner's Assault Force, which now included 300 warships and transport vehicles. The 5th Fleet commander also enhanced the size of Task Force 58, now led by Rear-Admiral Marc A. Mitscher. As a result, this unit possessed 12 carriers − collectively holding 715 fighters, dive-bombers, and torpedo-bombers − as support for the invasion. Mitscher then divided his command into four roughly equal Task Groups which were charged with keeping Japanese reinforcements away from the Marshalls.

Spruance, Turner and other senior officers sought to avoid the carnage that the Americans had seen during their one intense assault on the Gilberts. Thus, they resolved to pick off important islands one by one, ignoring all areas deemed unnecessary. To carry out this objective, the V Amphibious

Force received new units, including the 4th Marine Division under Major-General Harry Schmidt and the 7th Army Division under Major-General Charles H. Corlett. Altogether, 53,000 ground troops were to attack targeted islands, while 31,000 reserves stood by to occupy and consolidate American control over subdued areas.

In late January, Operation Flintlock began. The 5th Fleet bombarded the atolls of Wotje and Maloelap, while the V Amphibious Force prepared to land on Kwajalein atoll to the west. For about two weeks, the naval group kept Japanese forces pinned down with about 6000 aircraft sorties that dropped over 1000 tonnes of bombs on Wotje and Maleolap. South-east of these areas, without opposition, Spruance occupied Majuro atoll, a superb natural naval base that Nimitz would use for future campaigns to the west. Meanwhile, the amphibious force began their attack on Kwajalein on 31 January.

On the northern tip of the atoll, the 4th Marine Division conquered the islands of Roi and Namur within a day. In the south-

ABOVE
Originally intended to be a light cruiser, the USS Princeton was redesigned after the battle of Pearl Harbor to serve as a light carrier capable of holding 24 fighters and nine torpedo bombers. During the battle of Leyte Gulf, a Japanese dive bomber damaged Princeton badly enough to force the Americans to abandon and sink the vessel.

LEFT
American warships and transport vessels in convoy approach Tarawa atoll, an area that became the site of some of the most vicious combat in the Gilbert Islands. In November 1943, the 2nd Division, United States Marine Corps secured the archipelago after over-powering the occupying Japanese forces.

east corner of the atoll, during the first week of February the 7th Army Division secured control of Ebbaye and Kwajalein islands. By the end of Operation Flintlock on 7 February, American casualties were comparitively low – 400 dead and 1600 wounded – whereas Japanese losses exceeded 8000 men killed in action, including the commander of the Kwajalein garrison.

With the eastern Marshalls now safely in American hands, the 5th Fleet prepared to unleash Operation Catchpole, an assault on Eniwetok atoll which lay 580km (360 miles) north-west of Kwajalein. Before this assault could be conducted, enemy counter-measures had to be blocked. Accordingly, Admiral Mitscher dispatched nine fast carriers, six battleships, 10 cruisers and 28 destroyers from Task Force 58 to Truk in the Caroline Islands – 1240km (770 miles) west of the Marshalls – which was the site of a large Japanese air and naval base. In a two-day raid, christened Operation Hailstone, Task Force 58's warplanes sank an incredible three destroyers, seven fleet auxiliary vessels, six tankers and 17 cargo ships. Its pilots also shot down about 50 Japanese aircraft and demolished at least another 200 that were sitting on their runways. Meanwhile, the submarine *Skate* sank the Japanese light cruiser *Agano*, and

battleships from the 5th Fleet sank the destroyer *Maikaze* and the light cruiser *Katori* while these vessels were trying to elude Mitscher's aircraft.

Eniwetok conquered

Taken completely by surprise, the Japanese defenders at Truk did not land any significant counterpunches against the US force. Altogether, they shot down only 35 American aircraft and damaged the fleet carrier *Intrepid* with a torpedo. After the attack, because Truk was such an important point in Japan's defensive strategy, the commander-in-chief of the Imperial Combined Fleet, Admiral Mineichi Koga, dispatched the remaining warplanes from Rabaul to the island. However, this move effectively left Japanese troops on New Guinea without air support against General MacArthur and his allied forces. Back in Tokyo, General Hideki Tojo used the Truk debacle as a pretext for firing his navy chief-of-staff, Admiral Osami Nagono.

The task of conquering Eniwetok atoll fell into the hands of reservists from the V Amphibious Force, which included the 22nd Marine Regiment and 106th Regimental Combat Team, 27th Army Division. On 18 February, these units stormed Engebi island and took it after a two-day fight. Days later,

BELOW

Marine reinforcements arrive on Tarawa to aid their comrades in the conquest of the atoll. In four days of combat, the battle for the cluster claimed the lives of over 1000 Americans and around 4000 Japanese defenders.

LEFT
At Tarawa, a Marine, armed with a carbine and a bandolier of bullets, prepares to charge an enemy position, while his comrade tosses a grenade to help cover their upcoming attack.

they seized Parry and Eniwetok islands, securing control of the atoll by 23 February. During the fighting, the American regiments suffered 195 killed and 521 wounded personnel. As usual, Japanese casualties were much higher: 2677 out of the 2741 defenders on the atoll had fought to the death.

To minimise their own casualties, the Americans stuck with their island-hopping strategy, allowing remnants of the Japanese forces to remain stranded on Wotje, Moleap and Mili atolls for the rest of the war. With the Marshalls now in the possession of the Central Pacific Fleet, Admiral Nimitz was in a good position to continue pressing against the boundaries of the Japanese Empire. The Marshalls would serve as a good launching

point for further incursions to the west, as they were 4800km (3000 miles) west-southwest of Pearl Harbor, 1062km (660 miles) north-east of Truk island in the Carolines and 1600km (1000 miles) south-east of Saipan in the Marianas.

The situation in Burma

While the Americans pushed into Japanese-held areas within the Pacific Ocean, British and colonial forces made another effort to retake parts of Burma. After the failure of the First Arakan Campaign in May 1943, senior British military officers were forced to reorganise the command system of the Burma front. General Lord Archibald Wavell, commander-in-chief of British

BELOW
In Burma and other parts of the Far Eastern theatre of World War II, the Royal Air Force relied upon the Hawker Hurricane as its primary fighter, fighter-bomber and reconnaissance aircraft. Although not as fast as the Supermarine Spitfire and other Allied aircraft, the Hurricane was a tough and manoeuvrable warplane capable of reaching a speed of 540km (336 miles) per hour.

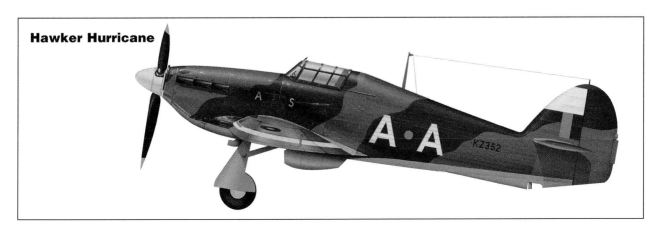

Hawker Hurricane

armed forces in India, became the Viceroy of the subcontinent so that he might have more authority over civilian aspects within the colony. From this position he would be better placed to suppress pro-Axis activity by any nationalist groups. With his headquarters in Ceylon, on 25 August 1943 Lord Louis Mountbatten assumed the role of Allied Supreme Commander of the South-East Asia Command. From the Middle East, Sir Claude Auchinleck arrived to replace Wavell as commander-in-chief in India.

Mountbatten and Auchinleck's new command structure centred around a new 11th Army Group, headed by General Sir George Giffard. Within this was a new 14th

Army, led by Lieutenant-General William Slim, which was responsible for operations in Burma. Within the 14th Army, Lieutenant-General A.F.P. Christison assumed command of XV Corps, which would be the primary unit involved in a second campaign against Japanese positions around the Arakan Yoma mountain range. Initially this corps consisted of the 5th and 7th Indian Divisions, as well as most of the 81st West African Division. Later, Christison would receive three more divisions for the campaign, which was scheduled to begin in December 1943.

General Auchinleck's first task in India was to establish effective administrative and training facilities that would create crack

Bristol Beaufighter

troops capable of better soldiering than had been seen in the First Arakan Campaign. Unlike the tough veterans who had distinguished themselves in North Africa, the Indian soldiers under Auchinleck's command tended to be green and demoralised. Most of them were from arid regions in north-west India and were unaccustomed to the jungles of Burma. Moreover, they rarely interacted with their British officers and thus felt little loyalty to them. Undaunted by these obstacles, Auchinleck and his senior commanders initiated reforms that would eventually turn the 14th Army into a first-rate organisation.

Firstly, Auchinleck's generals formed their forces into brigades, each with three battalions: one British, one Indian and one Gurkha. With this formation, the generals hoped that the professionalism of the British soldiers and the courage of the Nepalese Gurkhas would influence the inexperienced Indians. Secondly, Auchinleck implemented training regimens in jungle, riverine and night-time combat, as well as in rationing, so that the soldiers would become accustomed to deprivation when

situated in remote areas for extended periods. Thirdly, the 14th Army tackled the problem of malaria, a disease that was disabling several times more troops than combat wounds. Its commanders established forward malarial treatment centres, which would preclude the need to evacuate afflicted soldiers to distant hospitals. These treatment centres would be well supplied with mepacrine.

As a final reform, the British made plans to exploit their growing air superiority to its fullest. For several months, heavy losses of aircraft in Pacific Ocean battles had been forcing Tokyo to divert many warplanes from Burma. In December 1942, the Japanese 5th Air Division possessed only 50 fighters and 90 medium bombers. Within a year, this air force would possess only 80 aircraft altogether. In contrast, by the time of the Second Arakan Campaign, No. 224 Group of the Royal Air Force (RAF) in Chittagong alone possessed 14 fighter and fighter-bomber squadrons, numbering altogether about 200 Hurricanes, Spitfires, Beaufighters and Vengeances. Other available units included elements of the

OPPOSITE

Marines occupying a large beach on Tarawa. Collectively, almost 17,000 Americans participated in the invasion of the atoll, suffering a casualty rate of 17 per cent.

BELOW

In their defence of Tarawa, Japanese forces employed 203mm (8in) Vickers naval guns that had been brought in from Singapore. Before the war, the Japanese government had purchased many such artillery pieces from the British. Here the guns have been retaken by the Americans.

ABOVE

*In the aftermath of the
battle for Tarawa, Marine
Corps Major-General Julian
C. Smith and Admiral
Chester W. Nimitz inspect
smashed Japanese pillboxes.
In the background, Army
Lieutenant-General Robert
C. Richardson climbs onto
the remains of one of
the pillboxes.*

United States Army Air Force (USAAF) and the RAF Strategic Air Force. The architects of the Second Arakan Campaign also had access to Brigadier-General W.D. Olds' USAAF and RAF Troop Carrier Command. With this air power at their disposal, Auchinleck and his senior officers decided to use the RAF aggressively against enemy ground forces in a capacity similar to artillery support. With good reason, they determined that their forces would be better off using support from the sky, rather than dragging a large collection of large howitzers through the Burma jungle highlands. Not surprisingly, the invasion force would rely upon air supplies while campaigning in remote locations.

The Second Arakan Campaign

Combined with this air superiority, Auchinleck's administrative reforms for the 14th Army would prove crucial to the outcome of the Second Arakan Campaign. By the summer of 1943, the British and colonial forces in India had completed this reform, replenishment and reorganisation. In preparation for the upcoming operation, XV Corps received more divisions, including the 25th and 26th Indian, and the British 36th, bringing its total strength to six and a half

divisions altogether. It also possessed the No. 3 Special Service Brigade, which contained four commando units and a detachment of engineers charged with maintaining lines of communication and constructing airfields. Meanwhile, the Service Corps and flotillas of boats from the Royal Navy (RN) were to maintain supply lines in Burma.

Along with the depleted 5th Air Division, the Japanese presence in Burma consisted of the 54th and 55th Divisions of the 28th Army. Under the command of Lieutenant-General Tadashi Hanaya, the 55th Division was the only ground force to face XV Corps in the Arakan region; the 54th Division held back to defend coastal areas south of Akyab Island. A significant weakness in Hanaya's command was his fragile communication lines that went by track across the Arakan Yomas to Pakokku in the north-east and down to Prome in the south-east.

Late in 1943, Christison's XV Corps moved down the Mayu Peninsula. By mid-January, it was in place to strike the heavily fortified Maungdaw-Buthidaung Line. Meanwhile, the Japanese high command decided to launch a counter-offensive on the Indian state of Assam. For several months, Japanese generals in Burma had wanted to mount an invasion into India, and were all too delighted when Tokyo granted permission to do so. Thus, Lieutenant-General Renya Mutaguchi received orders to lead his 15th Army in an offensive across the Chindwin Hills to sever the communication lines of IV Corps at Imphal and crush British forces in the area. To lure as many British and colonial forces as possible away from north-east India and into the Arakan coastal region, Hanaya planned to start the HA-GO Offensive against XV Corps. This was to begin on 3 February 1944.

By this time, Christison's divisions – supported by 26th Indian and 36th British Divisions – were attacking Japanese positions along the Tunnels Road, which ran from the coast to Buthidaung. With support from armoured units, three brigades from the 5th Indian Divison fell upon Razabil and Maungdaw. Several miles inland in the Mayu Valley, three brigades from the 7th Indian Division assaulted Buthidaung. Even further east, Major-General C.G. Woolner's 81st West African Division advanced along the Kaladin River, seeing little action.

General Hanaya met this invasion by deploying four battalions into defensive positions. One battalion remained on the Mayu peninsula to guard the coast, while two more performed a similar function on Akyab island. Between the Bay of Bengal and the Mayu River, two battalions – later known as the Doi Column – formed a defensive

line along the Tunnels Road. Hanaya then dispatched a reconnaissance regiment to the Kaladan Valley near Myohaung to keep watch over the activity of the West Africans.

Japanese countermeasures

This deployment left the 55th Division with five battalions and an engineer regiment to serve as a penetration force in the execution of the HA-GO Offensive. Containing 5000 men altogether, it would fall under the command of Major-General T. Sakurai, and thus be known as the Sakurai Column. Its mission, planned for the night of 3 February, was to punch through the 7th Division near the Kalapanzin River, capture Taung Bazar, head west, cross the Mayu River and cut the

BELOW
During the battle of the Marshall Islands, a burning Japanese torpedo bomber plunges into the Pacific Ocean. The crewmen of the aircraft were trying to sink an American carrier when gunners aboard the vessel opened fire and shot down the warplane.

LEFT
A photograph taken from an Avenger torpedo bomber offers a bird's-eye view of Marcus Island in the aftermath of an American attack on a Japanese base. During the raid, the Japanese lost many storage tanks and warplanes.

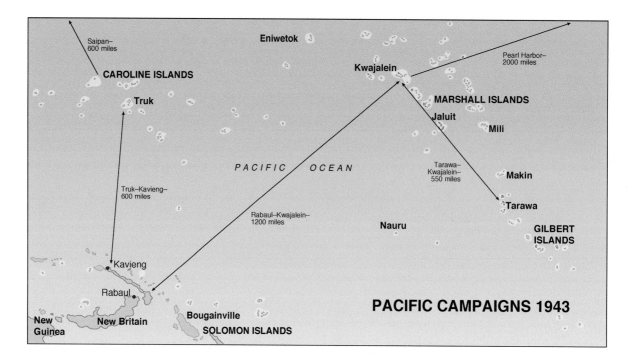

Saipan–
600 miles

Eniwetok

Pearl Harbor–
2000 miles

CAROLINE ISLANDS

Kwajalein

Truk

MARSHALL ISLANDS

Jaluit

Mili

PACIFIC OCEAN

Tarawa–
Kwajalein–
550 miles

Makin

Truk–Kavieng–
600 miles

Rabaul–Kwajalein–
1200 miles

Tarawa

Nauru

GILBERT
ISLANDS

Kavieng

Rabaul

PACIFIC CAMPAIGNS 1943

New
Guinea

New Britain

Bougainville

SOLOMON ISLANDS

communication lines of both Indian divisions. Meanwhile, the Doi Column was to pressure the Indian divisions from the south.

At first, the operation went well. The Sakurai Column reached Taung Bazar on the morning of 4 February and, by 5 February, was completely behind the 5th Division. While a detachment occupied Briasco Bridge on the coast road, the main part of the Sakurai Column overran the division's headquarters at Wabyin and assaulted XV Corps' Administrative Area at Sinzweya. This was crucial to the Japanese, who needed to capture the site in order to utilise its supplies and thus continue the offensive. Meanwhile, Hanaya committed all available air power to the area, launching about 350 bomber sorties against British and colonial positions.

RIGHT
American Marines surround two Japanese soldiers occupying a pillbox on Namur Island, located in the Kwajalein atoll of the Marshall Islands. In a battle that lasted a week, the Americans killed more than 8000 enemy troops before taking the atoll.

LEFT
Japanese prisoners captured at Kwajalein sit aboard a landing craft and prepare for transportation to a prison ship. During the battle for the atoll, the Americans captured 264 Japanese defenders.

BELOW
This Marine, of the 2nd Marine Division at Tarawa in November 1943, has captured two Japanese trophies: a sword and a water bottle.

However, by this time, the Indian troops' resistance had stiffened. While British aircraft dropped supplies to the two divisions, the brigades defending Sinzweya held their ground. General Giffard then ordered the 36th British Division from Chittagong to aid their comrades. Meanwhile, conditions worsened for the HA-GO Offensive when the 7th Division severed the Sakurai Column's communication lines and captured General Sakurai's code-book which contained radio frequencies and call signals. As a result, the column was now isolated and its commander unable to coordinate and command battles effectively. Hanaya responded to this problem by reinforcing the Doi Column and urging it to intensify its attacks from the south in order to take pressure off Sakurai's forces.

Aware that the Japanese offensive was doomed unless the Sakurai Column captured the Administrative Area – as well as the supplies the base was receiving from the air – General Slim ordered the 26th Indian and 36th British Divisions to help raise the siege on Sinzweya. Meanwhile, the RAF kept sending transports into the Arakan region, ensuring that the divisions from XV Corps were well supplied. Although the air force lost some aircraft during the campaign, its pilots delivered over 2700 tons of provisions to Christison's divisions.

East of the Administrative Area, General Hanaya had more luck against the 81st West African Division along the Kaladan River. On 18 February he assembled a unit that consisted of the 55th Reconnaissance Regiment, three infantry battalions and a regimental headquarters, placing it under the command of Colonel Tai Koba. Sent to meet the advancing West Africans, the Koba Force harassed General Woolner's troops with ambushes and flanking manoeuvres. These well-executed actions pushed them out of Kyauktaw and eventually out of the Kaladan Valley altogether.

On 24 February, General Hanaya persuaded his superiors that the attack on Sinzweya was an exercise in futility. Thus he gained permission to order the Sakurai Column to return to Japanese lines behind the Tunnels Roads. Although the Indian divisions had suffered about 3500 casualties during the HA-GO Offensive, they held their ground and enjoyed a significant boost in morale. However, Hanaya's forces boasted accomplishments of their own. In effect, one Japanese division had temporarily knocked two enemy divisions off balance and kept all six and a half divisions of XV Corps bogged down in the Arakan region. Meanwhile General Mutaguchi's 15th Army had marched across the Chindwin Hills and threatened Imphal. With just 8000 men, the 55th Division had prevented 27 Indian, 18 British, 7 West African and 5 Gurkha battalions from rushing to the aid of IV Corps.

In March, while the Japanese offensive on Imphal was just getting started, the 5th Indian Division captured Razabil, while the 7th Indian Division seized Buthidaung, thus securing a large portion of the Tunnels Road. On 22 March, General Giffard transferred these two divisions to north-east India to help defend Imphal.

The 26th Indian and 36th British Divisions then stepped in to occupy these newly acquired areas in the Arakan region. Later on, the 25th Indian Division replaced the 36th Division, which would be dispatched to northern Burma in order to give assistance to the Chindit brigades.

While Hanaya pulled his division back to more defensible positions and waited for the monsoon season to begin, Christison's divisions seized Maungdaw and Point 551. The Second Arakan Campaign effectively came to an end. From his new positions, Christison planned to launch a third campaign south of the Tunnels Road. Meanwhile, Major-General Charles Orde Wingate was executing the Second Chindit Campaign in the northern part of Burma.

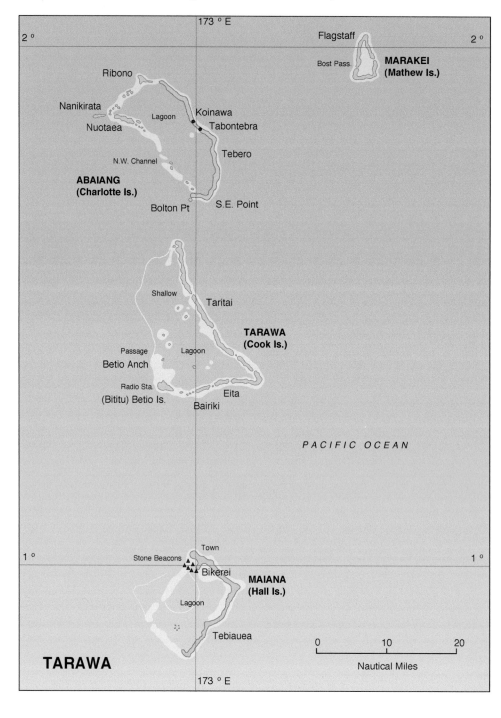

LEFT

After enduring two days of continuous combat on Eniwetok atoll in the Marshall Islands, American Marines sip coffee aboard a transport ship. The seizure of the atoll in late February 1944 completed the Allied conquest of the archipelago.

BELOW

British Spitfires return from a successful mission in Burma. The introduction of this fast and manoeuvrable fighter to the region helped ensure the continuation of Allied air superiority over the dwindling Japanese 5th Air Division.

Return of the Chindits

In November 1943, Roosevelt, Churchill and Chiang Kai-shek met in Cairo to discuss military and political priorities in Asia. Although the three political leaders disagreed over several issues, they managed to form a policy aimed at opening land and air routes between India and China. The result of this policy was an order directed at the commanders of all Allied forces in South East Asia. Beginning in February 1944, they were to initiate a campaign to seize northern Burma from the Japanese. All other military actions in the region would be in support of this objective. Churchill and Roosevelt both recognised the importance of securing the region, as it would maintain military ties and logistical lines to China. They feared that failure to do this would cause Chiang to drop out of the war and would enable the 26 Japanese divisions within the country to re-deploy against Allied forces elsewhere.

Although the First Chindit Operation had stalled on the Irrawaddy River in the spring of 1943, General Wingate and his superiors believed that they could secure northern

Burma if they perfected the formations and tactics of their irregular forces. Officially known as the 3rd Indian Division, the re-organised Chindits would form six brigades, known as Long-Range Penetration Groups (LRPG). The 14th Infantry Brigade, under Brigadier T. Brodie, contained the 1st Bedfordshire and Hertfordshire Regiments, the 7th Leicestershire Regiment, the 2nd Black Watch and the 2nd York and Lancaster Regiment. The 16th Infantry Brigade, led by Brigadier B.E. Fergusson, included four regiments: the 2nd Queen's Royal, the 2nd Leicestershire, the 45th Reconnaissance and the 51st/69th Field Regiment of the Royal Artillery. The 23rd Infantry Brigade, which was overseen by Brigadier L.E.C. Perowne, also contained four regiments: the 2nd Duke of Wellington's, the 4th Border and the 1st Essex, as well as the 60th Field Regiment of the Royal Artillery.

The other three Chindit LRPGs were officially designated as colonial brigades, although two of them actually possessed at least one British regiment. Brigadier J.M. Calvert commanded the 77th Indian Brigade,

Chinese troops cross the Salween River in eastern Burma. While the armies of Chiang Kai-shek pressured Japanese forces from the east, British-led Chindit Brigades invaded northern Burma from the west.

which included the 1st King's (Liverpool) Regiment, the 1st Lancashire Fusiliers, and the 1st Staffordshire Regiments, along with the 3rd Battalion, 6th Gurkha Rifles and the 3rd Battalion, 9th Gurkha Rifles. The 111st Indian Brigade served under Brigadier W.D.A. Lentaigne and contained the 2nd King's Own Royal Regiment and the 1st Cameronians, as well as the 3rd Battalion, 4th Gurkha Rifles and the 4th Battalion, 9th Gurkha Rifles.

Finally, Brigadier A.H. Gillmore led the 3rd West African Brigade, which included the 6th, 7th and 12th Nigeria Regiments. Each LRPG also contained a company of engineers, a detachment of Burmese scouts, RAF liaison officers, medical personnel and troops of light or anti-aircraft artillery.

With the Chindits thus organised, General Wingate implemented tactical policies aimed at promoting quick mobility and flexibility. He divided the regiments into eight 400-man columns. Each column was almost an independent unit, possessing its own mortars, machine-guns and support services. In addition, air force officers marched with these columns to ensure effective communication with fighter and bomber pilots. In the training programme for the Chindit brigades, General Wingate stressed the necessity of being able to break down into columns or even companies to manoeuvre and strike stealthily, then reassemble into regiments or brigades that could hold on to captured positions inside the Burmese countryside.

Within the country, the Japanese Burma Area Army group had three armies, along with several reservist and independent units. While the Japanese 28th Army occupied the Arakan region and the 15th Army moved on Imphal, it was the 33rd Army, under Lieutenant-General M. Honda, which guarded northern Burma, thus becoming the Chindit operation's primary adversary. To

ABOVE
Near Myitkyina, Burma, American troops fire shells from a 37mm (1.5in) anti-tank gun at a Japanese pillbox. In August 1944, the town fell to American and Chinese forces.

the east, Honda's divisions also had to deal with American and Chinese forces under Lieutenant-General Joseph Stilwell. Later, the 53rd Division would arrive from Formosa to help Honda deal with the Allied incursions. When available, the 5th Air Division could also help to defend northern Burma, although increasing Allied air superiority would render this task difficult.

In order to disrupt Japanese communication lines within northern Burma and to wrest control of the area, General Wingate developed a plan for his Chindit forces. While the 16th Brigade marched overland from Ledo, the 77th and 111th Brigades were to perform glider-borne landings at clearings near the Irrawaddy River. The three groups then would descend upon Indaw, the site of an important Japanese airfield and communication centre. If the capture of this area lasted more than two months, Wingate planned to rotate the brigades out and replace them with the other three.

On 5 February 1944, Fergusson's 16th Brigade began its 580km (360-mile) march. A month later, while Mutaguchi's U-GO Offensive on Imphal was under way, the brigade crossed the Chindwin River. On 16 March, these forces occupied Lonkin, about

160km (100 miles) north of Indaw. About 80km (50 miles) north-east of the objective, on the night of 5/6 March, Calvert's 77th Brigade began its landing on a site designated as Broadway field. Over a period of four nights, 12,000 men, 3000 mules, several small artillery pieces and large amounts of food and equipment reached the area without incident. South-east of Indaw, part of Lentaigne's 111th Brigade performed a similar feat at Chow-ringee field, although the group would later abandon this site after Lentaigne decided that his forces were in a remote location and too vulnerable to air and ground assaults. Thus, the rest of 111th Brigade landed at Broadway.

Indaw besieged

To protect Broadway field, Calvert left the 3/9th Gurkhas to serve as its garrison, while two columns from the King's Liverpool Regiment remained as a 'floater' unit that was to patrol the surrounding countryside and harass any Japanese forces that might attack Broadway field. The rest of the 77th Brigade advanced on Mawlu, a town just north of Indaw, planning to establish a blocking position on a railroad that ran from Indaw to Myitkyina, several kilometres to the north-east near China. After a brief skirmish, on 16

March 77th Brigade reached a position along the railroad 1.6km (1 mile) north of Mawlu and constructed a base that would be known as White City. The troops quickly constructed bomb-proof dugouts, gun emplacements, telephone lines and a network of barbed wire to keep the Japanese at bay. They also captured the lightly defended town of Mawlu with little difficulty before withdrawing, as it had no military value for them.

From Chowringee, Lentaigne led parts of his 111th Brigade north-west to aid Calvert in the offensive on Indaw. During this advance, Lentaigne detached a column from 3/4th Gurkhas and ordered it to act as an independent unit that was to destroy bridges along roads east of Indaw. Eventually known as Morris Force, this unit established a base in the Kachin Hills near the Chinese border and launched a three-month raiding operation on the Bhamo-Myitkyina Road, thus depriving the Japanese of the use of this artery for the transportation of supplies. However, they still had access to the Irrawaddy River.

While Lentaigne moved in to isolate Indaw from the south, Fergusson's 16th Brigade arrived to prepare an attack on the town. By this time, Brodie's 14th Brigade and Gillmore's 3rd West Africans had landed at Aberdeen field, near White City, to join the other Chindit units. However, before the 111th Brigade could reach their positions below Indaw, Japanese reinforcements arrived and, on 21 March, a relief column – which comprised three battalions from the 24th Independent Mixed Brigade joined with elements of the 4th Infantry Regiment – entered the town and took up defensive positions. Five days later, these defenders repulsed an attacked launched by Fergusson's battalions while more battalions arrived with artillery and engineer detachments. The Japanese garrison at Indaw was now a formidable obstacle.

By this time, Lieutenant-General Masakazu Kawabe and other senior officers in the Japanese Burma Area Army group were considering abandoning the U-GO Offensive on Imphal in order to expel the Chindits from northern Burma. Over Mutaguchi's protests, Kawabe diverted a battalion from the 15th Army to aid the 24th Independent Mixed Brigade at Indaw. The Burma Area commander also pulled the 5th Air Division from the Imphal front to provide air support for Japanese ground troops in northern

BELOW

Two B-25 Mitchell medium bombers from the 5th United States Army Air Force attack an airfield at Wewak on the northern coast of New Guinea. These planes held up to 1360kg (3000lb) of bombs and were capable of travelling at 442km (275 miles) per hour.

Burma. He also considered abandoning the U-GO Offensive altogether.

Meanwhile, the II/146th Battalion, 56th Division received orders from Honda to attack Broadway, but on the way to their objective the Japanese soldiers were spotted by a Burmese reconnaissance patrol and suffered substantial casualties in a harassing action. When they reached the base, they penetrated it only briefly before its Gurkha defenders repulsed them with 11.3kg (25lb) field guns.

After a few days of attacks and counter-attacks, the King's Liverpool Regiment struck the Japanese from behind and almost enveloped them, forcing them to withdraw with about 150 of their men killed in action. In addition to this, anti-aircraft crews and squadrons of Spitfires shot down several Japanese Oscars that were attempting to devastate Broadway field; and an assault by the III/114th Battalion, 18th Division on White City also ended in failure.

Deeper into Burma

On 25 March, Wingate perished in an airplane crash after leaving a meeting with Air-Marshal Sir John Baldwin, the commander of the 3rd Tactical Air Force, in Imphal. A charismatic leader among his Chindit warriors, his death created uncertainty about the success of the north Burma campaign. Two days later, Lentaigne assumed overall command of the 3rd Indian Infantry Division. The new leader of the Chindits now had to deal with more rigorous Japanese countermeasures against his positions near Indaw.

Days later, the 24th Independent Mixed Brigade received more reinforcements. Now the size of a division, it moved on White City. After an artillery bombardment against Chindit positions, three Japanese battalions struck the base on the night of 5/6 April. Since the Chindits enjoyed a clear view of the paddy fields to the south and west, the battalions attacked from the jungle cover north and east of White City. However,

BELOW

American soldiers from the 163rd Regimental Combat Team, 41st Army Division descend upon Wakde Island off the northern coast of New Guinea, on 18 May 1944. The action was part of the Hollandia Campaign launched by General Douglas MacArthur to push the Japanese into the interior of New Guinea.

stalled along the perimeter of the base, they suffered high casualties and fell back when Chindit mortar teams and machine-gun crews tore into them. Another attack just before dawn produced similar results.

The following morning, swarms of P-51 Mustang fighters and B-25 Mitchell bombers strafed and pounded Japanese positions near White City. Although these air strikes inflicted substantial damage, fresh troops from the 24th Brigade launched another attack that night. Although armed with Bangalore torpedoes to rip holes through barbed-wire emplacements and other obstacles, the attackers were repulsed yet again in two assaults during the night. Subsequent attacks by seven fresh battalions during the next three nights also proved to be costly failures. In the sky above, anti-aircraft crews in White City and Allied fighters effectively neutralised the 5th Air Division during the Chindit campaign.

Meanwhile, Chindit 'floater' columns flanked around the 24th Brigade. While the 7th Nigerian Regiment severed Japanese communication lines between Mawlu and Indaw, the 3/6th Gurkhas and the 45th Reconnaissance Regiment attacked from the south-east, overrunning the brigade's headquarters, administrative areas and several artillery emplacements. Now squeezed between White City and a fierce counter-attacking force, the Japanese assaulted the

base in a last desperate charge that killed their commander. From the base, soldiers from the 6th Nigerian Regiment then rushed the brigade from the north, while the Gurkhas and Reconnaissance troops continued pressing from the south. In addition, 27 Mustangs swooped down from the sky and strafed Japanese positions relentlessly.

Although the Chindits might have been able to annihilate the 24th Brigade completely, Calvert allowed its survivors to retreat south. On 18 April, the Chindits managed to occupy Indaw. They then continued their campaign of destruction throughout the area. Later in the month, soldiers from Brodie's 14th Brigade demolished 21 supply and ammunition dumps, incinerated 68,200 litres (15,000 gallons) of gasoline and severed the railroad at 16 places south of Indaw. They also left booby-traps and mines wherever they went. This activity inflicted significant damage to Japanese communication lines running from Burma to the divisions attacking Imphal and Kohina.

At the end of the month, South-East Asia Command ordered the Chindits to abandon Indaw, Mawlu, White City, Aberdeen and Broadway and to head north-east to help General Stilwell capture Myitkyina and Mogaung. Specifically, the 111th Brigade was to establish a blocking position at the Indaw-Myitkyina railroad near the town of Hopin.

Calvert's 77th Brigade would then follow and protect the east side of this position, while the 3rd West African guarded the west side. At this point, the Chindits were to clear an airfield that would be known as Blackpool.

The Chindits suffered from many problems during this phase of their campaign. Blackpool was not located directly on the railroad. Instead, the field was on a nearby spur that protruded into a valley, thus rendering a defensive position there vulnerable to an artillery bombardment. Moreover, the arrival of the monsoon season had flooded the surrounding lowland, which would deter the 77th Brigade from reaching Blackpool in the event of an enemy attack. Finally, the 111th Brigade was inexperienced in the construction of fortifications, increasing the base's vulnerability in an assault.

BELOW

A US Private from the Indian Army Group in Burma, March 1944. This sniper is loaded down with water bottle, ammunition pouches, wire cutters attached to his belt and rucksack. His weapon is the M1903 sniper rifle fitted with the M73 B1 (Weaver 330c) telescopic sight.

On to Myitkyina

On 25 May, these fears came to fruition when the Japanese 53rd Division, under the command of Lieutenant-General K. Takeda, arrived from the recaptured town of Indaw and attacked the 111th Brigade in Blackpool. At the time, there was no support: the 77th Brigade was stranded by the floodwaters, and other Chindit brigades were diverted several kilometres west to Indawgyi Lake, guarding Catalina flying boats that were evacuating wounded and malaria-stricken soldiers. Thus isolated in a badly constructed fortification, the 111th Brigade were forced to evacuate Blackpool when enemy troops overran its perimeter.

Merrill's Marauders and a Chinese regiment captured Myitkyina's airfield on 17 May. However, after the collapse of Blackpool, Stilwell became concerned about the arrival of enemy reinforcements which would protect the rest of the town and Mogaung. Accordingly, he brought in 30,000 more troops from China to help him seize all of Myitkyina before any more

Japanese forces could arrive. Meanwhile, Lentaigne ordered the 77th Brigade to attack Mogaung. He also urged the Morris Force to assail Japanese garrisons along the eastern bank of the Irrawaddy River.

The task of defending Mogaung, Myitkyina and other areas in northeastern Burma had fallen into the hands of Honda's 33rd Army, which now included the 53rd Division. In the Hukawng Valley, the army's 18th Division in Kamaing resisted efforts by Stilwell's forces to dislodge it. However, a Chinese regiment severed Japanese communication lines and, after a fierce battle, the Allies seized the town and practically eliminated the 18th Division as an effective fighting force. To the south-east, a battalion

from the 56th Division slipped past 12 Chinese divisions to help defend Myitkyina from Merrill's Marauders. Outnumbered 15 to one, the 3000 Japanese soldiers held their ground for 76 days.

An Allied victory

In early June, Calvert's brigade reached Mogaung and attacked the Japanese garrison there with 2000 men. Unsupported by aircraft or artillery, they overran a hospital and ammunition cache and captured 50 prisoners before being stalled at a bridge that crossed a deep stream. This bridge was important, as it led to the rest of the town. After the fighting, the 3/6th Gurkhas located a ford, enabling the brigade to cross it during

the night and attack the Japanese defenders at the other side of the bridge. Now confronted with the likelihood of seeing Mogaung swamped by the Chindits, Honda ordered the 53rd Division to concentrate on the town's defence. With Mogaung thus reinforced, Calvert's brigade became the object of heavy artillery bombardment. However, 27 Mustangs from a nearby USAAF base soon came to their rescue, striking the Japanese batteries, while Chindit mortar teams pummelled Mogaung relentlessly, and on 17 June the Chinese 114th Regiment arrived with a battery of 25-pounders. After nine more days of intense combat, the 77th Brigade finally captured the town, suffering 1500 casualties in the process.

ABOVE
At Aitape, New Guinea, American soldiers interrogate Japanese prisoners-of-war. In April 1944, MacArthur's forces seized the town in a battle that claimed the lives of 19 Americans and 525 Japanese troops.

ABOVE

Soldiers from the 41st
Division relax in the
aftermath of the battle
for Aitape. The seizure
of the area around the
coastal town provided
the Americans with two
more airstrips to use in the
conquest of northern
New Guinea.

With Mogaung now in Allied hands, Stilwell planned to deploy the heavily depleted 77th and 111th Brigades against Myitkyina. By this time, however, Mountbatten had decided that these two Chindit groups had endured enough sacrifice and had them evacuated. Fortunately for Stilwell, the Japanese battalion defending Myitkyina was worn down. It evacuated the area in early August and his forces seized the town without opposition. The capture of both Mogaung and Myitkyina effectively completed the Allied conquest of northern Burma, enabling General Stilwell to secure a safe land and air passage between India and China.

Later in August, the remaining Chindit brigades in Burma captured more areas. On 9 August, the 3rd West Africans took Sahmaw. Three days later, they joined with the 14th Brigade to seize the railway town of Taugni, near the site of the ill-fated Blackpool garrison. Toward the end of the year, Stilwell sent three divisions west to occupy the old ground upon which the Chindits had operated. Severely weakened and demoralised, the surviving remnants of the Japanese 53rd and 18th Divisions withdrew from the region. By December, Stilwell's forces controlled Indaw and all areas north of it.

While the Central Pacific Fleet seized japanese-held islands in the east and Allied ground troops captured parts of Burma

in the west, General MacArthur's forces attacked Japanese positions in the south at New Guinea. In late March, MacArthur met with Nimitz and the commander of the 5th USAAF, Major-General George C. Kenney, in Brisbane. There they formed a strategy aimed at securing Burma's northern shore as a stepping-stone en route to the Philippines and Formosa. To ensure the success of this campaign – known as the Hollandia Operation – Nimitz offered to send carriers from Task Force 58 to provide air cover for MacArthur's amphibious landings, although he did express misgivings about the vulnerability of these vessels to Japanese aircraft. However, with some justification, Kenney claimed that this fear was unfounded; his warplanes had decimated enemy air power throughout the area.

When the Hollandia landings began, the Allies caught the enemy off guard. The Japanese had been expecting an assault, but at a later date. In late March, the commander of the Second Area Army, General Korechika Anami, suspected that an enemy attack would begin in western New Guinea; thus he ordered Lieutenant-General Hatazo Adachi to dispatch elements of the 18th Army to aid in its defence. Although Adachi thought MacArthur would strike Wewak and Hansa Bay in the eastern part of the island, he followed his orders, sending two regiments from Wewak on an arduous 338km (210-

mile) trek through crocodile-infested jungle to Hollandia. At that point, Allied naval supremacy above New Guinea prevented Adachi's regiments from riding transport ships to the area.

Thanks to an intercepted radio communication, the Americans were aware of Adachi's mistaken assumption, and so they launched naval and aerial bombardments against Wewak and Hansa Bay to act as decoys. The ruse was an unqualified success. When three attack forces from the American 6th Army landed west of these areas on 22 April, there were no enemy forces ready to meet them. East of Hollandia, the 163rd Regimental Combat Team, 41st Division landed on Aitape, the site of an air base, and overwhelmed a tiny garrison comprising mostly pilots and ground crewmen.

The assault on Hollandia

At Hollandia itself, the rest of the division surprised 11,000 Japanese servicemen in their garrison – most of whom were not combat soldiers – and chased them into the interior. Meanwhile, the 24th Division landed at Tanahmerah Bay, 35km (22 miles) west of Hollandia. From their landing sites, these two American divisions converged upon an air base near Lake Sentani and captured it in a four-day battle. The seizure of Hollandia turned out to be an almost effortless operation in which only 152 Americans died. The Japanese losses were much higher – about 3300 killed and another 600 captured – and their survivors fled west to a base at Sarmi.

The fall of Hollandia and Aitape placed the Japanese 18th Army in what MacArthur described as a 'loop of envelopment', with American forces to its west and Australians to its east. Isolated and suffering from diseases and dwindling supplies and provisions, Adachi's forces prepared for a desperate counter-attack on Aitape. Leaving 20,000 of his men at Wewak to protect that garrison from the Allies, Adachi led the remainder of his army to his objective. By late May, his 35,000-man expedition reached the eastern perimeter of Aitape and began a campaign to retake the base that would last for over two months.

Meanwhile, the Allies completed their conquest of the northern shore of New

BELOW
Australian troops cross a river deep within the rugged countryside of New Guinea. While MacArthur sent his American forces north to conquer the Philippines, Australian forces remained on the island to clear out pockets of enemy resistance.

Guinea. On 17 May, an assault group called
the Tornado Task Force – primarily the 163rd
Regimental Combat Team – landed near the
village of Toem. One part of the task force
attacked an airfield near Maffin Bay and the
other attacked Wakde Island. However, on
this occasion Japanese resistance was tough.
Wakde Island fell only after a fierce four-day
battle. At Maffin Bay, 10,000 well-entrenched
Japanese soldiers from the 36th Division, 2nd
Army fought tenaciously until September,
only overcome when reinforcements arrived
to help the Americans capture the airfield.
Losses during these engagements were again
uneven: whereas 440 Americans were killed,
the Japanese lost 5000.

The Allies' next objective was Biak Island,
320km (200 miles) north-west of Maffin Bay.
Occupied by about 4000 Japanese troops and
many more support personnel, the island
was riddled with caves and rugged features,
rendering it very difficult to conquer.
Nevertheless, at the end of May the 41st
Division landed on Biak and, after 11 days
of combat, secured an airfield. Fighting
continued for several more weeks until 20
August, when the commander of the 6th
Army, General Walter Krueger, declared the
island secure. By the time the operation was
over, 400 Americans were dead and over
2000 wounded in action. Japanese losses, as
usual, were much higher: 4700 men had been
killed and 220 captured.

West of Biak, the 158th Regimental
Combat Team landed on the island of
Noemfoor, the site of more Japanese
airfields. On 6 July, after intense bombings
upon Japanese positions by the 5th Air
Force, the regiment and 1400 men from
the 503rd Parachute Infantry captured the
island. The battle for Noemfoor killed 63
Americans and 2328 Japanese. However, the
seizure of Noemfoor, Biak, Maffin Bay and
Wakde gave MacArthur the airfields he so

**Type 95 Kyugo
Light Tank**

vitally needed for adequate air support for the offensive on the Philippines.

Vogelkop

At the end of the month, a newly assembled group from the 6th Division called the Typhoon Task Force landed in the Vogelkop peninsula on the western end of New Guinea. Faced with little opposition, the task force consolidated its control over the area, isolating the Japanese 2nd Army's headquarters at Manokwari. The seizure of Vogelkop effectively concluded MacArthur's Hollandia operation by ensuring Allied control of the entire northern coastline of New Guinea. With this goal now accomplished, the Allies could focus on the liberation of the Philippines.

However, New Guinea still contained several pockets of Japanese resistance within its interior, the most significant of which was at Aitape. Here Adachi's forces were attacking a garrison occupied by the American XI Corps, which comprised 15 infantry battalions and two dismounted cavalry squadrons. Twice in July, Adachi launched two ferocious assaults on the Americans, only to be repulsed with heavy losses. After losing about 10,000 men, on 9 August he withdrew his forces, limped back to Wewak and remained there until May 1945. The Allied leaders' decision to allow the remnants of 18th Army to stay there was consistent with the successful island-hopping strategy; Adachi's command was now a spent force occupying an area with little military value.

From Washington, General George C. Marshall asked General MacArthur what he planned to do about other Japanese units that were still at large inside New Guinea. In response, MacArthur said that the issue was of little importance; he would leave the task of clearing out enemy remnants within the island to General Sir Thomas Blamey and his Australian forces. For the rest of the war, 12 Australian brigades performed this hazardous but relatively unglamorous duty, while, true to form, General MacArthur bowed out, proceeding northwards to join the attack on the Philippines.

LEFT
Australian soldiers aboard a motorised canoe begin a patrolling operation on rivers near their forward post in New Guinea. The shallowness of such rivers prevented these troops from using larger vessels.

CHAPTER SEVEN

TWILIGHT OF THE RISING SUN

At the Marianas and Philippine Islands, the Americans fought a series of decisive battles in the air, at sea and on land to determine who would control much of the Pacific Ocean.

In mid-June 1944, the US 5th Fleet approached the Marianas Island chain on the eastern end of the Philippine Sea. An impressive naval force that contained 535 warships and troop transports and was filled with 127,571 soldiers and Marines, it was poised to strike at yet another section of the Japanese Empire. Located 2092km (1300 miles) south-east of Tokyo and 2404km (1500 miles) east of Manila, the archipelago was an important objective for the Allies. Admiral Chester W. Nimitz and other senior officers in his command realised that by conquering key islands within the Marianas they could disrupt enemy supply lines and isolate Japanese forces at Truk and other far-flung areas. Moreover, this would provide the United States Army Air Force (USAAF) with bases that would enable B-29 Superfortress bombers to strike Japan.

Specifically, the Americans planned to capture Saipan, Tinian and Guam in an operation called Operation Forager. Among the three islands, Nimitz selected Saipan as his first target because it was the closest to Japan and thus the most attractive location for the B-29s. A well-developed area that contained a substantial Japanese civilian population, Saipan was about 23km (14 miles) long and 8km (5 miles) wide. Its military presence consisted of 25,469 soldiers from the 31st Army, under the command of Lieutenant-General Yoshitsigu

Saito, and 6100 naval forces, led by Vice-Admiral Chuichi Nagumo. The garrison on Saipan had not received any reinforcements for several months because the Imperial General Headquarters did not expect the Allies to attack the Marianas. Instead, diversionary air strikes on the Palau Islands had led senior Japanese officers to assume that an offensive would take place hundreds of kilometres to the south.

In preparation for the impending invasion of Saipan, battleships from the 5th Fleet bombarded Japanese positions on the island. Unfortunately for the Marines charged with the task of landing, US naval gunners lacked experience in striking land-based targets and thus missed many enemy positions, and so, when the invasion began on 15 June on the south-west coast, many Japanese mortar and artillery crews were still in position to disable some of 2nd and 4th Marine Divisions' amphibious tractors ('amtracs') as they landed. Nevertheless, about 20,000 Marines reached their destination, although they had already lost 553 men killed and another 1022 wounded on the first day of the assault.

Several hours after landing, the two US divisions repelled two night-time attacks launched by General Saito. Within 24 hours, the Marines occupied a large section on Saipan's south-western corner. Secure in their

The pilot of an F6F Hellcat prepares to take off from the deck of the USS Lexington and attack enemy warplanes over the Marianas Islands. In this region, Japanese air power suffered a crippling defeat, ensuring almost uncontested American control over the skies above the Pacific Ocean.

positions, they prepared for a campaign to subdue the rest of the island by pushing inland until they seized advantageous positions on high ground. Then the 4th Division was to turn east and capture Aslito airfield, while the 2nd Division headed north and occupied Mount Tapotchau in the centre. In the mean time, two regiments from the 27th Army Division arrived to seize terrain between the two Marine forces.

Battle of the Philippine Sea

Although momentarily beaten, General Saito was encouraged when he learned that Vice-Admiral Jisaburo Ozawa and his First Mobile Fleet was en route to Saipan and that Ozawa had several additional warships arriving with him, including *Yamato* and *Musashi*, two powerful dreadnoughts. Thus reinforced, Ozawa now had five battleships, 13 cruisers, 28 destroyers and nine carriers possessing 430 aircraft under his command. However, he had fewer warplanes than the Americans and inexperienced pilots operated his fighters and

dive bombers. Nevertheless, the approaching Japanese fleet meant that the seizure of Saipan would require a great naval battle.

Vice-Admiral Raymond A. Spruance, the commander of the 5th Fleet, knew about Ozawa's approach, thanks to reports from two submarines that had spotted the Japanese warships in the Philippine Sea. This revelation forced him to abandon his plan to invade Guam – initially scheduled to begin on 18 June – and to send the bulk of his vessels on a retreat eastward. This would leave Task Force 58 to deal with the First Mobile Fleet. Commanded by Vice-Admiral Marc A. Mitscher, the task force travelled to a point 290km (180 miles) west of Tinian and waited for Ozawa. On 18 June, the Japanese spotted Mitscher's warships and prepared an attack.

The following morning, 61 Zeroes and eight torpedo bombers took off from the Japanese fleet and headed for Task Force 58. At the time, several American pilots in F6F Hellcats which were engaged in a dogfight with Japanese aircraft over Guam were told to return to the task force to regroup and prepare to fight Ozawa's warplanes. Meanwhile, Mitscher's dive bombers pummelled airstrips on Guam in order to prevent the aircraft from the First Mobile Fleet from landing on the island to refuel. Later in the morning, the Hellcat pilots returned to the sky to duel with the Zeroes. The ensuing aerial combat turned out to be a spectacular victory for the Americans, who would refer to the engagement as 'The Great Marianas Turkey Shoot'. In their defence of the warships of Task Force 58, the Hellcat pilots shot down 42 of the 69 aircraft in Ozawa's first air raid. Some Japanese pilots manoeuvred past the American fighters to damage the battleship *South Dakota*, killing 27 sailors. However, all of the fast carriers remained untouched.

Later in the day, Ozawa assembled another air-raid group of 53 dive bombers, 27 torpedo bombers and 48 fighters, and hurled it at the task force. The ensuing battle produced a result similar to the earlier dogfight.

The Hellcats shot down 70 more Japanese warplanes and ensured that every ship in Task Force 58 but one was unharmed. Only *Bunker Hill* sustained any damage, a minor amount from a torpedo that killed three men. Two more Japanese air assaults during the course of the day also failed, causing Ozawa to lose almost two-thirds of his warplanes altogether. Another 50 land-based aircraft also crashed on 19 June; a total of almost 300 Japanese warplanes had been destroyed in the bitter struggle over the Marianas Islands.

Below the waves, American submarines were also wreaking havoc on the First Mobile Fleet. On the same day as the 'Turkey Shoot', they sank two carriers, one of which was Ozawa's flagship, *Taiho*. However, the admiral and his staff escaped the sinking carrier on a lifeboat and reached another ship. Despite this misfortune, Ozawa kept his fleet near Tinian and prepared to launch another attack. Incredibly, he based this decision on the assumption that his missing warplanes had performed well and were refuelling on Guam

BELOW
An LCVP delivers American Marines to a landing beach on Saipan. By seizing this island, along with Guam and Tinian, Admiral Nimitz sought to disrupt enemy supply lines and place the Japanese homeland within the range of B-29 bombers.

and that when they returned his assault on Task Force 58 would resume.

Meanwhile, Mitscher gained Spruance's permission to launch a counter-attack on the First Mobile Fleet. On the afternoon of 20 June, Task Force 58 located Ozawa's warships and hurled 54 torpedo bombers, 77 dive bombers and 85 fighters at them. Reaching the enemy fleet at the end of the day, the Hellcat pilots pushed aside the few remaining Japanese fighters sent to intercept them, while the American bombers descended upon the vessels. When the fighting ended, the warplanes sank the carrier *Hiyo*, damaged several more ships and shot another 65 enemy planes out of the sky. Although the Americans lost 20 aircraft in the twilight raid, they sent the First Mobile Fleet limping back to Japan.

Ironically, the American pilots' most dangerous enemies turned out to be the darkness of the night as they returned to their carriers and the long distance back to the fleet. Many warplanes ran out of fuel and plunged into the Philippine Sea and some of the pilots who did reach their carriers crashed onto the decks. To make the landings less difficult, Mitscher ordered all of the lights on his ships to be turned on so that the pilots could see where to land. Even so, 80 of the 216 aircraft sent against the Japanese fleet wound up in the bottom of the sea.

The naval battle at the Marianas Islands was a serious defeat for the Japanese Navy. During the two days of fighting, Ozawa had lost three of his carriers and over 90 per cent of his aircraft. Many more Japanese warships sustained serious damage. In contrast, the Americans lost 130 warplanes and 76 airmen, but succeeded in preventing any outside help from reaching the beleaguered Japanese garrison on Saipan and the neighbouring islands.

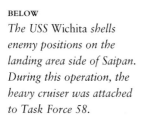

BELOW
The USS Wichita *shells enemy positions on the landing area side of Saipan. During this operation, the heavy cruiser was attached to Task Force 58.*

Yamato

By 21 June, the 2nd and 4th Marine Divisions had conquered most of the island's southern half. Continuing with their plan, the 2nd Division moved up the west coast of Saipan toward Mount Tapotchau, while the 4th Division headed east to the Kagman Peninsula. However, although the two Marine forces made substantial progress in their advance, they found themselves isolated and forced to dig in. Their supporting army regiments had failed to push forward in the centre; the commander of the 27th Division, Major-General Ralph Smith, was a cautious officer who preferred to engage in slow, methodical advances that inflicted fewer casualties. Dissatisfied with this style of combat, the commander of the V Amphibious Force, Lieutenant-General Holland Smith, persuaded Spruance to have the army general re-assigned to Europe.

Victory at Saipan

After this dismissal, the Americans on Saipan renewed their aggressive actions, and by the end of June had seized almost everything south of Mount Tapotchau. A week later, the Japanese found themselves pushed back to the northern tip of the island. Faced with an inevitable defeat, humiliated and ashamed, Saito and Nagumo committed suicide. The following day, on 7 July, their surviving troops launched a ferocious human-wave attack on the soldiers from the 27th Division at Tanapag Harbor. After overrunning two battalions and reaching a rear-area command post, the Japanese assault fizzled out, leaving over 4000 corpses strewn across the area.

On 9 July, the Americans declared Saipan secured. However, deadly carnage on the island persisted when hundreds of Japanese civilians opted for suicide over enduring American occupation. In vain, the Americans attempted to dissuade the local inhabitants

with assurances of humane treatment. Most of these civilians simply jumped into the ocean to drown, while others fell upon grenades. Among the combatants fighting for Saipan, 16,525 Americans were killed or wounded, compared to about 29,000 Japanese defenders who had fought to the death.

The seizure of Saipan provided the Allies with the airfields they needed to launch bombing raids on Japan itself. Back in Tokyo, news of the Marianas disaster forced Prime Minister Hideki Tojo and his entire cabinet to resign on 18 July. His replacement, Kunaiki Koiso, openly questioned the desirability of continuing the war. Both he and Emperor Hirohito now realised that the war would be coming home to terrorise their people and flatten their cities.

Lying just over 4.8km (3 miles) south-west of Saipan, the island of Tinian was another attractive target for the 5th Fleet. With a relatively flat surface, the island had

ABOVE

Without their own effective air cover, the Yamatos *– the biggest battleships ever seen – were vulnerable to attack from US carriers; as a result the Japanese command proved reluctant to deploy them. Nevertheless, the* Yamato *was sent to reinforce Vice-Admiral Ozawa's fleet, and survived the naval battle of the Marianas Islands.*

BELOW

An aerial photograph offers a bird's-eye view of the western Caroline Islands. The north-eastern corner of Peleliu is in the left centre of the photograph.

Spearheading the invasion of Saipan, a group of Marines huddles behind a sand dune and waits for reinforcements to arrive. Within a week, the Americans had captured much of the southern half of the island.

three airfields and the Japanese had been constructing a fourth landing strip when Operation Forager had begun. Finding a landing point on Tinian would be difficult because, despite its gentle interior terrain, it was almost completely surrounded by a rocky coastline. At first, the only practical point seemed to be an area of beaches surrounding Tinian Town on the south-west corner, which was well guarded by Japanese troops. However, navy frogmen soon discovered two unprotected narrow beach areas on the north-west corner of the island at which, apparently, the commander of the Tinian garrison did not believe a landing could take place.

Tinian assaulted

On 24 July, the 5th Fleet began its attack on Tinian with a massive bombardment, followed by the appearance of an invasion force off the coast of the town. After pretending to attempt a landing on the south-west beaches near Tinian Town, a group of transports pulled away as a diversionary manoeuvre, encouraging the

Japanese to think that the shore batteries had repulsed an invasion. Meanwhile, two regiments from the US 4th Marine Division descended upon the north-west tip of the island and established defensive positions 1.6km (1 mile) inland before the garrison at Tinian Town even knew they had landed. That night, the Marines were able to repulse a Japanese assault on their perimeter. Within a week, more Americans arrived, including tanks and infantry units from the 2nd and 4th Marine Divisions. From their north-western toehold, the invaders rolled across the island's level terrain, crushing enemy resistance with ease. By early August, they had conquered Tinian, bringing more airfields into Allied hands to enable long-range bombers to strike Japan. Meanwhile, another battle was taking place 160km (100 miles) to the south on the island of Guam.

The largest of the Marianas Islands, Guam possessed a rugged surface that was mostly covered with jungle-infested ravines and steep ridges. Although the island was 48km

(30 miles) long, most of the military objectives identified by the Americans occupied a small area on the west coast. These sites included the town of Agana, Apra Harbor, which possessed a navy yard and a large airfield on the Orote Peninsula. In their plan of attack, scheduled to begin on 21 July, American strategists decided to launch a two-pronged offensive. North of Apra Harbor, the 3rd Marine Division was to land and capture the navy yard. At the same time, the 1st Provisional Marine Brigade and a regiment from the 77th Army Division would strike south of the harbour and isolate Japanese forces situated on the Orote Peninsula.

Unlike Tinian, the battle for Guam began terribly. When the two invasion forces landed on the beaches, they found themselves being hit by artillery batteries from 29th Division gunners enjoying a bird's-eye view of the Americans from positions atop nearby cliffs and ridges. Although Guam had been an American possession for several decades, the 5th Fleet did not possess any accurate maps of the islands. The result of this carelessness was a stalled advance that inflicted heavy casualties on the American soldiers and Marines on the beaches. On 25 July, the 1st Marine Provisional Brigade finally broke this stalemate by seizing a road that crossed the base of the Orote Peninsula, thus cutting off the Japanese troops there.

The following night, the Japanese troops on the peninsula launched a desperate attack to break out of their trap. Drunk on alcohol to enhance their courage, they charged into an artillery bombardment that mangled most of them and sent survivors fleeing into a swamp. An attack 8km (5 miles) to the north led by Lieutenant-General Takeshi Takashina against the 3rd Marine Division went better for the Japanese, at least for a few hours. His troops charged the beach near Apra Harbor throughout the night and until the following morning, when the assault disintegrated into a fight so confusing and disorganised that it was like a riot. At that point, Takashina's forces withdrew, leaving 3500 dead Japanese soldiers on the beachhead.

By the end of July, the Americans had obtained possession of Apra Harbor and several kilometres of land around it.

For two more weeks, battles between the two belligerents persisted as the two American divisions swept northward, gradually pushing the Japanese to Ritidian Point and Pati Point. With their backs to the ocean, the soldiers of the 29th Division made a last stand, but on 10 August they were overwhelmed by superior numbers. Although pockets of resistance continued to carry out guerilla strikes against the Americans, the 5th Fleet was finally able to declare the island secure. The battle for Guam had claimed 1919 American lives, along with another 7122 wounded and 70 missing. Japanese losses were again much greater, amounting to about 17,300 killed and 485 prisoners taken.

With the Marianas Islands now in Allied hands, Nimitz and other strategists turned

BELOW
USS Tennessee *pummels enemy positions on Peleliu. Within the island, the Japanese garrison was well entrenched in a network of tunnels and caverns.*

During the last half of the war, the F6F Hellcat gradually replaced the F4F Wildcat as the primary carrier-based fighter of the United States Navy. Capable of reaching a speed of 610km (380 miles) per hour, the Hellcat was a formidable adversary for the A6M Zero and other Japanese fighters.

F6F Hellcat

After landing on Saipan, American Marines scramble for safety during an artillery bombardment. In the background, an amphibious tractor burns from a shell that had scored a direct hit on the vehicle.

their attention to two new objectives: the island of Mindanao in the Philippines and the Palau Islands in the western Carolines. Located 800km (500 miles) east of the Philippines and 1600km (1000 miles) west of Truk, the Palaus contained a large Japanese airbase situated on Peleliu Island. Admiral William F. Halsey, the commander of the South Pacific region, considered the seizure of this area an unnecessary objective in the drive to the Philippines. However, his superior officer, Nimitz, disagreed. He believed that Japanese forces there were a

potential threat to his fleet during the attack on Mindanao and Leyte.

On to the Carolines

Thus, Nimitz scheduled the invasion of Peleliu – called Operation Stalemate II – to begin on 15 September, also planning to launch a simultaneous attack on Mindanao. The 1st Marine Division, commanded by Major-General William Rupertus, received the honour of spearheading the Peleliu assault. However, on 13 September, Halsey approached Nimitz with information that

LEFT
On the USS Pennsylvania, *sailors pass ammunition to their guns, in preparation for a bombardment in the Palau Islands. During the attack on Pearl Harbor, this battleship had been in dry dock and suffered relatively little damage.*

he hoped might lead to a cancellation of Operation Stalemate II. During a mission to bomb Japanese air bases in the Philippines in support of the Peleliu invasion, pilots under Halsey's command had reported very weak enemy resistance in the air. Halsey inferred from this that Japanese air power in the Pacific region had collapsed in the wake of the disastrous routs suffered by their forces at the Marianas and other places. Although he persuaded Nimitz to cancel the attack on Mindanao, the invasion of Peleliu proceeded on schedule.

Since April, the Japanese garrison at Peleliu consisted of 6500 crack troops from the 14th Division. Commanded by Lieutenant-General Sadae Inoue, they were tough veterans from the Chinese theatre of combat. Unlike most other Japanese officers defending island strongholds from Allied invasions, Inoue had no intention of hurling his men into reckless frontal charges. Instead, he exploited the island's rugged terrain to develop an effective defence-in-depth system. The airfield was on the southern tip of the island, and above it was Umurbrogol Mountain, a steep series of ridges covered with thick vegetation and riddled with hundreds of caves. A Japanese-held island for decades, Peleliu was also honeycombed with a system of tunnels left behind from pre-war phosphate-mining operations. One hollowed-out area was large enough to shelter 1000 men while others had steel doors that opened to allow howitzers to fire and slammed shut between salvoes. Not surprisingly, Inoue ensured that

Taiho

ABOVE

Commissioned in March 1944, the Taiho *was a state-of-the art carrier protected with thick armour on its deck and hull. Nevertheless, the vessel sank on 19 June that year after an American submarine struck it with a torpedo during the Battle of the Philippine Sea.*

BELOW

Aviators photograph a Japanese airfield situated on the Opote peninsula in Guam. This site was one of many objectives that the Americans sought in the Marianas Islands to enable their bombers to reach the Japanese homeland.

these strongholds were well stocked with ammunition and rations.

In anticipation of the impending invasion, Inoue drilled his troops in new tactics aimed at preventing the heavy losses that had been sustained by Japanese forces on other islands. If his troops failed to prevent the Americans from landing and consolidating their positions on the beaches, they were to withdraw to prepare defensive positions and to fire mortars at pre-arranged targets. His men were also instructed not to commit suicide if the enemy overran their perimeters. Instead, they were to keep themselves out of sight until the Americans moved past and then attack the invaders from behind.

In late August, American bombers from New Guinea reached the Palau chain to initiate hostilities, hitting several islands with their explosive cargo. Shortly afterwards, warplanes from the carriers of Halsey's 3rd Fleet performed similar duty. Then a force of battleships, cruisers and destroyers under the command of Rear-Admiral Jesse B. Oldendorf descended upon the islands to initiate a three-day bombardment that smashed several targets on the surface of

Peleliu but inflicted little damage on Inoue's underground fortifications. At the time, the general was not on Peleliu. Instead, he was on another island directing the defences of the entire archipelago.

Carnage at Peleliu

On 15 September, the 1st Marine Division began its scheduled landing. En route to the beaches, the Marines on the amtracs were in high spirits, encouraged by the decimation inflicted by the 3rd Fleet upon Peleliu. However, when the amtracs reached a coral reef hundreds of metres off the shoreline, Japanese batteries, machine-gunners and mortar teams opened fire, showering the Marines with lead and steel. In the centre of the invasion force, the 5th Regiment landed relatively intact, but to the north the 1st Regiment suffered more injury from Japanese troops firing from a rocky point of land protruding into the beach. At the southern end of the landing area, the 7th Regiment was forced to proceed single-file through a narrow passage that was flanked by mines and obstacles, enabling the 14th Division's artillerists to fire at the amtracs with greater accuracy.

When the 5th and 7th regiments reached the beaches, the Japanese defenders withdrew into the interior to prepare for a counter-attack. The 5th Regiment took advantage of the pause in the fighting and occupied the southern edge of the airfield. Further south, the 7th Regiment was in a state of confusion because its amtracs had been forced to land at random locations. On the northern end of the invasion site, the 1st Regiment was pinned down in a firefight. During the approach to the shoreline, the Japanese had sunk most of the 1st Regiment's command group amtracs, depriving its commander, Colonel Lewis B. 'Chesty' Puller, of the use of any radios to call for help. On the northern flank of the Marine force, Puller's men confronted enemy units well placed within a coral ridge and

steel-enforced pillboxes that were shelling the entire beach.

In a nasty two-hour battle that wiped out almost an entire company, Puller's regiment disabled the Japanese positions to their left. Later in the day, the Japanese launched a counter-attack, bringing 13 light tanks into the field of battle against the Marine regiments. In response, the Americans introduced 12 Sherman tanks and a navy dive bomber to knock out the enemy's armoured units. This firepower proved too powerful for the thin-skinned Japanese vehicles; within minutes, the 14th Division veterans withdrew, losing most of their tanks in the assault.

Throughout the ensuing night and following morning, the Japanese bombarded the 1st Regiment with mortar fire, but later in the day the Marines in that group repulsed another ground attack. Meanwhile, the other regiments seized the airfield from the 14th Division and proceeded until they reached the

east coast of Peleliu, thus cutting the division in two. However, the Americans could not use the airfield because Japanese artillery crews in Umurbrogol Mountain would demolish any plane that came close to it.

Because the 5th and 7th Regiments were preoccupied with enemy forces around the airfield, the 1st Regiment received the dubious honour of storming Umurbrogol. A jagged, rocky site covered with decayed coral and thick vegetation, the mountain was difficult to climb even without a battle raging in the area. On 17 September, Puller's Marines reached the mountain and began their slow, agonising ascent up its ridges. With the help of bazookas and naval gunfire, they blasted several caves on their way to the peak, suffering heavy casualties in the process. After three days of fighting on Peleliu, the 1st Regiment had lost almost half of its men.

On 18 September, the Japanese on Umurbrogol launched a brutal counter-attack

On Peleliu, American Marines place a wounded comrade on board a C-46 Commando hospital plane. The battle for the island claimed the lives of more than 1500 Americans and 10,000 Japanese defenders.

that pushed the 1st Regiment partially off a ridge gained on the previous day. After two more days of trying to claw their way up the mountain, Puller's command was no longer a viable fighting unit. Sustaining 1700 casualties at what the Marines now called Bloody Nose Ridge, the survivors of the 1st Regiment needed reinforcements. Although the 7th Regiment stepped in to help, the offensive on the mountain was mired in a costly stalemate.

To break this stalemate, on 23 September the 321st Regimental Combat Team, 81st Army Infantry Division arrived to relieve the worn-out 1st Marine Regiment. Two days later, the 5th Marine Regiment snaked around the western side of Umurbrogol and conquered the northern section of Peleliu with little difficulty. Then this unit moved up the mountain's northern face, while the army regiment pressed the Japanese from the west and the 7th Marine Regiment from the south. Gradually, the three regiments battered their way through enemy defences and constricted the 14th Division's perimeter atop Umurbrogol. For several weeks, heavy fighting continued as opposing units captured and recaptured ridges from each other and the Americans blasted caves with explosives and

flame-throwers. By late October, the 5th and 7th Marine Regiments had sustained almost 50 per cent casualties, needing more army units to replace them. Thus, responsibility for the offensive on Peleliu passed into the hands of Major-General Paul J. Mueller, commander of the 81st Infantry Division. Unlike most Marine commanders, he was more methodical with his attack plans, preferring to minimise casualties when possible.

General Mueller used artillery, mortar and napalm bombardments to soften Japanese positions prior to infantry assaults. He also sent armoured bulldozers to clear routes for tanks to use, while engineers designed a long fuel pipeline that sprayed fire into Japanese fortifications. As a result, on 25 November the 81st Division all but annihilated the 14th Japanese Division and declared the Peleliu campaign over. Collectively, American casualties during the operation exceeded 1500 killed and over 6000 wounded. Japanese fatalities amounted to about 10,000 men.

Ironically, the American people back home in the United States paid little attention to the carnage on Bloody Nose Ridge because they were much more preoccupied with the reconquest of the Philippines.

For General MacArthur, the seizure of the Philippines was more than just a strategic action aimed at moving closer to Japan. In his view, the liberation of the islands was a necessary moral obligation to the inhabitants suffering under enemy occupation. Like many other Americans, he also wanted to restore national honour by retaking a US colony that the Japanese had captured in an act of brutal aggression. Memories of Bataan fed into this mindset. Impressed with MacArthur's forceful arguments in favour of a Filipino campaign, the Joint Chiefs of Staff scheduled an invasion of Leyte, an island north of Mindanao, to begin on 20 December 1944.

Return to the Philippines

The offensive on the Philippines began on 9 September 1944 when, under the command of Vice-Admiral Mitscher, Task Force 38 initiated a naval bombardment and carrier-based air assault on Mindanao. Over a period of several days, the warships then swept across other Philippine islands, inflicting substantial damage on Japanese positions. Encouraged by the success of Mitscher's mission, the commander of the 3rd Fleet, Halsey, proposed bringing the invasion of Leyte

forward to an earlier date. With the consent of Nimitz, Churchill and Roosevelt, Halsey and MacArthur rescheduled the operation to begin in October.

The Japanese garrison on Leyte consisted of under 20,000 men from the 16th Division, 14th Area Army. Led by Lieutenant-General Shiro Makino, most of them were inexperienced conscripts. In addition to a prospective invasion from the sea, they also had to deal with guerilla bands operating in the island's mountainous interior. These guerillas served as excellent spies and scouts for MacArthur, providing him with useful information about Japanese defences through radio transmissions.

At Hollandia and the Admiralty Islands, MacArthur and Vice-Admiral Thomas C. Kinkaid assembled an invasion force that included a variety of warships, carriers, tankers, transports, amphibious craft and floating dry docks. Collectively, about 50,000 sailors from Kinkaid's 7th Fleet manned 577 vessels, while 165,000 troops from MacArthur's 6th Army waited for battle inside the transport units. To protect this expedition, Mitscher and his task force swept from Okinawa to the Philippine Sea, destroying enemy shipping and any aircraft their

BELOW
American forces occupy the area around the main airfield of Peleliu in the southern part of the island. The structures seen in the background are the remains of Japanese hangars.

The USS Tennessee *provides cover fire for landing craft descending upon one of the Palau Islands. Like the Pennsylvania, the* Tennessee *had survived the attack on Pearl Harbor.*

American Marines march across the ruined landscape of Guam. The invasion of the island began with landings on the west coast near the towns of Asan and Agat in July 1944.

warplanes could find. Near Formosa, on 12 October they decimated the Japanese 6th Base Air Force in a large dogfight. During the course of the battle, Japanese torpedo-bomber pilots disabled the Australian heavy cruiser, *Canberra II*, and a light cruiser, *Houston*, both of which were towed to the Carolines for repairs. However, the Japanese lost over 500 warplanes in three days.

On 17 October, a small group of American warships reached Leyte Gulf and shelled the small island of Suluan. In a short fight, the 6th Ranger Infantry Battalion seized it from a small garrison. Just before Suluan fell, one of its defenders sent a radio message warning of an American invasion. The commander-in-chief of the Command Fleet, Admiral Soemu Toyoda, reacted by sending Admiral Takeo Kurita's First Striking Force from Singapore and the surviving remnants of Ozawa's Mobile Fleet from the Inland Sea to Leyte Gulf. Toyoda also dispatched all available submarines to the area.

The following day, the rangers seized two more islands called Dinigat and Homonhon and erected navigation lights upon each to

enable 7th Fleet to enter the gulf between them. Hours later, the battleship *Pennsylvania*, two cruisers and several destroyers shelled beaches south of Tacloban, the capital of Leyte. Meanwhile, diving teams scouted the beaches along the island to locate any mines or obstacles that might impede the transports. Finding none, they returned with the good news. Their landing craft had received only sporadic gunfire from Japanese troops on the shoreline.

On 19 October, the van of MacArthur's invasion armada reached Leyte Gulf. While warships bombarded the beaches below Tacloban, carrier aircraft struck every single enemy air base in the area, practically obliterating what was left of Japanese air power in the region. By the end of the day, the transports had arrived, prompting the ground troops aboard to prepare for their landings on Leyte. The following morning, six battleships and other vessels resumed shelling Japanese positions until the transports approached designated landing sites.

MacArthur on Leyte

On the northern tip of the landing site, the 1st Cavalry Division descended upon White Beach. Once ashore, the cavalrymen cleared the area of enemy sharpshooters, dynamited concrete

pillboxes and occupied most of Tacloban – which General Makino had abandoned – and part of a coastal highway. To their left, soldiers from the 24th Infantry Division landed on Red Beach and fought through stubborn Japanese resistance to reach the highway. At Orange and Blue beaches further south, the 96th Infantry Division encountered little opposition and advanced 1.6km (1 mile) before being bogged down in a fight with scattered enemy troops. On the southern end of the invasion area, the 7th Infantry Division fought a fierce battle at Violet and Yellow beaches but eventually captured the coastal town of Dulag.

Later in the day, a barge filled with officers and news journalists landed on Red Beach. Out of the vessel stepped General MacArthur, along with the new Philippine president, Sergio Osmena, and General Carlos Rumolo. Surrounded by the soldiers from the 24th Infantry Division, MacArthur spoke into a microphone, notifying the inhabitants of Leyte that he had fulfilled his famous promise to return to the Philippines as a liberator. Then he handed the microphone to President Osmena, who urged his people to cooperate with the Americans in the fight to expel the Japanese from the rest of the country. This exhortation proved to be unnecessary, as crowds of happy

ABOVE
At Peleliu, an F4U Corsair from the 2nd Marine Aircraft Wing bombs enemy positions near Five Sisters Peaks. Such tactical air strikes helped the 1st Marine Division to clear out pockets of resistance from the enemy, who had holed up in the caves which covered the hills of the island.

In 1934, the Japanese Navy constructed the heavy cruiser Mogami, *a warship that was equipped with 10 203mm (8in) guns. After surviving several damaging encounters during the war, the* Mogami *sank in the Surigao Strait during the battle of Leyte Gulf.*

Filipinos embraced MacArthur's soldiers and pledged support for the Allied war effort.

The three-day naval bombardment had driven most of the demoralised Japanese soldiers from the 16th Division inland; thanks to this, American casualties during the Leyte landings were low. With the loss of only 49 soldiers killed in action, MacArthur's forces now possessed a sizeable toehold in the middle of the Philippines. On the day after the landings, the four divisions pushed inland,

meeting only sporadic, disorganised resistance. By the end of the month, they consolidated their control over the north-eastern part of the island, while Makino divided his division into two sections. One held onto the north-western corner of Leyte, while the other retreated south.

Meanwhile, Admiral Kurita's First Striking Force approached the Philippines from the south-west, while Ozawa's Mobile Fleet rushed down from the north. A

Mogami

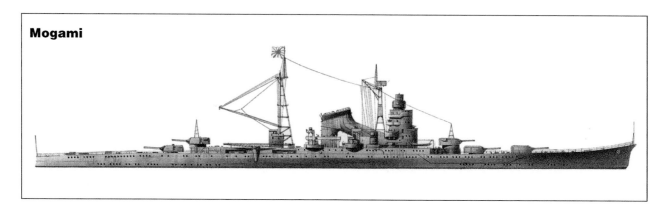

shadow of its former self since the Marianas debacle, the Mobile Fleet possessed only 116 warplanes, which were distributed among four carriers and two battleships that had been converted into semi-carriers. Kurita, however, possessed a more formidable group that included *Yamato* and *Musashi*, the two most powerful battleships in the world. He also had under his command five more battleships, 11 heavy cruisers, two light cruisers and 19 destroyers.

On 21 October, while steaming past Borneo, Kurita had received orders from Combined Fleet to enter Leyte Gulf and destroy American amphibious shipping there. His superiors suggested approaching the area in a two-pronged attack in which the main part of the First Striking Force would move along the northern coast of Palawan Island, pass through the San Bernardino Strait between Luzon and Samar and approach the gulf from the north. Meanwhile, the other group would veer to the right, sail through the Surigao Strait between Leyte and

Mindanao and assault enemy vessels from the south. Agreeing with this suggestion, Kurito placed two battleships and four destroyers under the command of Vice-Admiral Teiji Nishimura and sent this detachment on the southern route to Leyte. Kurita's plan called for the two groups to converge upon the gulf on 25 October.

The morning after Kurita received his orders, the two naval forces pressed on to Leyte. The following day, off the west coast of Palawan, two American submarines, *Dace* and *Darter*, spotted the main column of the First Striking Force and, in a surprise torpedo ambush, sank Kurita's flagship, *Atago*, and another heavy cruiser called *Maya*. The submarines also damaged a third cruiser, *Takao*, badly enough to force it to return to Borneo for repairs. Fortunately for Kurita, a destroyer was nearby to pull him and his senior staff officers out of the South China Sea.

Aboard his new flagship, *Yamato*, Kurita led the First Striking Force into the Sibuyan

Sea and, on 24 October, approached the San Bernardino Strait. Luck was not on his side. Spotted by an American reconnaissance plane, he feared that his fleet was now vulnerable to attack in the straits it was navigating, and thus requested air support from Manila. However, such assistance was not possible because, at that time, almost every available Japanese warplane was engaged in a massive battle with Mitscher's

Hellcats east of Luzon. Although a dive bomber managed to sink the light carrier *Princeton*, the Japanese lost several more aircraft during the fight.

When Halsey received news of Kurita's approach, he sent 24 fighters, torpedo bombers and dive bombers from *Cabot* and *Intrepid* against the First Striking Force. Although the American pilots flew valiantly through a barrage of anti-aircraft fire and hit Musashi with a bomb and a torpedo, the massive battleship seemed unaffected by the strikes. Later in the day, a second squadron of American warplanes hit it again with three more torpedoes but produced a similar result. However, only minutes later a third group of aircraft from *Lexington* and *Essex* appeared and inflicted substantial damage to *Musashi*'s hull, forcing the Japanese fleet to slow down so that the battleship could keep up at a slower speed.

In the afternoon, more American warplanes descended upon *Musashi*. Without Japanese aircraft to protect it, the battleship had to rely upon its own 460mm (18.1in) guns to repel the assault. However, the American pilots managed to evade the fleet's anti-aircraft fire, firing several more bombs and torpedoes into *Musashi*, severely damaging its port side and killing several officers and sailors. Throughout the course of the afternoon, the battleship gradually sank. Although escort destroyers rescued half of the ship's crew, its captain refused to go, electing to remain on board and sink into the Sibuyan Sea. The Americans also smashed the heavy cruiser *Myoko* badly enough to force it to return to Borneo for repairs.

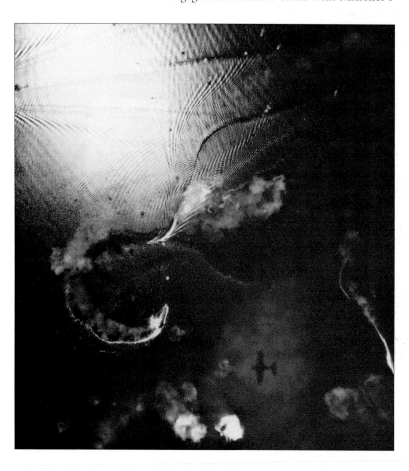

ABOVE

Japanese vessels attempt to evade United States Navy warplanes at Tables Strait in the Battle of Leyte Gulf.

RIGHT

Japanese warships depart Brunei to participate in the Battle of Leyte Gulf. They include the battleships Nagato, Musashi, Yamato *and the heavy cruisers* Maya, Chokai, Takao, Atago, Haguro, *and* Myoko.

The Battle of Leyte Gulf

Meanwhile, the Mobile Fleet approached the east coast of Luzon. To help Kurita pass safely through the San Bernardino Strait, Ozawa sent his two semicarriers *Ise* and *Hyuga* – as well as five other ships – south in order to lure the 3rd Fleet from the area. By this time, Halsey assumed that Kurita's command had been decimated to the point where it no longer constituted a serious threat; thus he took the bait. Assuming direct control of Task Force 38, he led most of his warships north to fight Ozawa and, not surprisingly, Kurita was relieved to learn about the 3rd Fleet sailing away from the strait. However, passing through and heading for Leyte Gulf, due to the devastating American air strikes in the Sibuyan Sea, he was behind schedule by about 12 hours. He notified Nishimura that the First Striking Force would be late for the attack on Kinkaid's 7th Fleet. Nishimura would have to launch the attack on his own.

Fortunately for Nishimura, help arrived from another direction. From the north-west, the Second Striking Force swept in behind his warships as they approached the Surigao Strait. Commanded by Vice-Admiral Kiyohide Shima, the group consisted of two heavy cruisers, one light cruiser and four destroyers. Unlike Kurita, Nishimura had to deal only with PT boats harassing his naval column as it passed into the strait, none of which did any significant damage.

In the early morning of 25 October, Nishimura's warships were almost through Surigao Strait when, suddenly, seven destroyers from the Kinkaid's fleet fell upon the column in a surprise attack. Firing 27 torpedoes, they blew the battleship *Fuso* in half and sank three Japanese destroyers. They also damaged Nishimura's flagship, the battleship *Yamashiro*, but not enough to prevent it from proceeding to Leyte Gulf. At this point, the surviving warships of the Japanese flotilla

ABOVE

LSTs operated by sailors from the United States Coast Guard line up along the shoreline of Leyte while men and material land on the island. Guardsmen in the foreground are filling sandbags to help protect gun emplacements on the beach.

included only the flagship, the heavy cruiser *Mogami* and the destroyer *Shigure*.

The commanders of the 7th Fleet met this determination by unleashing their cruisers and battleships upon the three vessels. Now hopelessly outnumbered and outgunned, Nishimura's warships withered under an intense bombardment. After a feeble attempt to return fire, *Shigure* and *Mogami* turned south and retreated. Out of 19 vessels under Nishimura's command, these two ships were the only survivors. Burning and crippled, *Yamashiro* attempted to follow suit, but capsized and sank with its captain and most of the crew on board. During this one-sided battle, the Americans lost only 39 men killed and another 114 wounded.

Shortly after the battle had ended, the Second Striking Force reached Leyte Gulf, only to find the remains of Nishimura's flotilla. Satisfied that he could do nothing more to challenge American control over the area, Shima gathered *Mogami* and *Shigure* and headed back the way he came, but during this retreat American cruisers, destroyers and PT boats wrecked one of his destroyers. After his naval force travelled beyond the range of enemy surface vessels, TBF-1 Avenger torpedo bombers fell upon *Mogami* and knocked out its engine, forcing Shima to abandon the ruined cruiser.

About 320km (200 miles) to the north, Kurita's warships passed through the San Bernardino Strait without incident and headed

BELOW
American troops manoeuvre around a tank trap left by retreating Japanese forces on Leyte. In October 1944, the United States 6th Army seized Tacloban, the island capital, and pushed the Japanese 35th Army steadily westward.

toward Leyte Gulf. East of Samar Island, the First Striking Force ran into Taffy 3, a group of vessels from the 7th Fleet that had been assigned the responsibility of providing air cover for amphibious shipping to Leyte. Commanded by Rear-Admiral Clifton A. F. Sprague, Taffy 3 possessed three destroyers, four destroyer escorts and six escort carriers. Aware of his substantial superiority in numbers and firepower, Kurita ordered an attack on the American warships. Sprague responded by launching fighters and torpedo bombers against the Japanese, before heading south towards two more groups, Taffy 1 and Taffy 2. When Kurita's pursuing warships seemed to be overtaking the Americans, Sprague ordered three destroyers to counterattack. In the ensuing battle, these American vessels kept the Japanese at bay long enough for aircraft from Taffy 1 and 2 to arrive and damage three heavy cruisers so badly that they were forced to retire. Believing that he was up against a much larger carrier group, Kurita decided to head north and aid Ozawa,

satisfied that he had inflicted enough damage upon the Americans. He was mistaken. In reality, his ships had sunk only two destroyers, one destroyer escort and one escort carrier, while losing one heavy cruiser during what would be the last surface naval battle of World War II.

Kamikaze!

An hour later, nine Japanese warplanes descended upon the five surviving escort carriers. Five Zero fighters with bombs attached to their wings piloted by fearless airmen dived at high speeds towards the enemy. Aboard the carriers, American crewmen watched in amazement when one Zero slammed into the side of *Kitkun Bay*. Two more pilots attempted to plunge into another carrier, only to crash into the sea before they could fulfil their mission. Although another Zero crashed into the flight deck of *Saint Lo*, causing the carrier to sink, the last two Zeros pulled back under heavy battery fire. After holding their own against the massive First Striking Force, the

ABOVE
Soldiers from the 7th Division, XXIV Corps, 6th United States Army ford the Wahrang River on Leyte Island. Landing at Dulag, the division quickly pushed deep into the interior of the island and captured the town of Burauen.

B-29 Superfortress

ABOVE

The largest bomber in the United States Army Air Force, the B-29 Super-fortress had a range of 6600km (4100 miles) and could carry up to 9070kg (20,000lb) of bombs. During the last months of the war, these warplanes wreaked havoc upon Japanese cities and industrial centres. Two of these bombers dropped atomic explosives on Hiroshima and Nagasaki.

RIGHT

An aerial photograph reveals considerable damage inflicted by American bombers upon a factory in Akashi. The acquisition of airfields on islands closer to Japan enabled the United States Army Air Force to strike such targets more frequently and with more devastating results.

sailors of Taffy 3 had the dubious honour of experiencing one of the first *kamikaze* attacks in the war. Nearby, Taffy 1 and 2 experienced a similar assault.

About 160km (100 miles) east of Luzon, the Mobile Fleet and Task Force 38 collided into each other. Before Kurita was able to reach the area to aid Ozawa, a battle ensued. Early in the morning of 25 October, Halsey hurled 180 fighters, dive bombers and torpedo bombers at the Japanese vessels. By this time, Ozawa possessed only a handful of aircraft and was unable to intercept this air attack. In a series of raids, the American pilots sank a destroyer and three carriers, including *Zuikaku*, Ozawa's flagship.

Later in the day, Ozawa also lost another carrier, two more destroyers and a light cruiser to Americans. Now aboard a cruiser – his new flagship – Ozawa decided to retreat, satisfied that his fleet had discharged its duty as a decoy force to lure Halsey from the First Striking Force. Nevertheless, he had lost all of his carriers in an action that did not prevent the Americans from stopping Kurita's advance on Leyte Gulf.

At the end of the day, Kurita also retired. Harassed by fighters and torpedo bombers and low on fuel, his fleet passed through the San Bernardino Strait and back to friendlier waters. This retreat ended one of the greatest naval battles in history, involving 244 vessels

altogether. During the fighting, the Japanese Navy lost 26 warships, rendering this branch of the armed forces ineffective for the rest of the war. The battle of Leyte Gulf also ensured that the Japanese 14th Area Army would be trapped on the Philippines without reinforcements or supplies from any other part of the Japanese Empire.

The war comes home

While the 3rd and 7th Fleets sent several Japanese warships to the bottom of the Philippine Sea, the USAAF initiated bombing operations against Japan itself. In October 1944, after the first B-29 Superfortress reached Saipan, Brigadier-General Emmett O'Donnell established the 73rd Bombardment Wing and initiated a training regimen for his fliers. A month later, on 24 November, he led over 100 bombers on a raid against an airplane engine plant at Musashino, 16km (10 miles) north-west of the Imperial Palace. Fewer than 50 bombs hit their intended target and damaged it only slightly, the rest of them landing on a dock and a nearby neighbourhood. In response, about 100 fighters attacked the bombers but brought down only one B-29.

Three days later, 62 bombers from the 73rd Wing attempted to strike the engine plant again, only to be thwarted by heavy cloud cover that forced them to hit secondary targets. Nevertheless, with the American presence over Japan, a disturbing realisation dawned on Japanese military leaders and citizens alike. They now knew that the war was coming home to bring them the same death and misery suffered by the people of China and the Philippines, among others.

In the last weeks of 1944, as the bombardments intensified, sorties against Tokyo, Nagoya and other urban areas could only reinforce this sense of dread.

BELOW
American troops load the corpses of fallen comrades on to a transport ship for a return home. The deceased men are some of the 3508 American soldiers killed during the battle for Leyte.

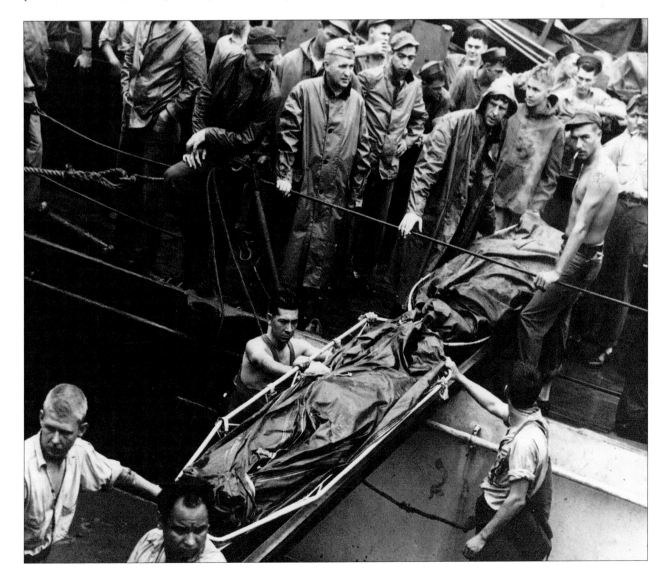

CHAPTER EIGHT

THE LONG ROAD BACK

While Allied forces waged a campaign to liberate Burma, the Japanese planned an ambitious offensive aimed at overthrowing British rule in India.

While Japan's land and naval forces struggled to maintain their possessions in the Pacific Ocean, their generals in the Burma Area Army devised a plan to topple British rule in India. By capturing the border towns of Imphal and Kohima with the aid of the pro-Axis nationalist, Subhas Chandra Bose, and his Indian National Army (INA), Lieutenant-General Renya Mutaguchi and other senior officers hoped to instigate a revolution in the subcontinent and thus bring it into the Japanese camp. For several months in 1943, the commanders of the Burma Area Army had been urging Tokyo to allow them to invade India. At the beginning of the following year, Imperial Headquarters honoured this request and ordered the 15th Army to seize Imphal and nearby areas in north-east India.

Months earlier, Mutaguchi, commander of the 15th Army, had been reluctant to go on the offensive until he saw how well the Chindits operated when they had first invaded northern Burma in February 1943. If these British commando brigades could operate deep in enemy territory, he reasoned that his army could employ similar tactics to push further into India after securing Imphal and Kohima. His chief operations officer, Colonel Tadashi Katakura, did not share this sense of optimism, however, warning that the 15th

Army would face serious logistical problems crossing formidable rivers and rugged mountainous terrain, especially with the shortages of ammunition, food and medical supplies that plagued the Burma Area Army. These warnings did not dissuade Mutaguchi from his plans.

The U-GO Offensive

Thus determined to invade India, Mutaguchi developed a plan for what would be known as the U-GO Offensive. In addition to the ambitious goal of overthrowing British rule in India, he hoped to fulfil a more limited objective. By applying pressure to Imphal and Kohima, the 15th Army might be able to force the British to abandon their second Chindit assault on northern Burma. Within the Arakan region, the Japanese 55th Division was performing a similar function while waging the HA-GO Offensive against the British XV Corps in February 1944.

When the British dispatched more than six divisions to the Arakan region to oppose the 55th Division, Mutaguchi became even more encouraged about the outcome of the U-GO Offensive. With so many Allied troops bogged down in the Arakan Yomas Mountains, he reasoned that, with their reinforcements preoccupied, the British would have a much tougher time defending

OPPOSITE

Veterans from the Chinese 6th Army fraternise with American officers and enlisted men aboard a transport aircraft. The Chinese 6th Army had seen a great deal of action in northern Burma before being sent home by Chiang Kai-shek to fight Japanese forces within China.

As the Burma campaign intensified, on Saipan in June 1944, American Marines look for enemy snipers operating in the densely wooded jungle. On the right, one of the Marines examines a Japanese gun emplacement that has just been captured.

north-eastern India. If Mutaguchi had launched his offensive in mid-February, he might have been able to exploit this situation to its maximum effect. However, he had to wait until his 15th Division returned from service in Thailand and so was forced to postpone the campaign to early March, when the HA-GO Offensive was winding down.

To the Imphal Plain

After reaching Burma in mid-February, the 15th Division was in a poor state. Badly equipped, underfed and demoralised from a long march, its soldiers needed time to be re-supplied and reinvigorated for the U-GO Offensive. Fortunately for Mutaguchi, his other two divisions were in a much better condition. Composed of tough veterans who had been fighting in China for several years, the 33rd Division possessed a tank regiment

and two artillery regiments. The 15th Army's other division, the 31st, also contained crack troops who had seen action in China as well as in the Pacific Theatre. For several months, both divisions had been fighting enemy forces in Burma and were thus accustomed to conditions in the area.

Mutaguchi's plan of attack for these divisions called for a three-pronged offensive against IV Corps, the British unit defending the Imphal Plain. On the right, the 31st Division was to split into three columns and advance along northern routes to Kohima, which was about 130km (80 miles) north of Imphal. In the centre, the main part of the 15th Division would move on Imphal itself while a detachment from its 60th Regiment turned south to harass the 20th Indian Division near Palel. Further south, the 33rd Division would handle the left flank of the offensive, being charged with the responsibility of containing the 17th Indian Division at Tiddim and Tonzang, then would turn north to cut a railroad track at Bishenpur, which ran west to Silchar. Meanwhile, a regiment-size armour column from the 33rd Division was to proceed further north into the Kabaw Valley and open a road for the 15th Division advancing from the east.

At the insistence of Prime Minister Hideki Tojo and Field Marshal Count Hisaichi Terauchi, Mutaguchi also incorporated an INA division into his expeditionary force. Although Bose's 'division' was in actuality only a brigade-size unit totalling 7000 men, Tojo and Terauchi hoped that its presence in India would provoke a pro-Axis uprising against British rule. Accordingly, Mutaguchi attached units from the INA to the 15th and 31st Divisions. With these Indian troops, he now had almost 100,000 men under his

command in the 15th Army. Collectively, his forces contained nine infantry regiments, three engineer regiments that were often employed as infantry units, two heavy artillery regiments and one tank regiment.

On the night of 7/8 March, Mutaguchi's 33rd Division crossed the Chindwin River and entered the mountains separating Burma from India. Within a week, the other two divisions would follow suit. On the other side of the border, Lieutenant-General William J. Slim, commander of the British/Indian 14th Army, suspected the possibility of long-range penetration attacks by enemy forces, but not on this scale. Instead, he anticipated no more than a brigade-size advance, and so he intended to wait until the Japanese reached the Imphal Plain, and then order IV Corps to counter-attack and destroy them while they prepared for their assault. For the time being, he was more preoccupied with the Chindit raids in northern Burma.

BELOW
A jungle conference in Burma. Air Vice-Marshal S. F. Vincent (left) commanding an RAF group on the Imphal front, and Air Marshal W. A. Coryton (right) commanding RAF Bengal and Burma, visit the jungle headquarters of the 14th Army in Burma to confer with General Sir W. J. Slim (centre).

Under the command of Lieutenant-General Geoffrey A.P. Scoones, IV Corps possessed three divisions, along with the Royal Artillery's 8th Medium Regiment and the 254th Indian Tank Brigade. While the 17th Indian Division occupied Tongzang and Tiddim 160km (100 miles) south of Imphal, the 20th Indian Division maintained positions along a road between Palel in India and Sittaung in Burma. At Imphal, Scoones held the 23rd Indian Division and the tank brigade in reserve. When the enemy attacked, he planned to withdraw his two forward divisions to the Imphal Plain and use his air, tank and artillery support to demolish Mutaguchi's divisions.

Further north, XXXIII Corps was concentrated on the Kohima-Dimapur sector, although few combat troops were actually garrisoned in Kohima. Commanded by Lieutenant-General M.G.W. Stopford, this corps included the 2nd and 7th Indian Divisions, the 23rd Chindit, 3rd Special (Commando) Service and Lushai Brigades and the 149th Regiment, Royal Armoured Corps. Collectively, Stopford's forces contained about 75,000 men. Its total infantry

strength consisted of 20 British, 11 Indian and three Gurkha battalions.

During the preparation for the Japanese invasion, Slim assured Scoones that IV Corps would receive the 5th Indian Division from the Arakan region. In addition, Scoones expected the 50th Indian Parachute Brigade to arrive. At its peak, his command included nine British, 16 Gurkha and 24 Indian infantry battalions, along with 120 tanks. Altogether, he led 120,000 ground troops during the campaign, in addition to the construction engineers and Royal Air Force (RAF) squadrons at his service.

The Japanese in India

Within a day after the start of Mutaguchi's advance across the Chindwin River, the 33rd Division reached the Manipur River and began encircling the 17th Indian Division. Commanded by Major-General D.T. Cowan, this outfit contained several crack Gurkha battalions. In the south, the Japanese 215th Regiment manoeuvred around Tiddim and occupied a position west of the town. The 213th Regiment followed and

ABOVE

Brigadier-General Frank D. Merrill, commander of the 5307th Composite Unit (Merrill's Marauders), led American ground forces in Burma. Like the Chindits, his Marauders functioned as mobile units that operated deep within enemy territory.

remained south of Tiddim. Meanwhile, the 214th Regiment marched north-west, then turned to assault Tongzang. Both regiments also established blocking positions on the Tiddim-Imphal Road.

On 13 March, Scoones ordered Cowan to pull the 17th Indian Division back to the Imphal Plain. A full day passed while these orders were communicated to every man in the unit, which then withdrew, pushing aside the Japanese roadblocks with little difficulty. Using Grant and Sherman medium tanks, Cowan's troops inflicted heavy casualties upon their enemies. As protection for 17th Division from ambushes in its 160km (100-mile) retreat, Scoones dispatched the 37th and 49th Brigades, 23rd Division, along with

a tank squadron, to Milestone 100, located 32km (20 miles) north-west of Tongzang.

While the main part of the 33rd Division attempted to keep Cowan's troops pinned down, an armoured detachment under the command of Major-General Tsunoru Yamamoto proceeded north to the Kabaw Valley to help the 15th Division reach Imphal. On 11 March, Yamamoto's column approached the right flank of the 20th Indian Division at Maw. Commanded by Major-General D.D. Gracey, the division quickly followed Scoone's instructions to retreat after destroying unnecessary supplies within the base. En route to the Shenam Heights, east of Palel, Gracey's troops fought past Yamamoto's troops at Nippon Hill.

On the night of 15/16 March, the main part of the 15th Division progressed towards their goal, crossing the Kabaw Valley and heading toward Ukhrul, a town located only about 32km (20 miles) north-east of Imphal. At the same time, elements of the division's 60th Regiment headed south-west to join Yamamoto's armoured detachment on their march along the Palel Road. On 21 March, five days after crossing the Kabaw Valley, troops from the 15th Division drew up to Ukhrul. However, the town was now occupied by the 50th Indian Parachute Brigade and therefore Mutaguchi ordered 15th Division to bypass the town and head for the hills north of the Imphal Plain. At the end of the month, they seized Kanglatongbi, a town roughly 16km (10 miles) above Imphal.

At the northern end of the U-GO Offensive, Lieutenant-General Kokotu Sato and his 31st Division had located good routes through the hills leading to Kohima and proceeded west in three columns at a surprisingly rapid rate. Sato's left column, comprising parts of the 58th and 124th Regiments (and under the command of Major-General Shigesburo Miyazaki), made contact with the 15th Division and swept elements of the 50th Parachute Brigade out of Sangshak, about 8km (5 miles) south of Ukhrul. Miyazaki's troops then moved north-west and reached Maram, a town about 24km (15 miles) south of Kohima. At this location, they established a blocking position on a road connecting the two towns to Imphal.

Kohima assaulted

East of Kohima, the remaining parts of the 58th and 124th Regiments which made up Sato's middle column seized Jessami on 1 April. Meanwhile, the 138th Regiment, Sato's right column, advanced along a track running from Tamanthi, Burma, to Kohima. Within a few days, the 31st Division was on the outskirts of Kohima and ready to attack it. East of the town, a company from the 138th Regiment established a blocking position on

a road leading to Dimapur, while the rest of the regiment surrounded the 161st Indian Brigade, 5th Division at Jotsoma. The ability of the Japanese to move so many troops to this location threw General Slim's defence plans into a state of disarray and forced him and other commanders to assist XXXIII Corps in its defence of the town and the adjacent railhead at Dimapur.

The 161st Indian Brigade had once served as the garrison protecting Kohima. However, Stopford had pulled these troops back to Jotsoma, where they were to defend a road running from Kohima to Dimapur, situated about 48km (30 miles) to the north-west. This move left Kohima in the hands of 60,000 unarmed administrative and supply personnel, along with a group of wounded and ill soldiers recuperating in a medical facility. Now the town's obvious vulnerability forced Slim to dispatch reinforcements to the area by rail and air in a frantic effort to save his army's only supply base. Meanwhile, the personnel trapped in Kohima formed a makeshift defence force to hold the town long enough for help to arrive.

However, the crisis at Kohima was only a part of a problem the British faced throughout north-eastern India. At that point, the Japanese seemed to be on the verge of conquering Imphal and the entire region. To prevent such a catastrophe, Scoones developed a defensive strategy involving the establishment of protective 'boxes' around those areas within the Imphal Plain that contained supply stores and airfields. Within each of these boxes, all available troops were to assemble and fortify their positions against Japanese attacks. During the course of Mutaguchi's invasion, this defensive strategy worked well, managing to hinder efforts by enemy troops to secure the supplies necessary for their offensive. However, as the Japanese assaults intensified, the defending troops often had to pull back. Some stores thus fell into enemy hands.

Fortunately for Scoones, the advantage of defending areas around Imphal enabled

BELOW

The senior officers of the British forces in India stand to attention. In the front row of the assembly, from left to right, they are: Lieutenant-General Sir William Slim, commander of the 14th Army; Lieutenant-General Sir A.F.P. Christison, commander of XV Indian Corps; Lieutenant-General Sir G.A.P. Scoones, commander of IV Corps; and Lieutenant-General M.G.W. Stopford, commander of XXXIII Corps.

British and colonial troops to resist enemy attacks more effectively. On this open plain, Japanese positions were easy targets and, in addition to his four divisions, Scoones enjoyed the support of 27 RAF fighter and fighter-bomber squadrons to strafe and pummel their enemy. This geographical advantage also prevailed to the north, where Sato's 31st Division became vulnerable to air strikes after marching past Litan on the way to Kohima. Like many other Japanese operations, Mutaguchi's invasion suffered from the growing air supremacy enjoyed by the Allies as the war progressed.

Meanwhile, Stopford quickly realised that he had made a mistake in pulling the 161st Division back to Dimapur, and soon another brigade was on its way to help it repel the 138th Regiment at Jotsoma. In this way, reinforcements were able to reach Kohima before the Japanese division conquered the entire town. Stopford also sought to blunt the Japanese offensive by sending the Chindit 23rd Brigade behind the 31st Division. Proceeding in their eight-column formation, the Chindits moved through footpaths to Ukhrul, fighting skirmishes with Sato's troops and threatening enemy communications. In addition, the 23rd Brigade destroyed Japanese railway supply lines and prevented about 300 trucks from reaching Japanese forces.

After five weeks of marching and attacking, Sato's units were running low on supplies, prompting him to advise Mutaguchi against continuing the U-GO Offensive. This request received an angry refusal. By this time, the defences around Kohima had stiffened. Meanwhile, the 5th Brigade, 2nd British Division arrived from Dimapur. On 14 April, it smashed a company-size roadblock established by the Japanese 138th Regiment south of Zubza and helped the 161st Brigade repel the rest of the regiment at Jotsoma. Four days later, the two brigades reached Kohima and aided in its defence.

A stalemate at Imphal

While Sato and his 31st Division troops despaired at the increasing difficulties they faced at Kohima, the INA column attached to their expedition headed south to Imphal. Surprised to see that the road to their objective was lightly defended, the INA column's commander urged Sato to abandon his siege on Kohima and join them in the attack on Imphal. However, Sato decided that his troops were already overburdened with their current mission and he refused. In reality, he was by now convinced that the U-GO Offensive had become an exercise in futility and was preoccupied with persuading Mutaguchi to allow his division to withdraw back to Burma.

When Subhas Chandra Bose heard about Sato's refusal to advance on Imphal, he was livid, accusing his Japanese allies of depriving the INA of a major victory in its homeland. Meanwhile, Mutaguchi was just as angered at Sato's pessimistic assessments and timid behaviour. As the Japanese position around Kohima deteriorated, and Allied reinforcements continued to arrive and push the 31st Division out of the area, messages between the two generals became increasingly hostile. On 1 June, Sato openly proclaimed his intention to pull his forces back to Burma. In response, Mutaguchi threatened to court-martial the division commander. Unfazed by this threat, Sato withdrew the 31st Division from Kohima after 64 days of brutal combat and, on his return to Burma, denounced his superior officer.

To the south, for the Japanese the attack on Imphal seemed to grow ever more promising. While the 15th Division occupied high ground north of the town, the 33rd Division pressed forward from the south. Confident that they would prevail, the Japanese division commanders requested Bose to deliver a radio address on Emperor Hirohito's birthday, offering Imphal to the sovereign as a gift. Bose

took offence. Still angry about the behaviour of Sato at Kohima, he now scorned the idea of a Japanese-led invasion of India. Only INA troops, he announced, could rally the people of the subcontinent behind an anti-British revolution; if the Japanese attempted this feat, it would only serve to provoke pro-British sentiment.

Not surprisingly, the INA 'division' near Imphal was too small for Japanese military commanders to heed Bose's prophecy. In fact, the U-GO Offensive was becoming increasingly difficult even for Mutaguchi's two divisions. Toward the end of April, troops from the 33rd Division attacked the 17th Indian Division at Ningthoukhong, only to be repulsed with heavy losses. To the south-east, a series of assaults on the 20th and 23rd Indian Divisions in areas near Palel produced similar results. North of Imphal, the 15th Japanese Division failed to push IV Corps past Sengmai and Mapao Ridge.

BELOW

Admiral Lord Louis Mountbatten visits an artillery crew on the Myebon peninsula. Appointed Allied Supreme Commander, South-East Asia Command, Mount-batten was the highest-ranking officer overseeing Allied operations in Burma.

ABOVE

Members of the 36th Armored Division evacuate a wounded Japanese captive during an offensive on Pinwe near the Irrawaddy River. Like many other wounded prisoners in the area, he went to the 60th American Portable Surgical Hospital for medical treatment and interrogation.

In June, the arrival of the 2nd British and 19th Indian Divisions from Kohima made the task of conquering Imphal seem impossible for Mutaguchi's forces. Allied strength in the area had now grown to the equivalent of nine divisions. Moreover, the RAF's total air superiority ensured that British and colonial forces would be well fed and supplied, while Japanese and INA troops sank into a state of deprivation. As the monsoon season blew in, conditions for the 15th and 33rd Divisions only worsened. Like Sato's troops in Kohima, their soldiers were suffering from malnourishment, disease and exposure to the elements. Monkeys, snakes, lizards, snails, grass and potatoes were their only food.

The offensive stalls

When Mutaguchi was preparing for the U-GO Offensive, the commander of the 5th Air Division had warned him that the 15th Army could not count on any air support after

its divisions had crossed the Chindwin River. This warning turned out to be accurate; every Japanese warplane was now wrapped up in the defence of northern Burma against the Chindits and other Allied forces. Luck was on the Allies' side. RAF transport planes were able to operate continuously without fear of attack from Japanese fighters and, from 18 April to 30 June, Allied pilots delivered over 18,000 tonnes of supplies and at least 12,000 troops to IV Corps at Imphal. During the same period, American and British transport aircraft evacuated about 13,000 casualties and 43,000 non-combatants. In areas around Imphal and Kohima, ground troops received most of their supplies from the air. Not surprisingly, Allied combat aircraft was also active during the U-GO Offensive. From 10 March to 30 July, the RAF 3rd Tactical Air Force sent fighters on almost 19,000 sorties, losing only 130 aircraft. At the same time, warplanes from the United States Army Air Force (USAAF) flew

ABOVE

As commander of the 7th Indian Division, Major-General Frank W. Messervy participated in the Second Arakan Campaign and the defence of Kohima. Promoted to Lieutenant-General later in the war, he led IV Corps during the offensive on Mandalay and Rangoon.

almost 11,000 missions, with 40 aircraft being lost in the campaign. In most instances, these sorties provided close air support for ground troops. During the same time period, aircraft from the Japanese 5th Air Division managed to fly a meagre 1750 missions.

From Tokyo, Lieutenant-General Hiko-saburo Hata, the Vice-Chief of the Army General Staff, led a group of staff officers to Burma to evaluate the progress of the U-GO Offensive. Returning home, he informed Prime Minister Tojo that the invasion was not going well and that it would probably fail; withdrawing from India was highly desirable. This evaluation did not sit well with Tojo, who was hoping that a successful invasion of India might distract public attention from the recent loss of the Marshall Islands. Accusing Hata of being a defeatist, he heaped verbal abuse upon the general in front of other senior officers.

Eventually, even Mutaguchi came to see the futility of carrying on the U-GO Offensive. On 5 June, during a meeting with the commander of the Burma Area Army, General Masakazu Kawabe, he hinted to his superior the need to order a withdrawal, but Kawabe ignored this subtlety. Days later, Mutaguchi was more explicit, requesting permission to withdraw his divisions to high ground 160km (100 miles) south of Imphal for the duration of the monsoon season. Kawabe rejected the suggestion, imploring the troops of the 15th Army to fight with more tenacity.

Fortunately for the worn-out Japanese soldiers near Imphal, the commander of Southern Army, Field Marshal Terauchi, agreed with Hata's assessment of the U-GO Offensive. Mutaguchi was now granted the all-important permission to withdraw from India and, in mid-June, the remaining two divisions of the 15th Army began to evacuate. A costly operation that had killed over 30,000 and disabled another 23,505 Japanese troops had now ended. British and Indian losses during the offensive amounted to about 16,700 killed and wounded; many casualties on both sides were the victims of disease, in particular malaria.

Return to Burma

It was the middle of monsoon season and, during their journey back to Burma, the 15th Army would suffer many more casualties. Struggling through washed-out trails that had become deep mud-pits, sick and wounded soldiers found it impossible to keep up with their units and often committed suicide. Many others drowned trying to cross the flooded banks of the Chindwin River. Ultimately, the U-GO Offensive would prove to be one of the most disastrous defeats suffered by the Japanese during the war, destroying the 15th Army as an effective fighting force and rendering Burma especially vulnerable to an Allied invasion. Not surprisingly, Tokyo relieved Kawabe, Mutaguchi and other senior officers in the Burma Area Army of their commands.

Back in India, General Slim reorganised his forces shortly after Imphal had been relieved. Moving his own headquarters to the border town, he sent IV Corps and the 50th Parachute Brigade away from the front for temporary rest. In addition, he ordered XXXIII Corps to pursue Mutaguchi's 33rd Division into Burma. By this time, Stopford's command now included the 2nd British, 11th East African, the 5th Indian and the 20th Indian Divisions. Like the Japanese soldiers being pursued, XXXIII Corps travelled through the wet, rugged terrain to Burma with difficulty Having used explosives to destroy several points on the tracks back to the Chindwin River, Stopford's forces were stymied and did not reach the river until early December.

To the east, Lieutenant-General Stilwell's Northern Combat Area Command (NCAC) was also active. Within northern Burma, its 36th British Division proceeded from Mogaung to an area 160km (100 miles) north of Mandalay. This advance effectively shifted the front in Burma, forcing the Japanese to confront a substantial Allied presence north of Kalewa and Tagaung. At the end of the

year, Lord Louis Mountbatten, Lieutenant-General Stilwell and other senior commanders were poised to unleash an offensive aimed at expelling the Japanese from Burma.

In Burma, Mountbatten had reorganised the Allied high command structure. Several months earlier, Stilwell had agreed to serve under the 11th Army Group and take orders from its commander, General Sir George Giffard. However, Stilwell had stipulated that this arrangement would only last until he captured Kamaing. This goal attained, he was now under the direct command of Mountbatten, the Allied Supreme Commander, South-East Asia Command.

To ensure the effective coordination of Slim's forces in the west and Stilwell's in the east, Mountbatten abolished the 11th Army Group and established a new headquarters to command all land actions in Burma. Called Allied Land Forces in South-East Asia

BELOW
At the Myitkyina airfield, Corporal Richard E. Herman of Detroit gives a haircut to Sergeant Harry Fragola of New York. In the background, the Americans are using the remains of a C-47 transport aircraft as a supply centre.

American troops haul their gear through the Burma countryside on their way to Myit. Their overall commander, General Joseph W. Stilwell, sought to bring the northern part of the country under Allied control in order to establish a supply route to Chiang Kai-shek's forces.

(ALFSEA), it required a commander who had experience leading American forces in the field. Mountbatten appointed Lieutenant-General Sir Oliver Leese to its command. Leese was an experienced combat soldier who had commanded the 8th Army in Italy, but his appointment effectively removed Giffard as a senior strategist in the Burma Theatre, despite his distinguished record in this region.

The march to Mandalay

In his effort to retake Burma from the Japanese, General Slim developed an invasion plan known as Operation Extended Capital. His scheme called for XXXIII Corps to advance along the Chindwin River from Kalewa to Mandalay, while Major-General Wynford Rees's 19th Indian Division headed east, crossed the Irrawaddy River and proceeded to the same objective. Presumably, the presence of this division between Stopford's divisions to the west and Stilwell's NCAC to the east would enable Rees to maintain effective communication lines between the two invasion forces. Meanwhile, IV Corps – under Lieutenant-General F.W. Messervy – was to advance south through the Gangaw Valley until Myitche, then turn east and head for Meiktila, an important communications and railroad centre that was located 130km (80 miles) south of Mandalay.

the Japanese 5th Air Division. The British and American Air Forces in the Burma area possessed 17 fighter, 12 fighter-bomber, 10 heavy bomber, five medium bomber, one light bomber and three reconnaissance squadrons. Collectively, the RAF alone had 4464 warplanes, while the USAAF added another 186 to the region. In addition, the Allies possessed 16 transport and four troop-carrier squadrons. By March, this number would increase to 19 transport squadrons, with yet another one added in May, bringing about 500 cargo aircraft into the Burma theatre. In contrast, at the start of the Allied invasion the Japanese had only 66 warplanes, relatively obsolete machines built back in 1942.

The distribution of forces

During his advance through the Gangaw Valley, Messervy placed the 28th East African Brigade and the locally raised Lushai Brigade at the front of his formation. To lure enemy forces to the area, these two brigades would appear as if they were engaging in Chindit-style commando operations on the 15th Army's left flank. If the Japanese took the bait, the 7th and 17th Indian Divisions and the 255th Indian Tank Brigade would then spring forward and join the brigades in a surprise counter-attack. By 10 January, IV Corps had moved past Gangaw along the Pondaung Range. Five weeks later, it reached its jumping-off positions along the Irrawaddy River at a place called Myiche.

After Kawabe's dismissal, command of the Burma Area Army had passed into the hands of Lieutenant-General Hoyotaro Kimura. In addition to the three armies under his command, Kimura also gained the services of the 49th Division, recently arrived from Korea, providing him with 10 divisions and two independent mixed brigades. However, the heavy losses sustained by the 15th Army during the U-GO Offensive had left this organisation with only 21,400 men able to fight General Slim's 14th Army.

Altogether, Slim's forces in Burma contained six divisions, two independent brigades, two tank brigades and several support troops maintaining supply and communication lines, bringing his army's total strength to about 260,000 men. To the north-east, the NCAC was also a formidable presence, consisting of five Chinese divisions,

Fortunately for General Slim, the end of the monsoon season arrived and Allied forces were to enjoy advantageous weather conditions during the execution of Operation Extended Capital. Advancing through a relatively dry region within Burma, his troops were able to move armoured units through the countryside without great difficulty. Moreover, the clear sky above the battlefields allowed RAF and USAAF aircraft to strike enemy positions on the ground with greater precision. With few Japanese warplanes to challenge them, British and American pilots could demolish enemy targets almost at will.

By January 1945, Allied air supremacy had become more than overwhelming for

BELOW
The figure shown here, in May 1945, is Sub-Lieutenant A. Lloyd Morgan, a member of the RNVR, who served aboard the submarine HMS Shakespeare in the Indian Ocean. The informal style of his uniform was typical of both Allied and Axis submariners, given the nature of these vessels.

the 36th British Division and the Mars Task Force. Collectively, Stilwell had 140,000 troops in his command. If necessary, he could also summon up to 12 more Chinese divisions stationed in Yunnan province.

Specifically, the NCAC included two Chinese armies. Based at Myitkyina, the New 1st Army possessed the 30th and 38th Divisions. Further south, the New 6th Army contained the 14th, 22nd and 50th Divisions. An irregular unit similar to Merrill's Marauders, the Mars Task Force consisted of the American 475th Infantry, 124th Cavalry and 612th Field Artillery Regiments, along with the Chinese 1st Regiment.

In north-eastern Burma, the primary enemy of these forces was the Japanese 33rd Army, with the 18th and 56th Divisions, in addition to the 24th Mixed Independent Brigade. Like the 15th Army, this command's divisions were severely depleted from earlier

battles with the Chindits and Stilwell's units. Although the 49th Division was supposed to be attached to the 33rd Army, Kimura dispatched one of the division's regiments to support the 15th Army on the Irrawaddy River. Meanwhile, the other two regiments remained at Maymyo as a reserve force.

On the coast of Burma, the Japanese 28th Army – consisting of the 54th and 55th Divisions, along with the 72nd Independent Mixed Brigade – was ordered to hold on to the area. Their task was to prevent Lieutenant-General Sir Philip Christison and his XV Corps from crossing the Ap and Taungup passes since, if they were allowed to cross these passes, Christison's divisions could move behind the other two Japanese armies and disrupt Kimura's communication system in the Irrawaddy Valley. By this time, the formidable XV Corps contained 120,000 men. Christison's command included the 25th

Landing Ship, Tank

and 26th Indian Divisions, the 81st and 82nd West African Divisions and the 3rd Commando Brigade. Eventually, he would also receive an East African Brigade to use against the 28th Army.

To enable General Slim to focus his attention on the Mandalay operation, Lord Mountbatten removed XV Corps from the 14th Army and placed it under the direct command of General Lees. Since Christison's forces were primarily concerned with combined coastal operations with the navy, they had little to do with the Extended Capital invasion. As an officer with experience in seaborne operations, Lees was a suitable commander to oversee such activity. In addition, Mountbatten relieved Slim of any responsibility for maintaining administrative or communication lines between the 14th Army and ALFSEA back in India, thus allowing him to concern himself only with his battles in Burma.

Down the coast

For good reason, some Allied commanders – including Lord Mountbatten and General Slim – were confident that the numerical superiority of their forces would overwhelm the Japanese. However, they were concerned about the logistical lines from Imphal becoming too long and thin to support so many divisions as they pushed deep into Burma. Thus, they sought to supply their forces from the south-west by ordering Christison's divisions to capture airfields along the Bay of Bengal, thereby enabling RAF cargo aircraft to fly shorter routes to troops on the field. To accomplish this mission, Christison worked closely with the Royal Navy in a series of amphibious landings. Fortunately for XV Corps, British naval supremacy in the Bay of Bengal would enable Rear-Admiral B.C.S. Martin and his Flag Officer Force W to provide ample support for the divisions charged with capturing coastal positions.

On 2 January, the 71st Brigade, 25th Indian Division landed unopposed on the island port of Akyab. Later in the month, Christison's 3rd Commando Brigade spearheaded an invasion on Myebon. After almost a week of fighting, XV Corps seized the town and surrounding areas. Meanwhile, the 71st Brigade reached the northern tip of Ramree Island and secured a beachhead with the help of warships and bombers that

BELOW
General 'Vinegar Joe' Stilwell enjoys a cigarette while cleaning his Thompson machine-gun. In October 1944, his disagreements with Chiang Kai-shek over strategic issues prompted Roosevelt to replace him with Lieutenant-General Daniel I. Sultan.

pummelled Japanese positions. Within a month, the rest of the division arrived, expelled the small garrison of Japanese defenders from the area and secured the island for RAF aircraft to use. Further inland, XV Corps applied more pressure on the 28th Army at Kangaw, leading to a long and bloody battle that kept Japanese forces in the area from aiding in the defence of Mandalay. During the course of these operations, Christison's divisions suffered a total of 1138 men killed and almost 4000 wounded.

While XV Corps moved into the coastal regions of Burma, the 14th Army continued pushing deeper into enemy territory. By sending XXXIII Corps to Mandalay and IV Corps to Meiktila, Slim hoped to ensnare the 15th Army with a pincer-like movement and then destroy it. However, the Japanese forces seemed prepared for this when, on 12 February, they spotted Stopford's 20th Division attempting to cross the Irrawaddy River at Myinmu. As a result, two weeks of fighting ensued, stalling the division's advance 48km (30 miles) west of Mandalay.

In the mean time, Messervy's 7th Division had better luck 145km (90 miles) to the south-west at Myiche, where it was able to cross the river and establish a bridgehead at Nyaungu. Within a matter of days, Messervy succeeded in bringing his remaining divisions to the other side of the river and proceeded to march on Meiktila.

Later in the month, Stopford's 2nd Division successfully established a bridgehead at Ngauzun, only 24km (15 miles) west of Mandalay. While XXXIII Corps kept the 15th Army preoccupied here, Messervy moved his divisions east, encountering very little opposition on the way to Meiktila. On 1 March, the 17th Division assaulted the town and captured it within two days. In a desperate series of counter-attacks, the Japanese attempted to retake the town, only to be thrown back with heavy losses. Altogether, the casualties of IV Corps during the campaign to take Meiktila included 835 killed, 3174 wounded and 90 missing. Messervy's forces also lost 26 tanks in the fighting.

To the north, Stopford's divisions succeeded in securing their bridgeheads and prepared for an assault on Mandalay. Their commander developed a plan in which the 19th Division would attack the city from Singu in the north while the 2nd and 20th Divisions hit Japanese positions from the south. During this offensive, these units made gradual but steady progress against the rapidly dwindling remnants of the 15th Army, now being pummelled relentlessly by heavy bomber attacks. On 20 March, the survivors of the annihilated Japanese army evacuated Mandalay and XXXIII Corps entered the city unopposed. Collectively, Stopford's command suffered 1472 killed, 4933 wounded and 120 missing.

The fall of Rangoon

East of this region, Chinese and American forces were consolidating their control over the areas between the Irrawaddy and Salween rivers. By mid-January, they had captured Namkham, Wamting and several other towns between China and Mandalay. These victories over the 33rd Army opened the land route that Chiang Kai-shek had so desperately wanted in order to connect China to India. Thus, on 4 February, the first supply convoy travelled down the Ledo Road to reach Kunming.

With this objective fulfilled, Chiang pulled his Yunnan armies out of Burma in order to deal with Japanese forces in his own country.

Meanwhile, the NCAC pushed further south. At the end of February, the Chinese 30th Division occupied Hsenwi, while the British 36th Division crossed the Shweli River at Myitson, despite an attack from the Japanese 18th Division. On 6 March, the Chinese 38th Division captured Lashio. Later in the month, when northern Burma was devoid of any significant Japanese presence, the NCAC disbanded, thus ending American involvement in the country. While the Mars Task Force returned to China in order to help train and reorganise Chiang Kai-shek's armies, the British 36th Division headed to Mandalay to join Slim's forces in the campaign to push the Japanese completely out of Burma.

By this time, the decimation of enemy forces in Burma had rendered the reconquest of the country a foregone conclusion. Not only was the Burma Area Army a worn-out, skeletal organisation but it was also surrounded by an enemy capable of landing more troops from the sea, even if Slim's army had any trouble reaching Rangoon by itself. From their positions south of

ABOVE

In an airfield in Burma, veterans of the Chinese 6th Army prepare to board Dakota transport aircraft that will take them over the 'Hump' to their homeland. The disintegration of Japanese Burma Area Army enabled Chiang Kai-shek to recall his troops for deployment in China.

RIGHT

The first convoy from India to China delivers supplies to Nationalist forces over the new land route through Burma. The vehicles are travelling across the Hwei Tung Bridge over the Salween River.

Mandalay, IV Corps and XXXIII Corps had about 565km (350 miles) to travel to the capital. At Pyabwe, Stopford's divisions stalled in their march to Rangoon when they had to clear the last remnants of the 18th Division out of the town. However, apart from this battle, the two corps faced little opposition in their advance. To the east, friendly Karen guerillas protected their left flank from Japanese troops.

Meanwhile, on 30 April a naval force consisting of two battleships, two escort carriers, four cruisers and six destroyers bombarded targets in and around Rangoon in preparation for a seaborne invasion on the city. The following morning, a battalion from the 50th Gurkha Parachute Brigade landed at Elephant Point, a peninsula near the mouth of the Irrawaddy River. After overwhelming a small group of Japanese soldiers there, the Gurkhas secured a beachhead for the 26th Indian Division to land. On 3 May, the division marched into Rangoon without meeting any opposition.

By this time, IV Corps had arrived and made contact with the amphibious forces responsible for securing the capital. To the west, XXXIII Corps captured Prome. With the significant towns and bases throughout Burma now in Allied hands, and with the Japanese Burma Area Army practically non-existent, Mountbatten's forces had little more to do than initiate mopping-up operations against residual enemy forces.

The only possible hindrance to these actions came from the 28th Army. This unit was now struggling across a range of hills east of the Irrawaddy River – called the Pegu Yomas – in order to reach the remnants of the other two Japanese armies beyond the Sittang River. However, their effect was minimal. From May until the end of the war, Stopford's Indian battalions hunted down scattered units of the 28th Army, killing or capturing most of its soldiers. Meanwhile, Mountbatten sought to bring order to Burma by directing the establishment of a viable civil government.

ABOVE
Admiral Lord Louis Mountbatten meets General Stilwell and Admiral Sir Bruce A. Fraser. At the time of the meeting, Fraser had recently been appointed Commander-in-Chief of the British Eastern Fleet.

CHAPTER NINE

BLOODY CONQUESTS

Like cornered animals, Japanese troops resisted ferociously as
Allied forces invaded their strongholds in the Philippines,
Iwo Jima and Okinawa.

General MacArthur had originally planned to start his invasion of Luzon in December 1944. The US 6th Army's divisions had stormed the beaches of Leyte and captured Tacloban in late October, so for a while it seemed he would be able to stick with this schedule. However, elements of the Japanese 35th Army continued to resist American forces on the island, and the subsequent lengthy mopping-up operation forced MacArthur to delay the invasion of the main island of the Philippines until 9 January 1945. From 22 October to 11 December, about 45,000 Japanese reinforcements from the 1st and 26th Divisions reached Leyte to help the garrison prevent a complete American takeover of the island. However, 35th Army was still badly outnumbered on Leyte; by early December, the American 6th Army had reached 183,000 men. Making matters worse, warplanes of the 5th United States Army Air Force (USAAF) had sunk several Japanese transport vessels ferrying soldiers from Luzon, Davao and Cebu.

Aware of his numerical disadvantage, 35th Army's commander, Lieutenant-General Sasaku Suzuki, attempted to form an effective defensive strategy. In an effort to keep X Corps contained, to the north he dispatched the 1st Division to Carigara and elements of the 26th Division to Jaro. The rest of his reinforcements went south to aid the 16th Division, now fending off an attack from XXIV Corps. Thus deployed, Suzuki's troops had managed to stop the Americans at Jaro and Limon, but on 10 November the likelihood of this resistance continuing grew remote. Field Marshal Count Hisaichi Terauchi and Lieutenant-General Tomoyuki Yamashita decided not to send any more reinforcements or supplies to Leyte; in their view, the island had become a burden that hindered their efforts to protect Luzon.

The struggle for Leyte

Yamashita also ordered the 35th Army to abandon its plan of defence and commit the 16th and 26th Divisions to an aggressive counter-attack on areas around Burauen. While Suzuki's divisions pressured XXIV Corps from the west, in late November and early December paratroopers from the 4th Air Army launched a series of airborne assaults behind enemy lines. At Dulag, Tacloban and Buri, the Americans beat back these badly coordinated raids with little difficulty; however, at the Burauen airstrip, Japanese paratroopers were more successful, setting fire to stores, ammunition, fuel and small aircraft before being killed off.

With his two corps stalled at Limon and Baybay, the commander of the 6th Army,

OPPOSITE
Two Marines of American Indian ancestry transmit a message in the Navajo language. The inability of the Japanese to understand this language made it an excellent code system for the Americans.

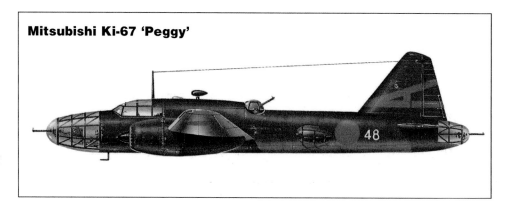

Mitsubishi Ki-67 'Peggy'

Lieutenant-General Walter Krueger, landed the 77th Division on the west coast of Leyte in an effort to split the Japanese divisions into two. Suzuki was now forced to shift his divisions and matters got worse when, on 10 December, the 77th Division moved up the island and captured Ormoc. Ormoc was an important base of operations for Suzuki and, from then on, organised Japanese resistance disintegrated rapidly. Krueger's divisions were now free to seize and occupy every town and area of military value on the island but, despite this, bands of dedicated Japanese soldiers continued to live off the land and harass American forces until the end of the war.

Ultimately, the battle for Leyte claimed the lives of over 80,000 Japanese soldiers, and roughly one-third of these deaths occurred during the mopping-up operations. During this period, the 6th Army captured 828 prisoners. American casualties included 3508 ground troops killed and over 12,000 wounded. Furthermore, on areas around the island, US naval forces lost several hundred men and two destroyers to *kamikaze* strikes while transporting troops and providing support for the 6th Army.

While Krueger's forces consolidated their control over Leyte, MacArthur prepared for his assault on the main island. At the end of 1944, the airstrips at Leyte could not be used due to flooding and, in order to provide the invasion with sufficient air support, the Americans first had to acquire decent airfields in close proximity to Luzon. An operation was devised to seize the island of Mindoro,

command of which fell into the hands of Brigadier-General William C. Dunckel. He was the leader of a landing party called the Western Visayan Task Force, consisting of two reinforced regiments.

Before Dunckel's task force could reach Mindoro, during its three-day ride from Leyte it was battered by harsh *kamikaze* attacks. The suicide pilots severely damaged the cruiser *Nashville* but could not prevent the invasion of Mindoro from taking place. Right on schedule, on 15 December, Dunckel's troops landed unopposed, before establishing a large beachhead and constructing two airstrips, which they finished in eight days. Although the Western Visayan Task Force still had to deal with isolated enemy units hidden deep in the interior of Mindoro, its airfields were now available for American planes to use from which to support the Luzon invasion.

The invasion of Luzon

On 2 January 1945, Vice-Admiral Jesse B. Oldendorf led a group of warships from the 7th Fleet out of Leyte Gulf to initiate a naval bombardment on Japanese positions at Lingayen Gulf on Luzon. While passing through the Sulu Sea, his vessels had to endure wave after wave of *kamikaze* attacks, one of which destroyed an escort carrier. As the flotilla steamed across the mouth of Manila Bay, the suicide raids intensified, damaging several American and Australian carriers, cruisers and destroyers. However, on arriving south-west of Lingayen Gulf, the Allied warships managed to sink two Japanese destroyers. They finally reached their destination on 6 January.

Oldendorf's strike force fended off yet more *kamikaze* attacks and positioned itself for the bombardment of Lingayen Gulf. Within a day, the suicide pilots sank three minesweepers and damaged several of Oldendorf's warships, including the battleships *New Mexico* and *California*. In the mean time, warplanes from Admiral William F. Halsey's 3rd Fleet had been battering Japanese airfields throughout Luzon, and soon the

ABOVE
Two LSTs upon the shoreline while their occupants move onto a beach. The island-hopping strategy of the American war effort in the Pacific Ocean led to the use of a wide variety of amphibious transport vehicles.

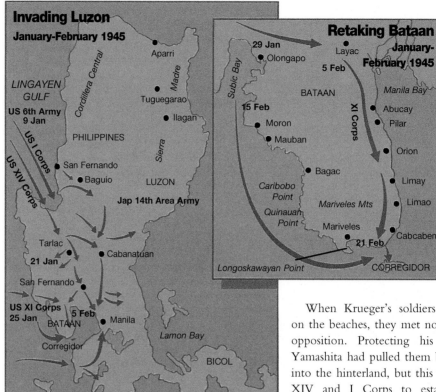

Invading Luzon
January–February 1945

Aparri
LINGAYEN GULF
Cordillera Central
Madre
Tuguegarao
Ilagan
US 6th Army 9 Jan
PHILIPPINES
Sierra
US I Corps
US XIV Corps
San Fernando
Baguio
LUZON
Jap 14th Area Army
Tarlac
21 Jan
Cabanatuan
San Fernando
US XI Corps 25 Jan
5 Feb
BATAAN
Manila
Corregidor
Lamon Bay
BICOL

Retaking Bataan
January–February 1945

29 Jan
Olongapo
Layac
5 Feb
Subic Bay
BATAAN
Manila Bay
15 Feb
Moron
XI Corps
Abucay
Pilar
Mauban
Orion
Bagac
Limay
Caribobo Point
Mariveles Mts
Limao
Quinauan Point
Mariveles
21 Feb
Cabcaben
Longoskawayan Point
CORREGIDOR

Japanese were forced to withdraw all of their functional aircraft from the Philippines. Oldendorf's strike force was therefore able to soften Japanese defences. Ready for the invasion and right on schedule, Krueger's XIV and I Corps approached Lingayen Gulf aboard transports on the morning of 9 January.

When Krueger's soldiers landed on the beaches, they met no enemy opposition. Protecting his forces, Yamashita had pulled them back far into the hinterland, but this enabled XIV and I Corps to establish a beachhead that was 6.4km (4 miles) inland and 27km (17 miles) wide. With this feat accomplished, MacArthur made another publicised landing on the shore, reminding the world that he was about to liberate the Philippines. From here, Krueger's divisions prepared to cross the central plain of Luzon and capture Manila.

Before they could realise this objective, XIV and I Corps had to deal with the

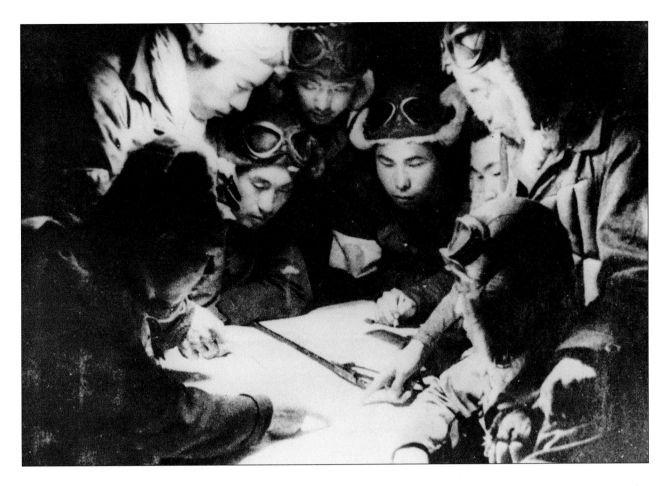

Shobu Group. This 152,000-man force was the largest concentration of Yamashita's three forces on Luzon. Entrenched in a line of positions stretching from the gulf to the Cabaruan Hills, it constituted a serious threat to the left flank of Krueger's forces. Accordingly, Krueger ordered Major-General Innis P. Swift, the commander of I Corps, to dislodge the Shobu Group and push it back further north while Major-General Oscar W. Griswold and his XIV Corps moved slowly toward Manila. Not surprisingly, Swift's forces experienced great difficulty carrying out their assigned task. Throughout January, the 6th and 43rd Infantry divisions, I Corps pummelled Japanese defences, but they made scant progress in their advance.

On to Manila

To the south, during their cautious march to Manila, Griswold's forces faced little opposition. However, because the attack on the Shobu Group had stalled, Krueger was reluctant to move XIV Corps too quickly. He had no real choice in the matter; on 17 January, MacArthur intervened, demanding a quicker advance on Manila to give his forces

a good port. In addition, he stated that he needed to secure Clark Field for the USAAF. Finally, MacArthur and other high-ranking officers were keen to liberate inmates held in prisons within the city before the Japanese were able to kill them or inflict further injury.

To neutralise enemy threats to Krueger's left flank, MacArthur dispatched the 25th and 32nd Divisions to Lingayen Gulf to help I Corps. By the end of the month, after a tank battle at San Manuel, Swift's forces had finally defeated the Shobu Group and pushed them into distant high ground. Two weeks later, I Corps reached the east coast of Luzon, isolating these Japanese troops from the rest of Yamashita's command. As a result, for the remainder of the war, Yamashita and most of his Shobu Group would be confined to the island's northern part, while the rest of his command struggled with the 6th Army in areas closer to Manila.

Meanwhile, Griswold's forces confronted the 30,000-strong Kembu Group. Led by Major-General Rikichi Tsukada, it was based in the Zambales Mountains, west of the central plain of Luzon. On 23 January, the Kembu Group and XIV Corps clashed at

ABOVE

Japanese kamikaze *pilots receive instructions the night before a sortie. Named after a 'divine wind' that had destroyed a Mongol invasion fleet attempting to attack Japan in the 13th century, these suicide squadrons began operating against American warships in the Battle of Leyte Gulf.*

ABOVE

Manned by the United States Coast Guard, a group of landing barges delivers the first wave of American ground troops to Luzon. The invasion of the island began at Lingayen Gulf, just over 160km (100 miles) north of Manila.

Bamban and, after a week of intense combat, the Americans pushed the Japanese back and seized Clark Field. During the fighting, Tsukada lost more than 2500 men.

West of the Kembu Group, the American 8th Army's XI Corps landed at San Antonio, just above the Bataan peninsula. Commanded by Major-General Charles P. Hall, these troops were to capture the Olongapo naval base and then join the drive on Manila. For

two weeks, they fought their way through Japanese defenders. Meanwhile, further south, most of the 11th Airborne Division, 8th Army descended upon Nasabugbu in an operation aimed at holding back Japanese forces in southern Luzon and opening another route to the capital. On 3 February, the rest of the division parachuted into Tagaytay Ridge and joined the offensive on Manila.

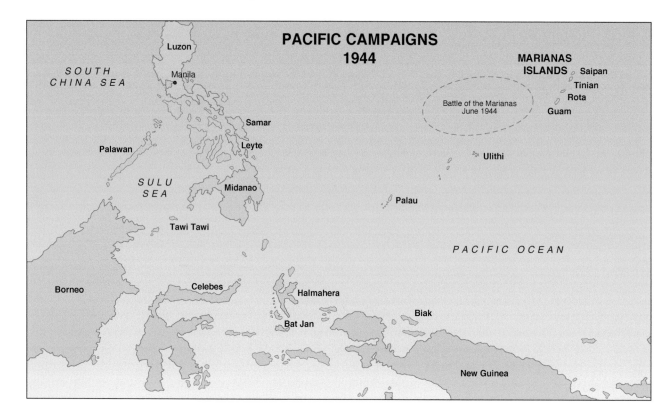

PACIFIC CAMPAIGNS 1944

That same day, XIV Corps approached the capital. By this time, the 1st Cavalry Division had arrived and spearheaded an assault on a civilian internment camp at Santo Tomas. While the cavalrymen liberated the prisoners, the 37th Infantry Division seized the Old Bilibid Prison and freed 1300 more civilian and military inmates. While these thrusts placed all of the northern suburbs of Manila into the hands of XIV Corps, the Americans still had to defeat the 17,000 naval troops who were now guarding the capital.

Urban warfare

Yamashita had no intention of sacrificing his own soldiers in a fruitless effort to hold Manila. However, the Japanese sailors and Marines occupying the city were not under his command. They were led by Rear-Admiral Sanji and were determined to fight to the last man. Accordingly, Iwabachi divided his forces into combat groups charged with defending specific sections of Manila. In what would be the only urban battle in the Pacific Theatre, a month-long struggle ensued, during which the Americans were forced to destroy entire buildings in order to neutralise enemy units which were using them as bunkers. After over a week of intense fighting, XIV Corps pushed the Japanese into Intramuros, the old inner city

of Manila. To the south, the 11th Airborne attacked Japanese naval units. These units were protected by solid defensive positions at Nichols Field but, aided by artillery support from XIV Corps, the paratroopers fought through in a series of brutal, hand-to-hand combat matches before seizing the base and linking with the 1st Cavalry Division on 12 February. Despite these American gains, Japanese resistance at Intramuros and other

ABOVE

The light cruiser USS Boise *and other warships fire anti-aircraft projectiles into the sky during the landings at Lingayen Gulf. Command of the naval bombardment against enemy positions in the area was in the hands of Vice-Admiral Jessie B. Oldendorf, a senior officer in the 7th Fleet.*

LEFT

American landing craft approach the Cebu Islands in the Philippines. A pre-invasion bombardment from the 7th fleet left behind a veil of smoke that obscures the objectives.

sections continued. Unfortunately for the residents of the capital, Iwabachi refused to evacuate any non-combatants, and many of them were condemned to suffer the same fate as his sailors. On 3 March, MacArthur's forces finally crushed the last remnants of the Japanese naval force holding the city. The price of this costly victory was over 1000 Americans killed and another 1550 wounded; in addition, civilian casualties approached 100,000. Not surprisingly, the vast majority of Iwabachi's sailors chose to die rather than surrender to the Americans.

Bloodshed in Luzon

Fighting also persisted in other parts of the Philippines. On 14 February, IX Corps assaulted Japanese positions in the Bataan peninsula and, after a week of fierce combat, seized the area. To the south, they fought a savage battle against well-entrenched defenders on the island of Corregidor. Having rooted out enemy units lodged in underground positions, American paratroopers secured the island at the end of the month. In mid-April,

MacArthur's forces took the islands of Caballo and El Fraile, attacking Japanese positions by incinerating them with diesel oil, TNT and phosphorus shells. Finally, the island of Canabao fell without a fight after the Japanese had evacuated it. All of Manila Bay was now in American hands.

After three months of combat, MacArthur's divisions had driven the 14th Area Army out of central Luzon and captured the capital of the Philippines. However, the Japanese presence on the island still constituted a significant threat. Yamashita had 172,000 soldiers on Luzon and occupied large areas in its northern and south-eastern regions, and he also held most of the country's dams and reservoirs, thus controlling much of Manila's water supply. Finally, his units possessed artillery pieces that had enough range to hit the capital.

Before MacArthur and Nimitz could plan another operation that would move their forces closer to Tokyo, they had to render the rest of Yamashita's army so weak that it could not threaten the American occupation

BELOW

American soldiers gather near Intramuros, the walled section of Manila, just before the Japanese garrison released 3000 civilian hostages. After the release, hundreds of Japanese troops made a final stand and forced their enemies to destroy the entire area.

of Luzon. East of Manila, Lieutenant-General Shizuo Yokoyama's Shimbu Group was the most noticeable menace to the capital. Arrayed in the southern end of the Sierra Madre range, from Ipo Dam to Laguna de Bay, Yokoyama's command contained about 80,000 men. On 6 March, USAAF bombers struck these areas in preparation for a ground assault which was to be conducted by XIV Corps two days later. Near Laguna de Bay, the 1st Cavalry, 6th Infantry and 43rd Infantry Divisions punched a hole in the centre of the Shimbu Group's lines before being relieved by XI Corps. The 43rd Division then headed south and pressured Yokoyama's left flank. To the north, the 6th Division had more trouble,

carrying out unsuccessful attempts to capture the Wawa and Ipo Dams. In late April, the 43rd Division arrived to join the offensive.

While the two divisions prepared for an assault on the northern part of the Shimbu Group, the USAAF initiated a three-day campaign of saturation bombing, dumping 1,136,600 litres (250,000 gallons) of napalm on enemy positions. On 6 May, the 43rd Division launched its attack, while, in support, Filipino guerillas harassed Yokoyama's right flank. Eleven days later, the Allies captured Ipo Dam and, to the south, the 38th Division relieved the 6th Division and began to wear down the Shimbu Group. By this time, Yokoyama's forces were starting to disintegrate.

ABOVE
Although General Tomoyuki Yamashita was willing to allow the Americans to take Manila without a fight, Japanese naval units acting independently of his 14th Area Army were determined to defend the Philippine capital at all costs. This stubbornness led to a vicious urban battle that inflicted a great deal of damage upon the city.

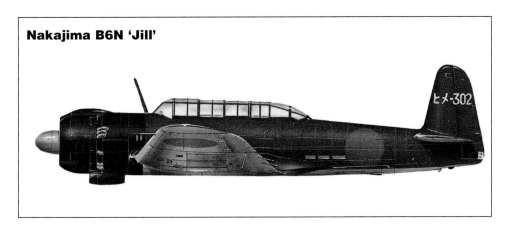

Nakajima B6N 'Jill'

LEFT
Designed to be a carrier-based torpedo bomber, the Nakajima B6N 'Jill' was eventually used as a kamikaze aircraft after the Japanese had lost several carriers during the course of the war. The B6N could reach a speed of 480km (300 miles) per hour and carried one torpedo weighing 800kg (1764lb).

A Landing Signals Officer of the USS Princeton. *Although the ship was one of six sunk at the Battle of Leyte Gulf, the Japanese came off far worse, losing four carriers, three battleships, six heavy and four light cruisers, 11 destroyers and a submarine. The action also led to a serious reduction in Japanese ground-force strength in the Philippines, with some 135,000 Japanese soldiers being marooned behind the American advance.*

At the end of the month, the Wawa Dam fell into American hands; meanwhile, the remnants of the Shimbu Group fell back to a position on the east coast and stayed there for the rest of the war. West of Clark Field, the 40th Division, XIV Corps dealt with the Kembu Group. The Kembu Group had retreated to coastal high ground when the air base had fallen to the Americans and, well entrenched in its advantageous terrain, it managed to hold out for two months. Two more American divisions arrived to dislodge it, on 6 April finally hammering the Japanese positions badly enough to force Major-General Tsukada to disband his forces and direct his soldiers to carry out guerilla war. Below Manila, throughout southern Luzon, the 1st Cavalry Division, the 158th Regimental Combat Team and Filipino irregulars crushed bands of Japanese soldiers and sailors. By the end of April, the area was effectively pacified.

In the north-eastern corner of the island, Yamashita's Shobu Group remained a formidable threat, but Krueger was preoccupied with the other two Japanese organisations to the south and west of Manila and could only spare three divisions to use against it. By late April, he was able to send more divisions north, since the 6th Army had neutralised the Shimbu and Kembu Groups, by which time American soldiers had become so enraged at the abusive treatment of the San Tomas prisoners they had liberated that they were keen to slaughter as many of Yamashita's men as possible.

The southern Philippines

In two months of fighting, Swift's I Corps forced the Shobu Group out of Balete Pass and Bambang before moving into the Cagayan Valley. In late June, American paratroopers landed in the northern end of the valley and connected with the 37th Division at Tuguegarao. Although Yamashita still had 65,000 able-bodied men in his command, most of them were now pinned to the northern part of the Sierra Madre range east of the Cagayan River, while other units held small, scattered areas between Bontoc and Bambang. The Shobu Group held these positions until the end of the war but never again threatened Allied control of Manila or any other areas south of Lingayen Gulf.

From northern Luzon, MacArthur and Krueger were now able to stabilise and consolidate their control over the whole island, thus ending the six-month battle. As usual, the two armies' casualties were unmatched. Collectively, the Japanese lost about 190,000 men, while the Americans suffered 8000 killed and 30,000 wounded. To the south, savage fighting also took place on Mindanao and other islands in the Philippines.

The task of conquering the central and southern Philippine islands had fallen into the hands of Lieutenant-General Robert L. Eichelberger and his 8th Army. From February until April, his 24th, 40th and Americal divisions defeated isolated enemy forces and occupied Samar, Burias, Siniara, Romblon, Tablas and Masbate in the area around the Visayan Passages. With the conquest of these islands, Allied vessels were now able to pass through the Philippines without fear of enemy artillery bombardments. Further west, beginning on 28 February, the 186th Regimental Combat Team, 41st Division captured Palawan in a week-long battle against a total of 1750 Japanese soldiers and sailors.

On 10 March, the main part of the 41st Division landed on the western tip of Mindanao, the second largest of the Philippine islands. For two weeks, Suzuki and the 43,000 troops in his 35th Army kept the Americans contained on a small area on the Zamboanga peninsula. To the south, elements of the 41st Division attacked Suzuki's garrisons in the small islands of the Sulu Archipelago. While Basilan fell with little difficulty, the 163rd Regimental Combat Team had to fight 4000 Japanese defenders for three weeks at Jolo before crushing organised resistance on 9 April. Moreover, scattered resistance in the interior of the island persisted until as late as July.

Mindanao subdued

Above Mindanao, Eichenburger's forces also invaded Panay, Negros, Cebu and Bohol. On 18 March, the 40th Division landed on Panay, surprised a small garrison and conquered the island within 10 days, thanks in part to help from local guerillas. At the end of the month, the division stormed western Negros, and found itself fighting 13,500 Japanese troops commanded by Lieutenant-General Takeshi Kono. After a battle that lasted until late May, Kono pulled his remaining 6000 soldiers into the mountainous interior of the island,where they held out until the end of the war.

To the east, on 26 March, elements of the Americal Division landed on mined beaches

at Cebu before fighting a 10-day campaign to secure the island. Even after overcoming organised resistance, their struggle was far from over, and the ensuing mopping-up operations lasted until June. On 11 April, other members of the division had better luck invading Bohol and, within the space of two weeks, they had managed to crush all enemy units and joined the 40th Division in its assault on Negros.

Meanwhile, the fight for Mindanao continued. Although sizeable, the Japanese garrison at Mindanao controlled only a small percentage of the island. While Suzuki's troops occupied populated areas, local insurgents under the command of Colonel Wendell W. Fertig dominated the countryside. In April, the situation worsened for the Japanese when Suzuki perished during an enemy air strike. His successor, Lieutenant-General Gyosaku Morozumi, now faced the enormous problem of dealing with these guerillas while keeping the 41st Division in check at Zamboanga as well as preparing for another American invasion.

On 17 April, X Corps stormed Mindanao at Illana Bay and moved inland at a quick pace. Within 15 days, they travelled 185km (115 miles) and entered the town of Davao, which fell on 3 May. Unfortunately for X Corps, this rapid advance stalled, since the Americans had to fight for several more weeks against enemy forces entrenched within the island's interior highlands. On 10 May, the 108th Regimental Combat Team landed on the north coast of the island near Macajalar Bay in an effort to help split Morozumi's forces into two smaller groups. A month later, a battalion from the 31st Division hit the beaches at Butuan Bay and proceeded to join the fight.

By the end of June, the Americans had battered the main part of the 35th Army badly enough to force its soldiers to disperse and carry out guerilla warfare in remote jungle areas. In the extreme southern part of Mindanao, 2000 Japanese soldiers continued to resist. However, on 12 July, a battalion from the 24th Division reached Sarangani Bay and assisted local irregulars in an effort to liquidate the enemy force. This mopping-up operation was the last action in MacArthur's campaign to liberate the Philippines. He had now succeeded in establishing another base of operations in the drive to Tokyo.

Iwo Jima

While MacArthur's Army divisions fought their way through the Philippines, Lieutenant-General Holland M. Smith and his Marine Corps divisions assaulted a target in the Bonin Islands hundreds of kilometres to the north-east. Weeks before the invasion on Leyte, Vice-Admiral Raymond A. Spruance and three army generals had persuaded the Joint Chiefs of Staff to authorise a campaign to capture Iwo Jima, a tiny, triangular piece of earth less than 8km (5 miles) long and 4km (2.5 miles) wide. Because the island was situated 1005km (625 miles) north of Saipan and 1061km (660 miles) south of Tokyo, they considered it an excellent base for long-range bombers en route to bombing missions on Japan. In addition, Spruance noted that Iwo Jima's location would enable P-51 Mustang fighters to escort B-29 Superfortresses on bombing sorties. The

BELOW
Late in the war, the United States Navy introduced a new class of submarine modelled after the USS Tench. By the time these new weapons reached Japanese waters, there were few enemy targets to sink apart from a few merchantmen attempting to elude the American blockade.

USS *Tench*

ABOVE

A swarm of American landing craft approaches the eastern shoreline of Iwo Jima. In the centre of the photograph, Mount Suribachi dominates the landscape of the island.

RIGHT

To defend themselves from the American invasion, Japanese forces on Okinawa relied upon a network of caves and dugouts. This hollowed-out area is situated on a riverbank.

Major-General Harry Schmidt command of V Amphibious Force. An organisation that included the 3rd, 4th and 5th Marine Divisions, V Amphibious Force would carry out the ground assault on the island.

Unfortunately for the Marines obliged to spearhead the attack, Iwo Jima possessed few accessible areas on its coastline. The wide, northern end of the island was a high plateau with a steep, rocky shore. Only in the south, near an extinct volcano called Mount Suribachi, did any accessible sites exist. During planning, Smith and Schmidt selected a large beach on the eastern shoreline for their divisions to assault and occupy, but senior officers in the Japanese armed forces had by now anticipated an American attack and thus ordered its garrison to construct fortifications and to set minefields.

The assault begins

Since early 1944, when the Japanese had lost the Marshall Islands, Imperial Headquarters had been reinforcing Iwo Jima so that it would have a substantial garrison by the time the Americans arrived. In addition, the Japanese had constructed an airfield near Mount Suribachi and began another in the central plateau. By June 1944, the island's defence force was armed with 13 artillery pieces and at least 200 machine-guns. Around this

invasion of the island was scheduled to begin on 19 February; Spruance assumed overall command, while Rear-Admiral Richmond K. Turner became the Joint Expeditionary Force leader. Meanwhile, the oversight of ground troops on Iwo Jima fell into the hands of 'Howlin' Mad' Smith, who delegated to

time, the commander of the 109th Division, Lieutenant-General Tadamichi Kuribayashi, arrived to take charge of the troops. The garrison also had a naval unit under Rear-Admiral Toshinosuke Ichimaru equipped with 14 coast-defence guns, 12 large howitzers and 150 anti-aircraft guns.

A cautious officer, Kuribayashi chose a defence-in-depth strategy over one involving reckless counter-attacks on enemy forces at the beaches. Having ordered the small civilian population of Iwo Jima to evacuate, he instructed his troops to build a defence network of 800 pillboxes and 4.8km (3 miles) of underground tunnels connecting fortifications beneath the island's volcanic rocks. Eventually, the garrison would receive more reinforcements, enabling it to achieve a peak strength that included 13,586 soldiers and 7347 sailors. However, Kuribayashi had problems with his senior officers over his defence-in-depth scheme. Many, including Admiral Ichimaru, recoiled at the idea of allowing the Americans to take the beaches above Mount Suribachi, especially since they would then be able to seize Airfield No. 1. Needing the cooperation of the naval units and their ample supply of munitions, Kuribayashi offered a compromise: in exchange for half of their supplies, he would let them construct pillboxes near the beach. However, he insisted that all Japanese forces must hold their fire

until the Americans advanced 450m (1500ft) from their coastal positions. Ichimaru and his officers agreed to this proposal.

Soon after Kuribayashi's arrival, American carrier aircraft descended from the sky, thus initiating hostilities. For the rest of the year, these attacks persisted, culminating in a bombing campaign that lasted 74 days which was carried out by B-29s and B-24 Liberators based in the Marianas. Three days before the ground assault began, Spruance sent six battleships and several other vessels to bombard Japanese positions on Iwo Jima. Despite the high number of munitions fired into the island, the shelling caused few casualties; most Japanese troops were in their underground positions. However, this bombardment became more effective on its third day, when the Americans hit enemy pillboxes and blockhouses near the south-eastern beach areas with greater precision, tearing many structures from their foundations.

On the morning of 19 February, V Amphibious Force began its ground assault on schedule. To the left, the 5th Division landed near Mount Suribachi. Led by Major-General Keller E. Rockey, these Marines were to isolate enemy positions on the mountain and assail the southern end of Airfield No. 1. Further north, the 4th Division, under the command of Major-General Clifton B. Cates, was to help capture the airfield and

ABOVE

A Marine Corps rocket unit pummels enemy positions on Iwo Jima. The assault began on the southern part of the island near Airfield No. 1 and advanced steadily across Mount Suribachi and northward to Kitano Point.

A member of the 4th Marine Division inspects the remains of a Japanese Type 97 medium tank. During the Battle of Iwo Jima, the Japanese converted most of their tanks into makeshift bunkers by partially burying these vehicles in gullies.

a ridge leading to the Motoyama plateau. Meanwhile, Schmidt held Major-General Graves B. Erskine and his 3rd Division back to act as a reserve force.

Mount Suribachi

Following Kuribayashi's orders, there was little opposition on the beach area. However, the amphibious tractors (amtracs) transporting the Marines soon became mired in the loose, black sand which covered the landing site, and were forced to exit and cross the rest of the beach on foot. Furthermore, when the Marines reached a collapsing terrace hundreds of yards inland, the Japanese opened fire with machine-guns, mortars and rifles from concealed caves, blockhouses and pillboxes. This rude greeting from the garrison

inaugurated what would become one of the bloodiest campaigns in the history of the United States Marine Corps.

Later in the morning, V Amphibious Force deposited several tanks on the landing site. Like the amtracs, these vehicles were bogged down in the black sand and were vulnerable to Japanese anti-tank crews, who destroyed several of them. Not enough of the tanks were available to assist the 4th Division in its assault on Airfield No. 1 and, as a result, these Marines were forced to use flamethrowers and explosives to destroy enemy forces lodged in several pillboxes and blockhouses. By the end of the day, Schmidt had landed about 30,000 Marines on Iwo Jima. Out of that number, 536 were already dead from enemy mortar and machine-gun fire,

LST Mk 3

while the survivors had to endure a night of harassing artillery bombardments.

Despite the intensity of the Japanese counter-attack, the 5th Division's 28th Regimental Combat Team fulfilled part of its objective when it crossed 640m (2100ft) of sand to reach the other side of the island and, by the end of the day, isolated Mount Suribachi. The following morning, two battalions gained 183m (600ft), while a third was held back as a reserve unit. Within a day, aided by 40 warplanes that strafed and bombed Japanese positions on Mount Suribachi, the battalions reached the base of the mountain. To the north, the 4th Division pushed through Airfield No. 1 and located Kuribayashi's first major defence line, which ran just below Airfield No. 2 on Iwo Jima's central plateau. On 21 February, the Marines pushed further into this area, assisted by tank units that manoeuvred well on the plateau.

The Americans were dealt a blow when, that evening, Japanese warplanes appeared and launched a vicious *kamikaze* attack on the large carrier *Saratoga*. After five of the suicide pilots smashed their vehicles into the vessel, five more enemy aircraft swooped from the sky to finish it off, while its crew tried putting out the fires that were burning out of control. Although the Americans shot down four of them, the last plane's bomb ripped a large hole into the flight deck of the carrier. Badly damaged, *Saratoga* had to abandon the fight for Iwo Jima and return to the United States for repairs. Nearby, other *kamikaze* pilots managed to sink a small jeep carrier.

On 23 February, with the gauntlet around Mount Suribachi tightened, the 28th Regiment punched through Japanese defences to reach the top of the extinct volcano. Mid-morning, during a skirmish with a group of enemy soldiers, a patrol of 40 Marines under

ABOVE

All LSTs had British design roots, and American- and British-built ships operated successfully alongside each other. The British developed the Mk 3 simply because there were not enough of the American LSTs to meet demand. They had roughly the same dimensions as the US LSTs, but were much heavier, and thus more powerful. They were all launched between 1944 and 1945.

LEFT

During the Iwo Jima campaign, Vice-Admiral Richmond K. Turner confers with Major-General Clifton B. Cates and other senior officers of the 4th Marine Division. The Americans sought to capture the island in order to acquire its airfields for use by fighter escorts during bombing sorties over Japan.

ABOVE

Japanese prisoners-of-war gather on the deck of a Landing Craft, Tank (LCT). Their ultimate destination is a facility at Pearl Harbor.

Lieutenant Harold G. Schrier managed to hoist a small US flag on the lip of its crater. Caught on film, this became one of the most enduring images in Marine Corps history and, after this, the Marines staged more photographed poses with the national flag, thus boosting the morale of those who were still locked in combat to the north.

Around this time, Schmidt went ashore with the reservist 3rd Division to launch a three-pronged attack on Kuribayashi's remaining defences. In his plan, he called for the 3rd Division to assail Airfield No. 2 in the centre, while the 4th would advance on the right and the 5th on the left. For two days, the Japanese fended them off, until two battalions from the 21st Regiment, 3rd Division pushed through enemy lines and overran the airfield. As a result, by 25 February most of the facility and one-third of Iwo Jima were in American hands. Four days later, the rest of the division breeched Kuribayashi's second main defence

line and captured the ruined town of Motoyama. To the south-east, in early March the 4th Division drove Japanese forces out of Hill 382.

By this time, Kuribayachi was beginning to recognise the inevitability of defeat. On the day Hill 382 fell, he radioed his superiors in Tokyo, apologising for his inability to hold on to Iwo Jima and regretting that the loss of the island would render Japan much more vulnerable to bombing campaigns. Nevertheless, his forces continued to resist the American juggernaut, forcing the Marines to earn every centimetre of ground taken. Kuribayachi wanted to stick to his plan of defence-in-depth, but insubordinate officers in his command defiantly led suicidal banzai assaults, which did little more than get many brave Japanese fighters killed quickly. On 8 March, one attack against the 4th Division saw 650 troops slaughtered, caught as they had been on open ground without artillery support.

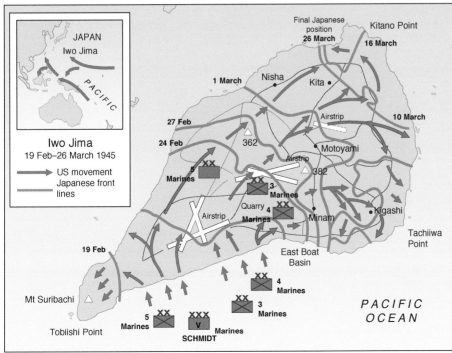

Inset map:
JAPAN
Iwo Jima
PACIFIC

Iwo Jima
19 Feb–26 March 1945
US movement
Japanese front
lines

Final Japanese position
26 March
Kitano Point
16 March
1 March   Nisha   Kita
Airstrip   10 March
27 Feb
24 Feb   362
Motoyami
Airstrip   382
5 Marines   XX
3 Marines   XX
Quarry   4 Marines   XX
Airstrip   Minam   Kigashi
19 Feb   Tachiiwa Point
East Boat Basin
4 Marines   XX
Mt Suribachi
3 Marines   XX
5 Marines   XX   Marines   XXX   V
Tobiishi Point   SCHMIDT
PACIFIC OCEAN

ABOVE

Marines from the 5th Division show their colours at the top of Mount Suribachi. Located at the southern tip of Iwo Jima, the mountain was an extinct volcano that the Japanese had converted into a fortress.

Now Japanese resistance began to crumble, and the battle for Iwo Jima turned into yet another mopping-up operation for the Americans. The following day, a patrol from the 3rd Division reached the north-eastern end of the island and, by 11 March, the Marine divisions had confined enemy forces to scattered areas in the island's northern tip.

On 14 March, high-ranking Marine Corps officers stood over a destroyed enemy bunker, proclaiming the conquest of Iwo Jima. Deep inside their underground fortifications, Kuribayashi, Ichimaru and other Japanese commanders contemplated how they would make their last stands. On 26 March, near Kitano Point, 350 half-naked, savage-looking Japanese soldiers and sailors launched a desperate surprise attack on an encampment of American Air Force, Marine Corps and Navy Seabee engineers. After half a day of fierce, hand-to-hand combat, the Americans repulsed their attackers with heavy casualties.

The following morning, Kuribayashi and two of his staff officers committed suicide and, later in the day, Ichimaru and 10 of his men accomplished a similar feat by charging

BELOW

Artillerymen from the 15th Regiment, 6th Marine Division push a 105mm (4.1in) howitzer into position during the battle for Okinawa. On the southern end of the island, the Japanese occupied well-constructed fortifications and offered fierce resistance to the Americans.

headlong into enemy positions and collapsing under a spray of machine-gun fire. By the time the fighting was over, the Battle of Iwo Jima had claimed the lives of roughly 18,000 Japanese soldiers and sailors. Among the 3000 survivors, only 216 emerged from their underground labyrinth to surrender to V Amphibious Force, the rest of them remaining hidden like hunted animals for the rest of the war. Although not nearly as high, American casualties were also substantial and included 5931 Marines killed and over 17,000 wounded. The battle also claimed the lives of 363 American sailors.

Okinawa

While the battle for Iwo Jima was winding down, another American invasion force prepared for an assault on Okinawa, an island in the Ryukyu Archipelago. This was much closer to Japan; in fact, most Okinawans considered themselves Japanese and had political representation in the national Diet. Since April 1944, the 32nd Army with its three divisions and one brigade had been serving as the island's garrison. Commanded by Lieutenant-General Mitsuru Ushijima, the army also had a tank regiment, several artillery units, a local militia and even teenage volunteers. In addition, 10,000 naval personnel were stationed on Okinawa under the command of Rear-Admiral Minoru Ota.

Above the southern cities of Naha and Shuri, Ushijima erected a defence-in-depth network consisting of concentric fortresses, blockhouses, fortified caves and other structures connected with tunnels. Anticipating an American invasion on the south-west coast, he placed most of his forces below the Kadena Airfield. While two divisions manned the defence network north of Naha, the third division and the 44th Independent Mixed Brigade took up positions on the southern tip of the island. However, only two battalions guarded the northern region.

As expected, the Americans planned to land their troops on the Hagushi beaches south of Zampa Point. Christened Operation Iceberg, this invasion would be led by General Simon Bolivar Buckner Jr, commander of the 10th Army and the son of a Confederate general. His assault force consisted of three Army and three Marine Corps divisions. On 24 March, Buckner's troops initiated hostilities in the area by seizing the Kerama Retto Group, a small collection of islands 24km (15 miles) west of Naha, thereby providing an anchorage

ABOVE
Marines from the 8th Regiment, 2nd Division march across the Naha airfield en route to the front. South of the Okinawa capital, fighting on the island settled into a bloody stalemate similar to that of the Western Front in World War I.

Soldiers from the 7th Infantry Division, 10th Army find shelter behind a bullet-scarred monolith while observing enemy activity. During the Battle of Okinawa, the 7th Division assaulted the eastern end of the Shuri line.

for British and American warships and a base for seaplanes. On the same day, a week-long naval bombardment upon Okinawa began in preparation for the ground attack.

The Shuri line

Despite the intensity of the naval bombardment, Ushijima's defences were still mostly intact when two Army and two Marine divisions landed on 1 April. Not confronted with any opposition, by the end of the day the Americans had placed 60,000 combatants on the Hagushi beaches, with only 28 dead and 27 missing. From the coast, the divisions moved rapidly, meeting only scattered enemy units that were easily pushed aside. Within two days, the 7th and 96th Infantry Divisions, XXIV Army Corps had swept across the slender island, reaching the east coast before heading south toward Kuba. To the left, the 1st and 6th Marine Divisions, III Amphibious Corps performed a similar feat before turning north at Kin Bay. By 4 April, central Okinawa and its two airfields were securely in American hands. Thus far, Operation Iceberg was going better than expected and was way ahead of schedule.

Almost a week after the landings, the two Army divisions approached Ushijima's defensive network above Shuri. It was at Kakazu Ridge that they suffered their first setback. Japanese forces occupying the ridge

abruptly halted the advance with intense fire; for three days, the Americans launched a series of assaults, only to be thrown back with heavy casualties. By this time, news of President Roosevelt's death reached Okinawa, depressing the Americans' morale. The Japanese reacted by printing propaganda leaflets which gloated over the tragedy. However, their jubilation was to be short-lived; Buckner's divisions repelled several counter-attacks launched between 12 and 14 April.

To the north, the 6th Marine Division was having an easier time against much weaker resistance. Marching along both shorelines, its members isolated enemy forces in the Motubu Peninsula on 8 April. Later in the month, the Marines smashed the main Japanese position at a ridge called Yae-Take in a three-day battle, effectively bringing northern Okinawa under American control. However, bands of enemy guerillas continued to operate in remote hills.

While American and Japanese ground troops slaughtered each other on Okinawa, the warships of the 5th Fleet surrounding the island confronted waves of *kamikaze* strikes. On a single day in mid-April, 185 of these suicide warplanes, along with 150 fighters and 45 torpedo bombers, swept in from Japan. Behind them flew eight twin-engined bombers, each carrying a new weapon called the *oka*, a torpedo-shaped glider packed with explosives that the pilot was to use like the *kamikaze*. Although the American warships shot down 383 enemy aircraft, the Japanese managed to sink six vessels and to damage another 24. On 7 April, 386 American warplanes sank the dreadnought *Yamato* and four escort destroyers which were steaming through the East China Sea to Okinawa.

Off the coast of the Motubu Peninsula, on 16 April the 77th Infantry Division invaded Ie Shima – a small, oval-shaped island containing three airstrips – so that from here Buckner could intensify air strikes upon enemy positions on Okinawa. Although 77th Division faced 2000 well-entrenched defenders who occupied underground positions, by 24 April, after a week of bloody combat, its forces had secured the island. Meanwhile, Buckner decided to try stealthy tactics to penetrate the Shuri defence line.

He ordered XXIV Corps' 27th Division to manoeuvre around such strong points as Kakazu Ridge and to push through Japanese lines at more vulnerable locations. On 19 April, the division sustained 720 casualties from enemy artillery and mortar crews guided by carefully measured zones of fire and this assault – and another launched the following day – failed. During the last week of the month, XXIV Corps was more successful, pushing Ushijima's forces further south. On 24 April, the soldiers from the 7th, 27th and 96th Divisions finally captured both Kakazu and Skyline ridges, thereby cracking the outer shell of the Shuri line. Three days later, the Americans seized another Japanese stronghold that they called 'Item Pocket'. On 30 April, Buckner replaced the depleted 27th Division with the 1st Marine Division; by this time, his divisions had gained about 8km (5 miles)

of land, seizing Machinato and Yonabaru Airfield in the process.

Meanwhile, Ushijima's subordinate officers cajoled him into launching another counter-offensive, this time in order to pierce 10th Army's centre and drive its fragments into the sea. Accordingly, on 4 May he initiated a complicated attack with amphibious landings on the east and west coasts, hoping to divert the Americans while three regiments from the 24th Division spearheaded the assault on the centre of Buckner's forces. Although the Americans quickly annihilated the amphibious units landing behind their lines, a 600-man Japanese battalion managed to punch a hole through enemy lines and recapture Tanabaru Ridge. However, the Americans quickly battered this unit until it received orders to fall back behind the Shuri line. On 7 May, only about a dozen survivors from the battalion managed to reach friendly forces.

During the fighting over Tanabaru Ridge, the combatants on Okinawa had received news of Nazi Germany's surrender to the Allies. Japan was now struggling against its enemies completely alone. By this time, Ushijima's forces were wearing down, forcing the 32nd Army commander to commit the last of his reserves to the Shuri line. Believing victory to be in his sights, Buckner resumed offensive actions on 10 May. After 10 days of combat, the 7th Division pushed back the

eastern end of Ushijima's line. However, hopes for a breakthrough quickly faded when the retreating Japanese defenders held their positions on land further south.

Although the invasion of southern Okinawa seemed to have settled into a bloody stalemate – similar to that of northern Europe during World War I – 32nd Army's heavy losses at last began to take their toll. On 21 May, Ushijima saw that he did not have enough manpower to maintain the Shuri line and decided to retreat further south. By the end of the month, his divisions had withdrawn to new defences at the Yaeju-Dake Ridge, just above Kiyan and Mabuni.

The way was now open for the 10th Army to seize Naha, Shuri and Jonaberu, but Japanese resistance continued to be tenacious. Although Ushijima, his division commanders and most other officers had given up hope of defeating the 10th Army, they still wanted to inflict as much damage on the enemy as they could. On the Oroku Peninsula, just below Naha, the 6th Marine Division was forced to fight the isolated remnants of Rear-Admiral Ota's naval force for 10 days before obliterating them on 15 June; meanwhile, along Yaeju-Dake Ridge, the Americans encountered opposition that was as stubborn as ever. For five days, the 10th Army had to blast and burn the enemy units that were holding out in their caves and fortifications.

By 17 June, Buckner's divisions had cornered the remnants of the 32nd Army at an area near Mabuni. While the Japanese prepared for a last stand, Buckner sent a message to his adversary, pleading with Ushijima to surrender before any more lives were lost in an unnecessary battle. Ignoring this request, on 21 June Ushijima and his chief of staff eventually committed ritual seppuku. On the same day, the battle for Okinawa reached a bloody conclusion at Hill 85. The 10th Army demolished the last element of organised resistance, and Operation Iceberg was effectively over.

The Japanese collapse

In the defence of Okinawa, the Japanese had lost about 110,000 troops, including local civilians. While the 32nd Army was in its death throes, only 7400 combatants chose to surrender to the 10th Army. Additional casualties included almost 1500 *kamikaze* pilots who had been sacrificed by Imperial Headquarters. During air and naval engagements around the island, 7800 aircraft and 16 warships were also lost. The massive destruction of their armed forces, combined with the American conquest of the Ryukyu Islands, forced the Japanese Government to contemplate the likelihood of total defeat. With Okinawa subdued, the Allied forces were now within 563km (350 miles) of the Japanese island of Kyushu.

However, Operation Iceberg was a costly victory for the Americans. Collectively, they suffered over 49,000 casualties. One of the fatalities was General Buckner, who perished on 18 June when an artillery shell landed near him, sending a jagged piece of coral into his chest. In the defence of Okinawa, the Japanese had also managed to destroy 763 Allied aircraft and 36 vessels. Furthermore, although the Allies were now well within striking distance of Japan, they knew that its conquest would require yet more slaughter and destruction in the Pacific theatre.

BELOW
The surviving remnants of Japanese forces charged with defending the Ryukyu Islands surrender to the United States 10th Army. To the left, Sherman and Pershing tanks line the roads at the surrender ceremony on 7 September 1945.

CHAPTER TEN

REAPING THE WHIRLWIND

To bring Japan to its knees, the Americans unleashed two terrible weapons upon Hiroshima and Nagasaki.

In April 1945, as the Okinawa campaign was just getting started, General MacArthur and Admiral Nimitz developed a two-phase plan for invading Japan. The first phase, Operation Olympic, scheduled to begin on 1 November 1945, would involve an attack on the southern island of Kyushu by three Army Corps and one Marine Corps amphibious force. After subduing Kyushu, the Americans were to use it as a staging area to launch phase two, Operation Coronet, an even larger campaign aimed at conquering Honshu which would begin on 1 March 1946. With some justification, high-ranking American officers anticipated that these operations would lead to high numbers of casualties for both sides.

Expecting an invasion of their homeland, senior Japanese military commanders formulated Operation KETSU-GO. This was designed to crush enemy forces on the beaches with 2.35 million troops organised into 53 infantry divisions and 25 brigades. In addition, several million bureaucrats and civilians would be organised into militias, armed with muzzle-loading rifles and sharpened bamboo sticks. Even if most Japanese people were exhausted from the war in the Pacific Ocean, they still seemed motivated to engage in a fanatical struggle for their homeland. Confronted with this determination, the Americans needed an alternative method of ending the war without sacrificing so many troops in a ground assault.

The Australians on Borneo

While the American 10th Army gradually subdued Okinawa, Lieutenant-General Sir Leslie Morshead and his Australian I Corps assailed Borneo, now one of the last significant Japanese possessions in the Pacific Ocean and garrisoned by a group of naval detachments and about 16 battalions from Lieutenant-General Masao Baba's Japanese 37th Army. General Sir Thomas Blamey and other senior commanders of Australian forces in the theatre questioned taking what now seemed to be a remote and irrelevant piece of land, and General Marshall believed that the seizure of Borneo would have little effect on the Pacific War. However, General MacArthur insisted that the island be returned to the Dutch East Indies colonial authorities.

With help from the US 7th Fleet and several bombers carrying out tactical air strikes, Morshead was able to land two divisions on Borneo's northern and eastern regions. In Sebuku Bay, the 2nd Brigade Group overwhelmed a small garrison on the island of Tarakan and seized Tarakan town on 5 May. After a month of combat, the Australians cleared Japanese forces out of the interior and

OPPOSITE

Anchored in Tokyo Bay, the USS Missouri *served as the location for the surrender ceremony ending the Pacific War. One of the four largest battleships in the world, the vessel had sustained minor damage from a* kamikaze *attack during the Okinawa Campaign.*

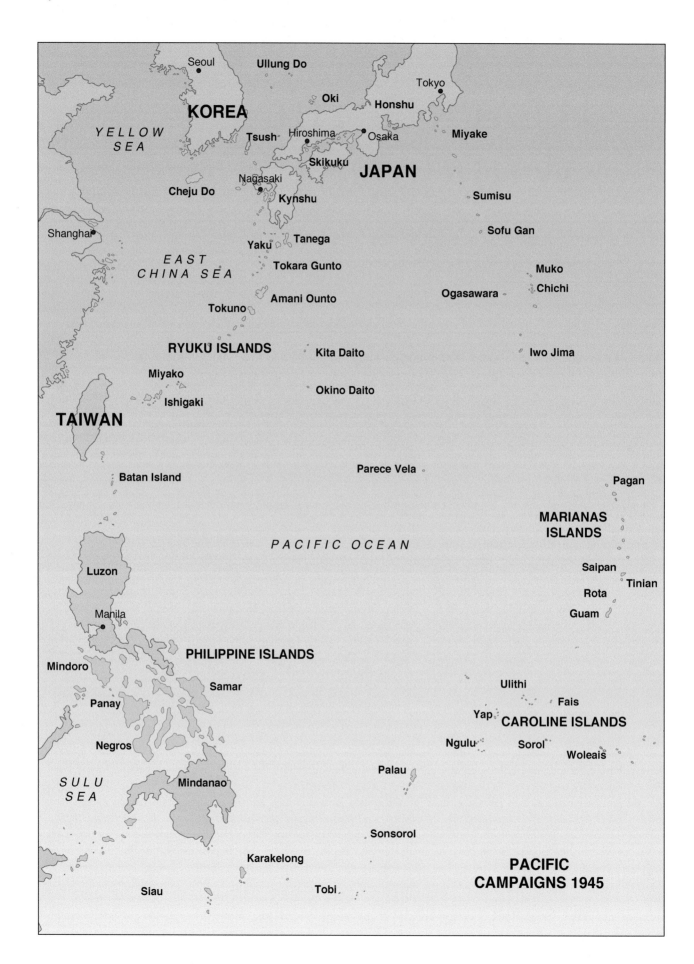

PACIFIC CAMPAIGNS 1945

A Japanese destroyer breaks in two during an American air strike on a convoy attempting to bring supplies to Ormoc, Leyte. While four B-25 Mitchell medium bombers pounded enemy vessels, escorting P-38 Lightning and P-47 Thunderbolt fighters shot down 16 Japanese warplanes.

secured the entire island, which contained little more than a worn-out airfield. During this battle, the Australians lost 225 killed and 669 wounded out of 13,000 troops in the brigade. Almost the entire Japanese garrison, numbering 1540, had died.

On 10 June, the Australian 20th and 24th Brigades, 9th Division landed at the British colony of Brunei Bay in an effort to capture the town of Brunei and several nearby oilfields. The 56th Independent Mixed Brigade was concentrated at Jesseltown, but within the town of Brunei itself only 1500 Japanese troops remained to oppose the 9th Division. Thus, the Australians faced little resistance and captured Brunei town, nearby islands in the bay and surrounding inland areas within four days. By the end of the month, the Japanese 37th Army had pulled back from the bay area, leaving the soldiers of the 9th Division and their commander, Major-General George Wootten, to consolidate their control and

A Japanese submarine sits atop the waves of the Pacific Ocean. Unlike their German allies, the Japanese did not use their U-boats in an aggressive manner against enemy convoys, enabling the Americans to move large amounts of supplies and manpower from island to island throughout the ocean.

to repair damaged oil facilities as well as other structures.

On the east coast, on 1 July Major-General E.J. Milford and his 7th Division went ashore near the towns of Balikpapan and Klandasan. In addition to three brigades, Milford's forces included three tank squadrons and an artillery unit. Fortunately for the Australians, 16 days of naval bombardments and air raids against enemy coastal positions near the invasion site had helped deter serious resistance. Within three days, the 18th Brigade captured the two towns, while the 21st and 25th Brigades headed north and seized several hills and two nearby airstrips. By 9 July, the 7th Division had attained all of its objectives and initiated aggressive patrolling movements that led to several skirmishes with nearby Japanese forces. These persisted right up until the end of the war.

Japan blockaded

With the acquisition of key positions on Borneo, the Allied high command decided that the complete conquest of Borneo was unnecessary. Morshead received orders to abstain from further penetration into the island and to allow the 37th Army to wallow in isolation while American land, naval and air forces tightened their grip on Japan. With

some justification, Blamey protested at what he considered to be a misuse of his troops when they could have been deployed in the Philippines, Okinawa or other areas more crucial to the war effort. Since by now the Allies controlled the waterways between Borneo and Kyushu, they did not have to worry about the Japanese transporting oil or other raw materials from Brunei to Tokyo.

Hundreds of kilometres to the north, Admiral Halsey and his 3rd Fleet intensified the blockade of Japan. While Halsey's carrier-based warplanes struck harbours and airstrips, American submarines stalked the remnants of the Japanese merchant marine in the East China Sea and the Sea of Japan. At the same time, B-29 Superfortress bombers dropped mines throughout the Inland Sea, inflicting hundreds of tonnes of shipping losses. By the summer of 1945, Japan's access to mainland Asia was practically non-existent, depriving the country of food and raw materials. Moreover, the inability to obtain petroleum products threatened to incapacitate the few warships that were still available to the Japanese Navy.

This isolation of Japan from its mainland possessions indicated that the construction and destruction of submarines had proved to be an important aspect of American naval

BELOW
Under construction at Sasebo, Japan, the carrier Ibuki *sits next to the submarines HA-105, HA-106 and HA-109. The carrier was still unfinished when the Japanese government surrendered to the Allies.*

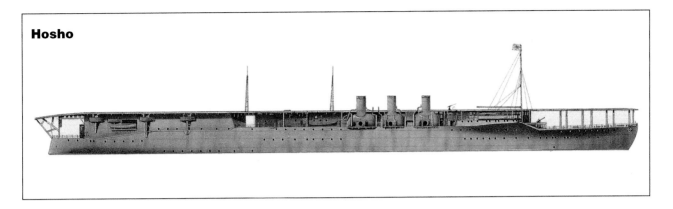

Hosho

supremacy. During the course of the Pacific War, the Japanese had built only about half, but had lost twice as many, submarines as the United States. Like the Germans in the Atlantic Ocean, the Americans in the waters around the Japanese Empire deployed their numerous underwater weapons in 'wolf-pack' patrols that aggressively preyed on both warships and transport vessels. Meanwhile, the small Japanese submarine fleet was performing an ineffectual defensive function. After the war, even General Hideki Tojo cited American submarine strategy as a crucial factor in the defeat of Japan.

Other factors helped ensure the success of the Allied submarine campaign. Since 1942, American crewmen had enjoyed the use of radar to locate enemy targets. In addition, the failure of the Japanese to develop an effective convoy system enabled these underwater predators to strike with impunity, sinking helpless merchantmen without much fear of reprisal from enemy warships. Finally, most US submarine commanders were skilled and dynamic leaders who became proficient at manoeuvring techniques that maximised their chances of striking their targets and escaping safely. During the course of the war, submarines were responsible for sinking almost 1200 merchantmen and destroying about 63 per cent of Japanese shipping.

As early as November 1944, American submarines were able to make their presence felt deep within Japanese waters. At the end of the month, *Archerfish* had been prowling the Inland Sea between Honshu and Kyushu when its crew spotted *Shinano*, a massive dreadnought similar to *Yamato* that had just been converted into an aircraft carrier. It was on its maiden voyage with three escorts when *Archerfish* fired four torpedoes into its hull. Although the carrier should have been strong enough to withstand these hits, its

crewmen were inexperienced and failed to enact damage-control measures to keep the vessel afloat. Within seven hours, *Shinano* sank with its captain and about 500 sailors. This debacle indicated that Allied control over the Pacific Ocean extended right up to the shoreline of the Japanese islands.

Like the *kamikaze* pilots and the dedicated soldiers fighting to the death against overwhelming enemy forces on the islands, the last remnants of the Japanese Navy adopted a desperate, suicidal strategy to defend their homeland. Specifically, Japanese warships were to take 'death rides' into Allied naval forces in an effort to damage and delay such targets as much as possible before facing inevitable destruction. On 6 April, the

ABOVE
Laid up in April 1945 for lack of aircrew to man her aircraft, Hosho *was thus one of the few Japanese carriers still in existence on VJ-Day. She was recommissioned as a transport to repatriate Japanese servicemen from all over the Far East.*

BELOW
The battleship Yamato *begins to sink after the attack by US Navy dive bombers and torpedo bombers in the East China Sea.*

ABOVE

Yamato *begins her career in the Imperial Navy while being fitted out in 1941. Armed with almost 200 guns of various sizes, the vessel was 263m (863ft) long and almost 39m (127ft) wide.*

dreadnought *Yamato*, a light cruiser and eight destroyers attempted such an action during the invasion to Okinawa. Like *Shinano*, these vessels travelled only a small distance before American submarines spotted them in the Bungo Strait between Shikoku and Kyushu.

The following morning, while *Yamato* was en route to aid the 32nd Army at Okinawa, Admiral Marc Mitscher hurled 386 dive bombers and torpedo bombers from Task Force 58 at the Japanese flotilla. Because Japanese air power was so depleted, *Yamato* was heavily armed with 146 anti-aircraft pieces, but even they were not enough to stop the waves of American warplanes that monopolised the sky over the East China Sea. Within hours, the bombers sank the heavy battleship and four destroyers, while the only injury suffered by Task Force 58 was a *kamikaze* strike that damaged the aircraft carrier *Hancock*.

Although the Japanese still had a few cruisers, battleships and carriers stationed in home waters, these were at the mercy of fuel shortages brought by the American blockade. To defend their country, the Imperial Navy only had 38 submarines and 19 destroyers that were operational. Not surprisingly, this contrast in sea power enabled American warships to tighten their gauntlet around Japan; by the summer of 1945, they were hitting enemy targets almost at will and with very little opposition.

In early July, three carrier groups from Vice-Admiral John S. McCain's Task Force 38 began a brutal campaign of air strikes against several airfields near Tokyo. Fortunately for the Japanese, most warplanes on the ground had been concealed. Later in the month, McCain's carrier groups terrorised northern Honshu and Hokkaido, sinking several coal-carrying transport vessels. Further south, on 24 July warplanes from Task Force 38 pounded the Koba and Kura naval bases, sinking three battleships and damaging three carriers and two cruisers.

The bombing campaign

While McCain's carriers pummelled air and naval bases throughout Japan, his surface ships bombarded manufacturing areas. By this time, battleships and cruisers from the British Pacific Fleet were there to help. At Kamaishi, three battleships and two destroyers immobilised an iron works factory. Meanwhile, a radar and electronics complex at Hitachi suffered a similar fate. On Hokkaido, another group of surface vessels hammered an iron and steel centre at Wanishi. By the end of July, only poor weather prevented the Allies from continuing their relentless attacks on Japan. On 9 August, while the Japanese were reeling from two atomic bombs dropped upon Hiroshima and Nagasaki, McCain's warships resumed operations, destroying about 250 enemy suicide bombers concealed at a facility in northern Honshu.

As the 3rd Fleet tightened its noose around Japan, the United States Army Air Force (USAAF) escalated its destructive bombing campaign upon enemy urban centres. In March 1945, the acquisition of Iwo Jima provided the USAAF with airfields that allowed emergency landings to and from the Marianas Islands and, in the last months of the war, 2251 crippled B-29s were able to take advantage of this. Unlike German cities, most Japanese urban centres did not have industrial districts. Instead, most Japanese factories and other manufacturing facilities were dispersed in residential areas, which prevented American bombers from hitting military targets without destroying entire neighbourhoods and killing many civilians. However, by 1945, most Americans were willing to do this to hasten an end to the war.

To inflict more damage upon Japanese industry, the commander of the 21st Bomber Command, Major-General Curtis E. LeMay, developed a new flight strategy. The B-29s woud fly low over their targets at night with few armaments in order to increase the bombing capacity of the aircraft. Upon reaching their destinations, they were to drop napalm canisters over wide areas, maximising the destruction inflicted upon enemy

BELOW
Amagi *sits capsized and sunk at the Kure Navy Yard. As Allied forces pushed closer to Japan, attacks on such targets became much more common.*

facilities. LeMay and other USAAF commanders knew this strategy would kill thousands of civilians but also knew it would deprive Japan of its ability to manufacture war materiel. To test its effectiveness, LeMay staged small-scale daylight raids on Nagoya and Kobe utilising his techniques. Satisfied with the results, the USAAF high command began the new bombing campaign.

Cities aflame

On the morning of 9 March, a large group of Superfortresses left their bases at Guam, Tinian and Saipan for Tokyo. Employing the method prescribed by LeMay, during this mission the 333 bombers only had tail cannons to protect them from enemy fighters but, with this sacrifice in firepower, each bomber was able to add an extra 1450kg (3200lb) of bombs to a total of six tonnes. At midnight, the pathfinders at the front of the formation reached their aiming points above

the capital and dropped incendiary bombs to burn a large 'X' upon an area, which the other bombers were supposed to hit. It was a downtown section filled with 750,000 working-class residents and several small, home-based factories.

As the pathfinders prepared to carry out their napalm drops, air-raid sirens sounded over Tokyo. However, few residents paid much heed to them; previous bombing sorties had done relatively little damage to the city. A short distance above the ground, the napalm canisters split apart, unleashing smaller containers filled with the explosive jelly that burst into flames when hitting the ground. With this mission accomplished, a large, blazing 'X' now covered the area, providing the other bombers with a clear target.

Before the B-29s in the main formation had dropped their bombs, the napalm dropped by the pathfinders started a conflagration, as strong winds caused the

BELOW

An aerial photograph reveals the extent of damage brought by a squadron of B-29 Superfortress bombers on Tokyo. In these and other raids throughout Japan, incendiary devices destroyed entire blocks of buildings and incinerated thousands of civilians.

flames to spread through blocks of buildings and houses. Flying at altitudes ranging from 1524 to 3048m (5000-10,000 feet) above ground, the rest of the bombers unloaded their napalm canisters and downtown Tokyo became a massive inferno. As the aircraft passed over the burning area, turbulence generated by the heat pushed many of them thousands of metres higher. Among the last bombers flying overhead, the odour of burning human flesh actually filled the nostrils of the crewmen, causing some of them to vomit. During the course of their mission, the Americans did not confront any enemy fighters and received only light anti-aircraft fire that shot down 14 bombers and damaged another 42.

The following morning, the surviving residents of central Tokyo emerged from their wrecked homes to see what was left of their neighbourhood. Not surprisingly, they found little more than a levelled, incinerated surface covered with ashes and concrete and steel ruins. Several victims had attempted to save themselves by plunging into the Kanda River but most of it was now evaporated and filled with bloated cadavers and personal

items. Most other victims were corpses in various positions left blackened by the fires. Altogether, the bombings had killed or wounded almost 130,000 people and destroyed over 267,000 buildings in about 41 square km (16 square miles), leaving over one million people homeless.

About 320km (200 miles) to the west, the following night another 285 bombers struck the aircraft-producing centre of Nagoya with napalm explosives. Although these Super-fortresses possessed a larger load of incendiary devices, they did less damage because winds were low that night and the city possessed an effective fire-fighting service. In addition, Nagoya had well-spaced firebreaks that discouraged the spread of any conflagration. Although the bombers missed the aircraft plants and damaged or destroyed only 18 industrial targets during the sortie, not one bomber was lost to counter-attacks, although a total of 20 aircraft suffered various amounts of damage.

On 13 March, LeMay's B-29s bombed Osaka, a city known for producing warships, army ordnance, electrical equipment and various types of machinery. Densely

ABOVE
A group of B-29 bombers from the 21st US Bomber Command receive maintenance service at a base in the Marianas Islands. On many occasions in 1945, hundreds of these gigantic vehicles dropped several tonnes of bombs on Japanese urban centres.

populated, with over two million people, the city had been spared the ravages of war until the Superfortresses appeared over it. In three hours, 274 bombers incinerated over 21 square km (8 square miles) in the city centre. Like Tokyo, Osaka sustained substantial damage, losing more than 130,000 houses and 119 factories. Almost 4000 people died.

Three days later, the B-29s struck the port city of Koba, another urban centre that had not yet suffered from significant devastation brought by the war. In just over two hours, 307 bombers dropped 2355 tonnes of magnesium thermite incendiaries on the city, despite being attacked by an enemy fighter squadron that failed to shoot down a single Superfortress. Altogether, the Americans lost three bombers during the operation. When

the sorties ended, roughly 7.7 square km (3 square miles) of Koba was in ruins, having lost 500 industrial buildings and almost 66,000 houses. One target that sustained heavy damage was the Kawasaki shipyard. During the bombings, civilian fatalities reached 2669, along with another 11,289 wounded.

Later in the month, LeMay's bombers flew another mission over Nagoya. On the night of 19 March, 290 Superfortresses dropped 1858 tons of bombs, incinerating 7.7 square km (3 square miles) and inflicting considerable damage to an arsenal and an engine factory. However, the Mitsubishi manufacturing plants remained almost untouched. This raid concluded 21st Bomber Command's productive 10-day campaign, during which the organisation had flown almost 1600 sorties and dropped over 9000 tons of bombs while losing less than 1 per cent of its crew. Not surprisingly, these results encouraged LeMay and other senior USAAF officers to launch another series of fire raids on Japan later in the year.

The destruction of Tokyo

Thus far, these bombings had destroyed about 83 square km (32 square miles) collectively in four cities. In addition to the deaths, and the destruction brought to the war industry of Japan, the campaign also created predictable hardships for civilians. Even before the start of the fire raids, the demolition of roughly 600,000 houses had rendered millions of urban residents homeless. Consequently, the destruction of entire neighbourhoods by incendiary devices exacerbated housing problems for those fortunate enough to survive such ordeals. Along with the catastrophe of war, many Japanese civilians also suffered from

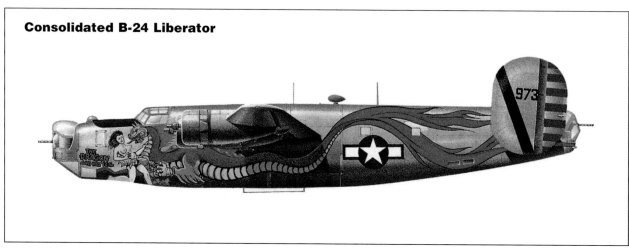

Consolidated B-24 Liberator

floods and earthquakes that destroyed another half a million houses throughout 1945.

For two months, the fire bombings on Japan halted. The USAAF was now preoccupied with providing air support for the 10th Army at Okinawa. During this campaign, LeMay noted how ferocious enemy resistance had been in the face of overwhelming American forces, realising that a ground invasion of the Japanese homeland would be much more deadly for both sides. Instead of fighting isolated pockets of army units, the Allies would be confronting more than 60 divisions and perhaps the entire population of Japan. LeMay therefore decided that the 21st Bomber Command should resume B-29 sorties over the country in an effort to force the Tokyo government to surrender before a ground invasion would take place.

Thus, on 14 May, LeMay sent 472 Superfortresses on a daytime bombing raid on Nagoya, each aircraft carrying 5.3 tonnes of incendiary devices. Flying at altitudes ranging from 3657 to 6096m (12,000-20,000 feet) above the ground, the bombers dropped over 2500 tonnes of napalm canisters on the city, incinerating a little more than 7.7 square km (3 square miles) and destroying many parts of the Mitsubishi manufacturing complex, in cluding a bearing plant. However, the formation lost 14 bombers during the mission. Two days later, another bombing squadron struck more industrial areas and docking facilities in the south of the city, this time going back to LeMay's strategy of night-time flying at low altitudes with few armaments, enabling each Superfortress to carry 8 tonnes of incendiary devices. During this raid, the Americans demolished almost 10.3 square km (4 square miles) and severely damaged a Mitsubishi aircraft factory, while their losses included only two bombers. This sortie was the last major action taken against Nagoya.

On 23 May, 520 Superfortresses destroyed over 13 square km (5 square miles) along the west side of Tokyo harbour with 3646 tonnes of bombs. During this mission, the flight crews had received instructions to avoid hitting the Imperial Palace. Planning for the future of postwar Japan, American officials

ABOVE
The devastation left behind after an Allied bombing attack on the Otake Oil Refinery.

ABOVE

The residents of Yokohama built huts among the ruins in the wake of a bombing raid launched by the US 7th Air Force. Unfortunately for Japanese civilians, the proximity of industrial facilities to residential areas led to widespread death and homelessness from such raids.

saw the survival of the Emperor and his family as desirable for US foreign policy in East Asia. In this raid, the Americans lost 17 bombers. Two days later, 502 more bombers carrying 3262 tons of explosives struck the government section of the city, an area closer to the Imperial Palace, this time creating an uncontrollable firestorm that obliterated almost 44 square km (17 square miles) of buildings, killed several thousand people and reached the Emperor's residence.

The victims of this attack included 62 Allied airmen detained in the Tokyo Army Prison. Although the palace was destroyed, the Emperor and his family fled to an underground shelter. The raid also incinerated the Prime Minister's house and buildings used by the Navy Department, Foreign Ministry and Greater East Asia Department.

Peace feelers

With 146 square km (56.3 square miles) of Tokyo now in ruins, LeMay decided that the fire raids on the capital had reached a satisfactory conclusion. However, bombardments of other population centres soon resumed. On 29 May, 517 Superfortresses demolished much of the nearby city Yokohama, after which the 21st Bomber Command unleashed its wrath upon Kobe and Osaka. During the May fire raids, LeMay's bombers had performed almost 4700

sorties and dropped more than 27,000 tonnes of explosives, losing 70 aircraft.

If LeMay's punishing air campaign was not doing enough to force the Japanese to surrender, it was at least eviscerating their urban infrastructure and thus depriving them of their ability to mobilise and prepare effectively for an invasion. By June 1945, more than half of Tokyo and Kobe were in ruins, as was almost half of Yokohama. Although Nagoya, Osaka and Kawasaki did not suffer quite as much devastation, over 25 per cent of these cities had become charred wastelands. Collectively, the Superfortresses and their napalm canisters had torched more than 272 square km (105 square miles) of urban areas during the month of May, demolishing over two million buildings and leaving at least 13 million people homeless.

From 17 June to 14 August, the 21st Bomber Command focused on smaller population centres. In this period, the B-29s flew over 8000 sorties and slammed more than 54,000 tonnes of incendiary devices into their targets, demolishing almost 166 square km (64 square miles) of urban sections. The total American losses in these missions included 19 bombers. To reduce civilian casualties and exacerbate the adverse psychological impact that the fire raids were inflicting upon the Japanese people, reconnaissance aircraft dropped leaflets warning residents to evacuate their neighbourhoods before the bombers arrived. In several instances, leaflets were dropped on cities that the Americans never intended to bomb, causing many people to flee into the countryside.

While this devastation was taking place, some members of the Japanese Government openly questioned their country's ability to continue fighting the war. Although Foreign Minister Mamoru Shigemitsu boasted that the whole country was willing to suffer incineration on behalf of the Emperor, many of his cabinet colleagues were not as defiant. Motoki Abe, the Minister of Home Affairs, observed that the May fire raids on Tokyo had induced a feeling of hopelessness in most of the Japanese people, who believed that the Americans could destroy as much of Japan as they wanted. Meanwhile, Prime Minister Kantaro Suzuki ordered his cabinet secretary, Hisatsune Sakomizu, to initiate a secret inquiry that would determine Japan's ability to continue the war.

Sakomizu's report confronted Suzuki with alarming revelations. Thanks to the bombings and the naval blockade, Japan had severe shortages of steel, aluminium, coal and other vital materials necessary to manufacture instruments of war. Moreover, Sakomizo predicted that the lack of fuel supplies would cripple shipping, railroads and other modes of transport within weeks, preventing travel between cities and collapsing important munitions industries. Finally, he anticipated the arrival of a famine due to an insufficient rice harvest. Suzuki issued copies of this report to members of his cabinet and called a meeting on 12 May to discuss possible actions for the government to take.

Based upon the information and conclusions drawn from the report, the Navy Minister, Admiral Mitsumasa Yonai, proposed turning to Russia as a mediator to end the war. When Suzuki responded favourably, the cabinet discussed possible methods of negotiating a peace settlement with the Allies. Some members accepted the idea of turning to a neutral third party to mediate, but doubted

BELOW
A group of SB2C Helldiver dive bombers and TBF Avenger torpedo bombers approach the coastline of Japan near Tokyo. The decimation of the Imperial Navy eventually enabled carrier-based aircraft to attack targets within Japan.

RIGHT
Piloted by Paul W. Tibbets, the Enola Gay was the first bomber in history to drop an atomic device upon an enemy target. Tibbets had named the B-29 bomber after his mother.

BELOW
An aerial photograph reveals the extent of damage caused by an incendiary raid upon a Mitsubishi aircraft plant in Nagoya, Japan. Such attacks eventually destroyed more than 12 per cent of the city.

ABOVE

A B-29 bomber unleashes a cluster of incendiary devices upon the waterfront of Kobe, Japan. A successful experimental low-altitude night raid on the city in February 1945 led the United States Army Air Force to repeat this procedure on other population centres in Japan.

that Stalin would be willing to fulfil such a role without receiving several territorial concessions from Japan, including the Kurile Islands. However, the Army Chief of Staff and the War Minister agreed with Yonai because they believed that Stalin would prefer to see Japan emerge as a viable power in East Asia to stand in the way of growing American influence in the region.

The Potsdam Proclamation

Impressed with this argument, Suzuki ordered Koki Hirota to initiate negotiations with the Soviet ambassador to Japan, Yakov Malik, who was staying at the resort town of Gohra, about 160km (100 miles) from Tokyo. Delayed by the 25 May bombing on the capital, Hirota did not reach Gohra until 3 June. During the two-day meeting, Malik assured Hirota that he would consider the request for Soviet help to end the war and asked for time to consider it. Encouraged by what he perceived to be a favourable reply, Hirota notified his government that the negotiations looked promising. Later in the month, the two men met again. On this occasion, Hirota made an ambitious proposition, effectively suggesting an alliance between Japan and the Soviet Union. Not surprisingly, this idea did not impress Malik, who was aware that most of the once-mighty Imperial Navy was at the bottom of the Pacific Ocean. During another meeting

held a week later, Hirota offered to sacrifice Manchuria and Japanese fishing concessions in Russian waters. Again, Malik professed little interest in these overtures but agreed to pass them along to Moscow.

By this time, the Emperor, who was as anxious to end the war as Suzuki, grew impatient. On 12 July, he persuaded a former prime minister, Prince Fumimaro Konoye, to accept an assignment to Moscow. As a special emissary to the Soviet government, Konoye was to appeal directly to Foreign Commissar Vyacheslav Molotov to help end the war without forcing Japan to surrender unconditionally. However, the Soviet government notified the Japanese ambassador to Moscow, Naotake Sato, that it was not interested in meeting with Konoye or in mediating a peace treaty between Tokyo and Washington. When he informed his superiors of this refusal, Sato urged them to accept any terms imposed by the United States that allowed Japan to keep its Emperor.

Back in Japan, few high-ranking officials paid any heed to this advice. Although most members of the Suzuki cabinet were eager to find a diplomatic solution to the war, they refused to accept the Allied powers' 'unconditional surrender' doctrine of the Casablanca Conference of January 1943, knowing that many senior military officers in Japan would never stand for such a capitulation.

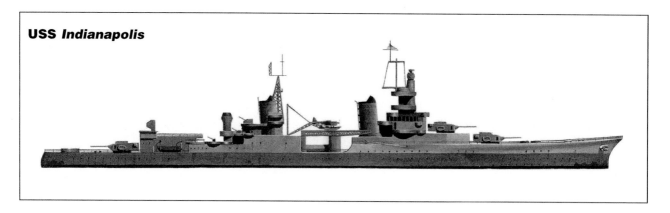

USS *Indianapolis*

ABOVE

The flagship of the US 5th Fleet, the USS Indianapolis *delivered the 'Little Boy' atomic bomb to the island of Tinian. With this task accomplished, the heavy cruiser headed for Leyte, only to be sunk by a Japanese torpedo. Although most of its crew survived the assault, subsequent shark attacks claimed the lives of almost 600 sailors clinging to life rafts.*

Unfortunately for the war-weary Japanese people, the Americans would not allow anything short of unconditional surrender.

At the time of Konoye's attempt to talk with Molotov, President Harry S. Truman and Prime Minister Winston Churchill were meeting with Stalin in Potsdam, Berlin. During this conference, Churchill suggested to Truman the possibility of permitting the Japanese some minor concessions to enable them to surrender with honour. Rejecting this advice, Truman claimed that the Pearl Harbor ambush had shown that the Japanese did not possess any honour and indicated his determination to force them to accept all conditions imposed by his government.

Therefore, he and Churchill issued the Potsdam Proclamation on 26 July.

Without mentioning any specific weapon of mass destruction, the Potsdam Proclamation warned the Japanese that, unless their government capitulated unconditionally, they would see their homeland completely destroyed. However, the manifesto also contained specific assurances guaranteeing the continued existence of the Japanese nation on its four main islands, as well as indicating that the Allied occupation of Japan would only last until order was restored and the Allies were satisfied that its war-making capabilities were gone. Finally, the Proclamation asserted that the Allies would allow the country to develop peaceful industrial projects that would enable the Japanese economy to thrive. Noticeably absent from this document was any assurance permitting the Japanese to keep their Emperor.

Within a day, the Japanese Government – still entertaining the prospect of Soviet mediation – received the details of the Potsdam Proclamation. Belligerent after several years of warfare, many senior military officers urged Suzuki to reject the document out of hand. While deciding whether or not to accept the terms imposed by the Allies, the Prime Minister allowed the major newspapers of the country to publish the Proclamation, with the proviso that they would not issue any editorial comments. However, many newspapers ignored the proviso and printed commentary that dismissed the surrender warning as a 'laughable matter', predicting that the country would become more resolved than ever to prosecute the war to a successful conclusion.

Not surprisingly, these defiant editorial policies angered and alarmed members of the Suzuki cabinet, who wanted to keep their options open and give the Allies reason to allow Japan to gain terms more favourable than unconditional surrender. Without hesitation, Foreign Minister Shigenori Togo accused the military of instigating this propaganda activity to trump any possible peace feelers. Dismissing this accusation, senior officers clamoured for Suzuki to issue an explicit rejection of the Proclamation. As a compromise, he agreed to ridicule the terms of the ultimatum without openly repudiating it.

'Little Boy'

Thus, in a public statement to reporters, Suzuki attempted to indicate that he had 'no comment' on the Proclamation. Unfortunately for him, most Americans interpreted this statement as an outright rejection of the Allies' terms. Satisfied that the Japanese would not surrender unless hit with enough force to bring them to their knees, Truman and his senior military officers had three options. The first was to continue with the brutal fire raids on Japanese cities, hoping that the destruction brought by these actions would eventually reach a point that would compel capitulation. The second was to launch a massive ground invasion.

However, Truman had already resolved to exercise his third option, which was to use atomic weaponry against Japan.

During the meeting at Potsdam, Truman learned that nuclear scientists working secretly for the US Government had successfully detonated an atomic bomb at Alamogordo, New Mexico. Told that an explosive device to drop upon Japan could be ready by early August, he and other American officials were especially interested in using such a weapon before Russia fulfilled its promise to join the war against Tokyo. If they could bring Japan to its knees before the Soviets intervened, they would not have to allow Stalin to play a major role in the reconstruction of postwar East Asia. Unlike Europe, this region would be left to the exclusive control of the Western powers.

On 26 July, the same day that Truman had issued the Potsdam Proclamation, the heavy cruiser *Indianapolis* delivered to the island of Tinian the first atomic bomb to be used in the history of warfare. Christened 'Little Boy', the device was 71cm (28in) in diameter, 304cm (120in) long and weighed 4082kg (9000lb), possessing the same destructive power as 15 kilotons of TNT. While technicians assembled Little Boy in an

air-conditioned hut on the island, Colonel Paul W. Tibbets Jr and his 509th Bomber Group received the honour of dropping the bomb on Japan. Specifically, his mission was to obliterate Hiroshima, a city located in western Honshu and the headquarters of the 2nd General Army.

In the early morning of 6 August, three weather planes took off from Tinian to monitor the three Japanese cities selected as candidates for destruction. If poor atmospheric conditions prevented a mission over Hiroshima, the Americans could bomb one of the other two cities. An hour later, Tibbets and his flight crew departed Tinian aboard their B-29, Enola Gay, with Little Boy secured in the fuselage. Accompanying the Superfortress bomber were two escort aircraft equipped with scientific and photographic equipment. During the flight to Hiroshima, the crewmen of Enola Gay learned that they were dropping an atomic bomb and received welder's goggles to shield their eyes from the blinding explosion that the device was expected to generate when detonated.

ABOVE

The domed Agricultural Exhibition Hall was one of the few buildings to remain standing in Hiroshima. After the war, the Japanese converted the structure into a monument for the city.

RIGHT

The Japanese delegation to the surrender ceremony aboard Missouri *prepares to sign the necessary documents of capitulation. Foreign Minister Mamoru Shigemitsu and General Yoshijiro Umezu stand at the front of the group.*

LEFT
General of the Army Douglas MacArthur, Supreme Commander for the Allied powers, signs the Japanese surrender agreement. Standing behind him are Lieutenant-General Jonathan Wainwright and Lieutenant-General A.E. Percival, the British delegate to the ceremony.

The eighth largest city in Japan, Hiroshima had about 365,000 residents. However, the government had evacuated 120,000 civilians into the countryside as a safety measure against possible fire raids. Two days before Enola Gay flew toward Hiroshima, American propagandists had dropped hundreds of leaflets on the city warning its people to expect terrible destruction of the area because of Japan's refusal to surrender unconditionally, but most of the residents seemed fairly unconcerned.

The death of Hiroshima

Later in the morning of 6 August, an American weather aircraft flying over Hiroshima caused air-raid sirens to sound in the city. Although some inhabitants fled to bomb shelters, most others on the ground continued with their daily routines. In the sky above, a radio operator from the weather plane advised Tibbet that conditions would permit him to unload his cargo. As they approached their target, the crewmen of Enola Gay prepared to put on their protective goggles when the countdown began.

At 0815 hours, the bombardier located the centre of Aioi Bridge, the designated aiming point for Little Boy, on the crosshairs of his sighting device. With ground zero thus established, the bomb-bay doors of the Superfortress opened and the bomb sailed downwards until it exploded 600m (2000ft) above the ground, producing a large fireball that melted metal and stone structures below. After this hot, brilliant flash of light came a loud concussion that demolished several buildings within a 3.2km (2-mile) radius. In a matter of seconds, Enola Gay had turned much of Hiroshima into a desolate wasteland.

Thousands of metres from the bomber, observers aboard the two escort airplanes studied, photographed and filmed the spectacle. Hiroshima residents who had survived the initial blast now faced several dangers to their lives. As the mushroom cloud blossomed into the sky, radioactive dust covered the area. From the west, fires were spreading throughout the city. Fifteen minutes after the blast, dirty, radioactive rain and foggy drizzle fell upon the area, caused by condensation from the mushroom cloud. Meanwhile, a cyclonic wind scattered flames all over, demolishing more buildings, bridges and trees. Altogether, the bomb had destroyed about 60 per cent of the city. Amid this apocalyptic environment, surviving victims wandered through the ruins, many of them

*Former adversaries gather
at Luzon for the Japanese
surrender. Although
the Allies aggressively
prosecuted senior officers
for alleged war crimes, they
allowed Emperor Hirohito
to remain as the titular ruler
of the country.*

suffering from horrible burns that peeled off much of their skin. Others permanently lost their eyesight from the initial flash of light.

As this terrible day was coming to an end, the fires died down and volunteers arrived to help care for the sick and wounded. Others set to work incinerating the remains of the deceased. Despite the diligent efforts of medical personnel, hundreds died every hour at first-aid stations. The bomb killed 86,000-100,000 people instantly and claimed another 100,000 victims who gradually perished from injuries, burns and radiation poisoning. This death toll included 22 American prisoners-of-war detained within the city limits.

The following morning, US Secretary of War L. Stimson released a statement from Truman explaining to the American people what had occurred in Hiroshima. Noting that the Japanese Government had chosen to ignore the Potsdam Proclamation, Truman proclaimed the necessity of unleashing a new, revolutionary weapon of unprecedented power. While Stimson publicised this statement, Truman himself was aboard the cruiser *Augusta*, returning from Potsdam. When he was notified that the bomb had been a success, the President immediately passed the news along to the ship's crewmen, who cheered loudly in response.

After a brief investigation conducted by the country's leading nuclear scientist, officials in the Japanese Government were satisfied that the destruction brought upon Hiroshima had been wrought by an atomic bomb. However, instead of capitulating, the Suzuki cabinet made one last attempt to persuade the Soviets to mediate an acceptable peace treaty for Japan. However, on 8 August, before Molotov had even received this request, he notified Ambassador Sato that a state of war now existed between Russia and Japan. As Stalin had promised, the Soviet Union entered the Pacific War exactly three months after the defeat of Nazi Germany.

The end

On the same day as the war declaration, more than 1.5 million Soviet troops poured into Manchuria and attacked the Japanese Kwangtung Army, which was only half the size, and by now severely under-supplied. For two weeks, three Red Army groups steadily pushed southwards, meeting the determined resistance that had confronted the Americans at Peleliu and Iwo Jima. Further east, Soviet amphibious forces landed on southern Sakhalin and the Kurile Islands. In the last major land campaign of the war, the Japanese were losing the remnants of their once-vast empire.

Senior Japanese officers sign a surrender document at a conference room in the Municipal Building in Singapore. Throughout East Asia, many Japanese units were still relatively intact when they capitulated to the Allies.

Three days after the bombing of Hiroshima, another B-29 appeared over the city of Nagasaki on the island of Kyushu. Called Bock's Car, the bomber carried a plutonium bomb that had been named 'Fat Man', a device measuring 335cm (132in) long and 152cm (60in) wide. During this mission, heavy cloud cover prevented Major Charles W. Sweeney and his flight crew from hitting their specific target in the commercial area of the city, and Fat Man missed the objective by 4.8km (3 miles), detonating over an industrial section at an altitude of 533m (1750ft). Although Fat Man was a much more powerful bomb than Little Boy, it killed fewer people because Nagasaki was located on an area covered with hills and valleys, preventing the radiant heat of the blast from covering as wide an area as it had done in Hiroshima. Estimates of casualties from the bombing of Nagasaki ranged from 23,000 to 35,000 people killed out of a total population of 195,290, and most of its factories were wiped out. In both cities, many more survivors gradually died from health problems caused by radiation exposure.

Hours after this second atomic bombing, Emperor Hirohito presided over an emergency meeting of high-ranking political and military officials. On this occasion, he transcended his figurehead status and acted as a genuine political leader. Satisfied that the Americans could produce all the nuclear weapons that they wished, the Emperor proclaimed that any further resistance would be an exercise in futility that would ultimately lead to the destruction of the whole nation. The next morning, Japanese diplomats in Sweden and Switzerland received messages from their government declaring its acceptance of the Potsdam Proclamation, although a formal declaration of surrender had not yet been made.

Chinese and Japanese delegates sign a peace treaty ending the war between their two countries. Two Nationalist Party flags flank a large portrait of Chiang Kai-shek on the far wall.

ABOVE

Japanese POWs ford the Sittang River in Burma en route to a hut where they are to surrender their arms.

BELOW

Developed too late to see action, the Japanese had constructed an ambitious new submarine class, with a range of 48,280km (30,000 miles), aimed at striking enemy targets around the Panama Canal and other distant areas.

On 15 August, the radio broadcast a recorded address by Emperor Hirohito in which he urged his people to capitulate and accept all terms imposed by the Allies. Two weeks later, the first group of British and American occupation troops arrived at Yokosuka. On 2 September, Foreign Minister Shigemitsu led a group of delegates aboard the battleship *Missouri* in Tokyo Bay, and he and MacArthur signed the official surrender document, officially ending World War II and ushering in a seven-year period of occupation for Japan.

Six days after the surrender ceremony, MacArthur entered Tokyo to begin his reign as the top commander charged with administering the occupation of Japan. During this period, which would last until 1952, General Hideki Tojo and other high-ranking Japanese officials who had led their country into the Pacific War stood trial for engaging in military aggression and committing atrocities on civilians and prisoners-of-war. Eventually, Tojo and many of his subordinates were executed, while others received long prison sentences. For the rest of the Japanese, American rule was more benevolent. After giving the people a democratic constitution and allowing them to keep their Emperor, the conquering Allies implemented a recovery programme that would enable Japan to become the most stable and prosperous nation in the Far East.

I-400

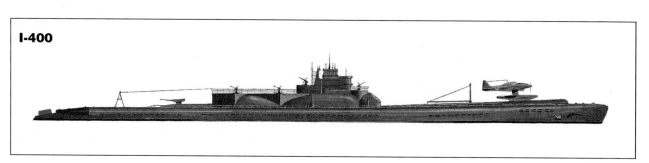

INDEX